HOW THE
LEFT
SWIFTBOATED
AMERICA

ALSO BY JOHN GIBSON

The War on Christmas: How the Liberal Plot to Ban the Sacred Christian Holiday Is Worse Than You Thought

Hating America: The New World Sport

HOW THE
LEFT
SWIFTBOATED
AMERICA

The Liberal Media Conspiracy to Make You Think George Bush Was the Worst President in History

JOHN GIBSON

HARPER

An Imprint of HarperCollins*Publishers*
www.harpercollins.com

HarperCollins books may be purchased for educational, business, or sales promotional use. For information, please write: Special Markets Department, HarperCollins Publishers, 10 East 53rd Street, New York, NY 10022.

FIRST EDITION

Designed by Renato Stanisic

Library of Congress Cataloging-in-Publication Data has been applied for.

ISBN: 978-0-06-179289-2

09 10 11 12 13   OV/RRD   10 9 8 7 6 5 4 3 2 1

Contents

Introduction: Swiftboating
for Fun and Profit

*"REMEMBER, THE POWER OF REPETITION. If you remember one thing
from the last four years of blogging about election debate rhetoric and what it takes to win,
remember this: WHAT WE REPEAT IS WHAT THE PUBLIC REMEMBERS."*
—JEFFREY FELDMAN, DIARIST FOR LEFT-WING WEB SITE THE DAILYKOS

S*wiftboating*, as it has come to be defined by the left, is the political trick of claiming to expose truth while in fact lying. The
left invented the word to counter the Swift Veterans and POWs for
Truth, an organization of former commanders of Vietnam era river
attack vessels called swift boats. Democrat presidential candidate
John Kerry was a swift boat commander in the Vietnam War. He
was the recipient of the Silver Star and other decorations for his service in the navy, including several Purple Hearts. In May 2004, the
Swift Veterans announced their opposition to Kerry's presidential
ambitions in a letter to him. The letter read, in part: "It is our collective judgment that, upon your return from Vietnam, you grossly and
knowingly distorted the conduct of the American soldiers, marines,
sailors and airmen of that war (including a betrayal of many of us,
without regard for the danger your actions caused us). Further, we
believe that you have withheld and/or distorted material facts as to
your own conduct in this war."

The Swift Veterans ran a series of ads questioning Kerry's war record, his decorations, but especially his involvement in the Vietnam Veterans Against the War, and the 1971 Winter Soldier project. As a part of those activities, Kerry had testified before a Senate committee alleging American soldiers committed atrocities in Vietnam, which especially angered the Swift Veterans.

The Swiftboat advertisements generated an enormous controversy about Kerry's war record and the Swift Veterans' affiliations with the Republican Party and various activisits assisting the campaign of George W. Bush. But *Washington Post* political analysts Dan Balz and Jim VandeHei wrote, "Privately, key Democratic strategists fear that attack ads against Kerry will *undermine the Democratic presidential nominee's character and credibility, no matter whether the charges are accurate*, because they dovetail with an argument Bush's campaign has tried to pound home in its advertising—that Kerry is unreliable and untrustworthy."

Swiftboating, used as a verb, came to mean just that: undermining character and credibility, no matter whether the charges are accurate. Supposedly too, this odious means of political combat was exclusively the practice of the right.

For many years, the left has accused American conservatives of building a well-oiled propaganda machine. David Brock, a onetime conservative firebrand, wrote a book called *The Republican Noise Machine* in which he outlined precisely how this mechanism worked: Think tanks cranked out position papers and arguments and opinions, which then found their way onto talk radio, and into newspaper and newsmagazine opinion columns, and eventually influenced the opinions and political outlook of the American voter. The left admired this powerful machine and made conscious efforts to reproduce it even as they denounced its baleful effects. By 2006, the left had consciously duplicated this imagined mechanism to push voters to the left. In the same way, the left adopted the perceived tactic of its political opponents in attacking George W. Bush.

The left's animus toward Bush was nurtured in the Florida sun in the thirty-five-day recount drama of the 2000 presidential election. Bush was scorned by the left even before Al Gore's agonizingly close electoral loss, but after the decision by the U.S. Supreme Court that gave Bush the presidency, he was forever viewed by the left as illegitimate. The objection that Bush was "selected not elected" soon became a common refrain and a fuming bumper sticker.

Bush entered office with a huge budget surplus, a country at peace, and in a climate of wedge-issue politics the left found more annoying than threatening. Then 9/11 changed all that.

After 9/11 the left began to realize—with mounting horror—that a man they regarded as a likable numbskull was taking on the near-heroic status of a national war leader. Worse, to attack him while the country itself was under attack would make them seem unpatriotic.

The answer was *swiftboating*. Undermine the president by a campaign of lies and ridicule. Thus Bush was mocked and scorned for continuing to read grade school kids a children's story while aides scurried for information on the attacks behind the scenes. He was later portrayed as a frightened president on the run when security demanded Air Force One fly from one Air Force base to another while the situation in the capital was assessed.

Swiftboating Bush involved attacking the president on several key fronts: on the disputed 2000 election, on his response to 9/11, on the Iraq War, on the national security initiative that involved warrantless domestic wiretapping, on enhanced interrogation techniques, on the surge, on uranium from Niger, on the number of deaths in Iraq, and on the federal response to Hurricane Katrina. After being relentlessly swiftboated by the left, these events turned into twisted versions of the truth: *the illegitimate president "selected" by the Supreme Court, the president who let 9/11 happen, the rush to war based on lies about WMD, spying on Americans, Abu Ghraib, Guantanamo, "watch what you say," the Downing Street memo, outing his own CIA spy, we killed a million Iraqis, Bush let New Orleans drown*—and many more.

Operating under that definition of swiftboating, and employing the maxim quoted above ("What we repeat is what the public remembers"), the left *repeatedly* assailed Bush, conservatives, the Iraq War, counterterrorism efforts, and the entire apparatus designed to keep America safe by defeating al Qaeda. The left said, "Here's the truth about failure of judgment, loss at war, incompetence at all levels." All this coalesced as the Case against Bush. The entire edifice was built of demonstrable lies masquerading as the truth. But through repetition the lies proved very effective.

Moreover, it must be acknowledged, Bush himself was woefully inadequate as an explainer and defender of his policies. That gave the left eight years to build an edifice of lies and distortions virtually unopposed by the president or his staff.

Polling tracked the disillusionment among Americans as the lies set in. "Wrong track" polling on President Bush finally ran into the 80-percent zone, and the credibility of the president was eroded into the low twenties.

Saddam had his Mother of All Battles and the left in America had its Mother of All Big Lies, namely this now widely accepted but erroneous idea that everything America has undertaken since 9/11 was wrong, based on various Bush lies, and was in fact criminal.

The left's Big Lie won them the Congress in 2006, and the hollow quality of the lies became immediately clear as the Democrats repeatedly declared the war was lost, opposed the surge, demanded an immediate withdrawal, slandered a general—and watched its own approval rating sink lower than even the hated George W. Bush.

The election of 2008 has proved that lies work. One only has to look at the charges leveled against the Bush administration by candidate Barack Obama to witness the success of this campaign. Obama ran and won on the left's extensive catalog of lies about George W. Bush.

The election also ensured that the levers of power in Washington, D.C., will be in the hands of Democrats for at least four years and perhaps longer. The left now has the White House, the Senate, and the House of Representatives, a lopsided leftist majority whose existence was founded on the Big Lie, the oft repeated and almost mythic tale that the War on Terror and the War in Iraq are failures and national humiliations.

Despite the fact that the left now owns the cranks of governmental power, and the media—the principal action switch of political power—the facts about the campaign remain in stark outline: the left played the War on Terror and the War in Iraq as political piñatas with the purpose of undermining and subverting the national effort. To Democrats in Congress, if America lost, they won. That calculus was their firm conviction, though they react in horror at the accusation.

They may deny they wanted America to lose, but it is obvious that American losses and setbacks in Iraq were wins for leftist domestic politics. The fact that they managed to grab power in 2008, at a time when America was demonstrably winning a war the left said was already lost, simply proves how effective their lies were. The American public grew disgusted and disinterested in a war they were winning because the left had convinced so many people that it was wrong from the start, and even if America were to win, it would still be wrong.

Electoral politics are now in a pause. The arguments of the last five years can now be judged without the left worrying about losing a presidential election it wanted so very badly to win. They won. Okay. What now?

It's time to render a verdict. Who was right and who was wrong in taking us into the Iraq War, and what followed in the elaborate and expensive efforts to protect America?

The answer may seem audacious to some, but it is the truth: The right was right, the left was wrong. Period.

The following chapters will prove it. In the last chapter I will also suggest how to win this argument with the 60 percent of your neighbors and friends whom probability theory suggests have already been taken in by the Big Lies of the left. Lies are lies, and they can and should be defeated.

Those lies about America come in a long list: the Iraq invasion and subsequent occupation were based on a lie, both were strategically and morally wrong, Saddam had nothing to do with 9/11 and he posed no threat to the United States, America built a gulag of torture centers starting with Abu Ghraib and Gitmo, bolstered by a chain of secret prisons, America spied on its own citizens by listening to their phone calls, invading their email, keeping lists of what they read at the library.

Where to start?

If the war was a failure, why are we "suddenly" winning, and why is it so hard to find that news in the *New York Times*? If Americans are to wail and weep over the loss of personal liberties, and have to endure the horrifying possibility a cell phone conversation might get scanned by spy satellites, how do they feel about the fact there has been no successful terrorist attack on the United States since 9/11?

Not that the terrorists haven't tried. In fact, listening to cell calls and watching email and heightened alerts have thwarted more than twenty terror plots on the United States. The much decried water-boarding of terrorist Khalid Sheikh Mohammad, the 9/11 master-mind, resulted in a gasping spew of dozens of active plots against the United States at home and abroad, the majority of which checked out. Lefties on the West Coast love to screech about impeachment and war crimes, but these methods actually saved thousands of Los Angeles office workers when KSM's plot to crash an airliner into L.A.'s Library Tower was thwarted.

A little water down his nose saved thousands and the left wanted Bush impeached.

This is called playing to lose. Lose a war, lose the will to fight, lose to terrorists who count on the softheads among us who na-ively facilitate their plans. If it's not actually criminal it certainly is condemnable.

By this method of swiftboating, the left accomplished a takeover of Congress in 2006, and had set its sights on the White House in 2008. The same Big Lie was the very centerpiece of the Obama cam-paign: The war was wrong.

In a general sense, the country has been in three wars since we were attacked: the Afghan War, the Iraq War, and one more—the war on the truth.

The left rewrote history as it was happening before our very eyes and, as they say about most wars, the truth was the first victim.

The left, as always, was bombastic in its assaults, and it employed all the tools of popular culture: cable news, Internet blogs, Holly-wood stars, popular musicians (they all would like to sing the perfect antiwar song), and every single comedian who ever stood before a camera or an audience. The left fielded an Army of the Outraged, massed on the media, howling at every twist and turn in all of Amer-ica's long and occasionally unsuccessful war strategies.

Success did not deter them in the slightest. We could win the war, but it was still counterproductive and wrong. We could kill al Qaeda, but we still hadn't captured bin Laden. We could keep America safe, but there were so many intelligent things we did *not* do. George W. Bush could stand on this record, but he was obviously an idiot. How could anyone say he is not?

The left simply borrowed a technique it imagined the right had used against John Kerry: *Swiftboating America*.

While the truth has been obscured, covered in mud and offal, it has remained intact for those who care to find it. The following chapters will lay out the story as an indictment of the left, and empower the right-thinking reader to fight back.

Chapter One

How Many Reasons Do You Need to Hate George W. Bush?

The torrent of abuse poured on George W. Bush for the Iraq War foamed and swirled right up to the end of his presidency and continued unabated even after. As much as the left wanted to see the Bush years end, they wanted desperately to hold on to their anger, even stoke it, right up to the last moment and beyond. A shameful spectacle, its fires burned right through the inauguration of the next president and into his new term.

On the eve of President Obama's inauguration, MSNBC's Keith Olbermann growled at the camera, spittle flying, "Prosecute, Mr. President-elect, and even if you get not one conviction, you will still have accomplished good for generations unborn . . ." Left unmentioned by this leftist cheerleader was the fact that on the very same day at the U.S. military base in Guantanamo Bay, Cuba, suspected 9/11 hijackers, testifying before a military trial, admitted their role in the plot, and the American left said, "So what?"

So what?

Why spoil the party? The September 11 attacks were ancient history, not to be mentioned in polite company. After all, that day stirred emotions in most Americans that the left wanted suppressed and ignored.

Bush's last day would provide no respite from the demonization and fevered hatred, from the dismal parade of charlatans and prevaricators who aimed to lose a war in order to seize power. It was swiftboating in action.

But of course, the left's swiftboating expeditions upriver in search of the Bush heart of darkness began the very day he was elected president.

"Bush was selected, not elected," rose the chant across the land, as the left bewailed the evil fate of Florida. California Senator Barbara Boxer, of the liberal charter jet set, was later asked what she would have done differently over the last eight years. She immediately blurted out, "If I'd known how things turned out I would have had everyone I knew move to Florida in 2000."

The Florida recount happened because the ballots were confusing, because elderly voters couldn't puncture the famous "butterfly ballot," and because something important and largely unnoticed happened almost four months earlier.

On a sunny morning, Friday July 21, 2000, Richard B. Cheney walked into the Teton County, Wyoming, courthouse and made his way to the Office of the Registrar of Voters. Cheney, the former high government official, presently CEO of Halliburton, and legal resident of Texas, walked to the counter unaccompanied and spoke to Sharon Nethercutt, a woman who was described as "very nice" by a reporter who called later that day. Cheney asked for a voter registration form, and checked the box that allowed Teton County to withdraw his registration to vote in Texas. Nethercutt promptly sent the document off for processing, and Dick Cheney was once again an official Wyoming voter.

Someone in the nascent Bush administration had read the Constitution of the United States. In setting out the rules for the Electoral College, the framers had mandated that electors would be forfeited if the president and vice president came from the same state. If Bush were to win with Cheney as vice president, the twenty-six electoral votes of Texas would be disallowed unless one of the two moved his residency out of Texas. And it wasn't going to be George W. Bush.

If Bush had been as stupid then as the left later came to believe, the great hubbub of Florida in November and December 2000 wouldn't have mattered. Even if he had won Florida by a wide margin instead of that official 157 votes (fewer than sit in the best seats behind home plate in Yankee Stadium), he would still have lost the election.

Bush and Cheney were smart then. They became evil imbeciles much later, after the left had spent years spinning virtually everything that happened during the Bush administration as an abomination worthy of impeachment.

On election night 2000, the states fell into the Gore column or the Bush column about as predicted. However, by early evening, producers in the network television control rooms were shouting into their phones, "It's Florida!"

All attention turned to Florida as both Republicans and Democrats rushed their teams of lawyers onto corporate jets and whooshed them to the land of palm trees, golf, and hanging chads.

The venerable Bush hand James A. Baker III took over as lawyer-in-chief for the Bush side, ably aided by election law litigator Ben Ginsberg. The Gore team featured the famous courtroom trial master David Boies.

The recount, undertaken at Gore's request, was confined to Democrat counties—Palm Beach, Broward, Miami-Dade, and Volusia—where Gore's lawyers thought he could win in the limited time available. This put Bush at an obvious disadvantage, so it should not have been surprising that at a certain point in the month-long process the Bush team demanded that the counting be stopped and certified, as required by law. The Gore team wanted an extension to "make certain every voter's vote counted," by which they obviously meant "every vote for a Democrat." But there was still a drop-dead date. The Constitution of the United States required each state to name its electors no later than December 12.

It was high drama, perfectly suited for television, and the three cable networks threw all the airtime at their disposal into a political story as charged with suspense as any in the country's history. Cameras sprouted in county recount centers and in the courtrooms of the state capitol, Tallahassee. Live coverage from seemingly everywhere in Florida brought national viewers more drama than anyone thought possible.

Television helicopters followed trucks carrying ballots to the state capitol, reminiscent of the OJ "slow-speed chase." A Republican-controlled committee in the state house heard testimony from angry voters who told of their "horror" upon realizing that the confusing ballot had led them to vote for right-wing Reform Party candidate

Patrick Buchanan, rather than Democrat Al Gore. Reverend Richard Harris, testifying before the committee, warned, "Listen to the voice of the people," and threatened that if the legislators appointed electors who would vote for George W. Bush, they would be regarded as "no better than thieves."

War veterans appeared before the committee to express their anger that the recount might be short-circuited. "Bush is trying to steal the election," one said to noisy cheers. Suspicions were raised even higher when Gore's supporters realized that the election would be validated by the state's governor—who happened to be George Bush's brother.

With the December 12 deadline fast approaching, newspapers speculated on what would happen if Florida's electors were not named in time. Even wilder speculation about a presidential election thrown into the House of Representatives raised the stakes even higher.

Immediate cries were raised in Democrat districts around the country that the Electoral College should be abolished. Some people learned for the first time that their individual vote did not directly elect the president, and were left wondering who those "electors" were and why there was an Electoral College in the first place.

(Feelings were still so raw among Democrats in Florida that eight years later on the eve of the Obama-McCain election, Democrat Senator Bill Nelson mounted yet another campaign to abolish the Electoral College.)

Gore actually led in the Electoral College going into the recount; but if Bush were to capture Florida's twenty-five electoral votes he would pull ahead and win by one.

The left could hardly believe what was happening. Frank Rich wrote in his *New York Times* column, "Democrats are having fits that Mr. Bush, whom they see as a nincompoop, has a serious shot at winning." If any single line foretold the venom that would spew forth from the left over the next eight years, this would have to be it. The respected *New York Times* was allowing the possible next president of the United States to be insulted in its pages. But there was much more to come.

Bush was under attack, the Electoral College system was besieged, and even the state of Florida was slimed. As the late gonzo-journalist Hunter S. Thompson said, "So many of its elected officials are so openly For Sale that politics in Florida is more like an auction than a democratic process. The state has no income tax and essentially no Law."

None of what transpired in that angry and bitter month is now contested. Gore won the popular vote by just over half a million. Bush won the state by just over 150 votes, giving him the electoral college victory by a margin of one.

It was Gore who took the case to the Supreme Court. And it was the arguments before the court that gave Bush his slim victory (a 5–4 decision). Therefore, despite later evidence that Bush had in fact won the election in Florida and therefore the national election, it was on this decision of the conservative banc of the court that the left focused its bile over the next eight years.

The SCOTUS decision said simply that an earlier decision on recount rules by the Florida Supreme Court violated the fourteenth amendment, which assures equal protection under the law. The Florida court had violated the equal protection clause by allowing different rules in different counties, or even within the same county. The court said Florida couldn't declare legal a situation in which officials could recount votes one way at one table and across the room at a different table allow the use of different rules. The recount was stopped and the state's twenty-five electors went to Bush.

It was that simple. The rules have to be the same for both candidates: That is all the majority of the court said.

Yet for the left, the SCOTUS decision in *Bush v. Gore* took on the contours of a plot, a coup conducted by a conservative court, some of whose members had been appointed by Bush's "daddy" and were therefore assumed to "owe" him or be "in his pocket." It was the theft of an election right before the nation's very eyes.

But the left's narrative about the dolt who stole the election started even before the SCOTUS decision. "Mr. Bush's Sunday night declaration of pseudo-victory, meanwhile, gave us the puppet without the puppeteer," wrote Frank Rich in the *New York Times*.

Jon Stewart, then in the dawn of his Bush-mocking career, joked, "The two candidates were said to have spent the evening poring over the complex and detailed Supreme Court ruling. But whereas Gore was poring over it with his eyes and mind, Bush was pouring a glass of juice over it because quote, 'I don't want to finish my juice.'"

David Letterman deadpanned, "Don't kid yourself. George W. Bush is very excited. He's already working on his first foreign-policy blunder."

A CNN/Gallup poll showed 34 percent of the nation was disappointed in the result and a solid 11 percent described themselves as "angry," and 18 percent said they would not accept George W. Bush.

It was so close that Ralph Nader, who had run as a Green Party candidate and took a tiny percentage of votes, became a target of inchoate left-wing rage. "I have been in the witness protection program for the last three weeks. I campaigned for Ralph Nader," joked liberal talk show host Phil Donahue. "I'm now living as a woman in Mississippi."

Still, despite all the carping, grousing, joking, and whining, Bush was inaugurated on January 20, 2001.

It later turned out that he wasn't "selected" at all. Within a year, a major study of the recount tallies in Florida was released by a consortium of news organizations. The *New York Times*, a member of the consortium, announced the same day that Bush would have won the recount even if SCOTUS had not called a halt. The long study of the actual Florida voting had determined that the Supreme Court "did not cast the deciding vote." In fact, the people of Florida had narrowly elected George W. Bush.

But the study also gave the Gore people a way to argue that Bush was not a legitimately elected president. The study showed that if a statewide recount had somehow been triggered, Gore would have won by 60–171 votes, whether counting "dimples" or using a more restrictive standard.

So Gore not only won the popular vote nationwide, but would have won Florida as well had it undergone a complete recount, instead of the limited one requested by Gore.

However, the *Times* also reported that the ballots of blacks seemed to have been declared invalid at a higher rate than should have been expected, fanning the flames of a long-held urban myth that blacks were prevented from voting by Republican dirty tricks.

In a "news analysis," the *Times*' Richard Berke expressed the bitterness that coursed through the living rooms and coffee bars (and newsrooms) of the left: Gore had more votes, he was ripped off, Bush stole the election. Looking forward to the possibility of a rematch,

Berke wrote, "If Americans are hurting financially in 2004, Mr. Gore could say he was cheated out of the presidency and that the people were cheated too."

Thus in the same edition on the same day the *New York Times* had confirmed the validity of the election and yet had called it "cheating." Ignoring one's own evidence constitutes a willful untruth. Since the attitude underlying the falsehood was pure hostility to Bush, why should we not call Berke's charge of "cheating" a lie?

But the lie was embraced by the left and Bush became the "illegitimate" president.

Respected journalist Pete Hamill put this stamp on Bush on the eve of his inauguration. "The coming presidency of George W. Bush should fill intelligent people with fear and trembling," Hamill wrote. "It was one thing to have presidents stained with illegitimacy in the 19th century; it is quite another to have an illegitimate president in full possession of the mightiest military machine in the history of the world. Rutherford B. Hayes, a mediocrity who lost the popular vote and became president in 1888, did not have the hydrogen bomb."

National Black leaders promised to fight the illegitimate president who had suppressed black votes in Florida (and would in 2004 be accused of doing the same in Ohio). At a Washington, D.C., "summit" the Reverend Al Sharpton promised, "Some say that it's over, that it's time to move on," he said, and added, "It's not over."

Sharpton alleged that New Jersey Governor Christie Todd Whitman, who was Bush's nominee to head the EPA, was the "queen of racial profiling" because New Jersey state troopers had been accused of pulling over motorists based on race.

The left-wing blog firedoglake.com posted on Inauguration Day 2001: "Backers of George W. Bush indeed stole the Presidency. We believe there is more than enough evidence that America inaugurated the wrong man on January 20th, 2001. Keep in mind; the theft of an election is a crime that borders on treason."

In 2005, following a speech by the president, left-wing bloggers were still calling Bush illegitimate, adding venom derived from 9/11, the watershed event of the Bush presidency. "Bush was a pathetic non-leader running around the country on his jet like a chicken without a head, scared shitless and flying from Florida to military bases in Arkansas and Nebraska," the "Down with Tyranny" blogger wrote.

"He was anything but heroic. He was the physical coward on 9/11 he had been his entire life. There is a big difference between being personally brave and heroic and being a cocky bully (when you're the commander of the most powerful military force in history)."

"Bush v. Gore gave us an illegitimate president. Bush presided over an outlaw government. If we sit on our asses, as we've done since that weird, soul-crushing day in late December of 2000, illegality will be hardwired into the U.S. government," left-wing political cartoonist Ted Rall wrote in 2008. "A gangster regime presiding over the trappings of law and order is a vicious joke—illegitimate and ultimately doomed."

The avowedly left-wing Thinkprogress.org gleefully reported in April 2008 that the city of San Francisco was planning to "honor" George W. Bush by naming a sewage plant after him. "The enterprising Presidential Memorial Commission of San Francisco is looking to rename Oceanside Wastewater Treatment Facility to the 'George W. Bush Sewage Plant,'" the blog reported. "The group explains it seeks to 'select a fitting monument to the president's work' and to 'honor George W. Bush for his eight years of honorable public service. . . . No other president in American history has accomplished so much in such a short time,' the group notes."

If such claims had come only from anonymous bloggers, the hubbub might have faded away. But name-brand writers in respected magazines and newspapers also jumped in. Hendrik Hertzberg, senior editor at the *New Yorker*, told *Washington Post* columnist Howard Kurtz, "Bush lost in the vote of the people, and his legitimacy is hard to accept." Hertzberg had been a speech writer for Jimmy Carter, a Clinton supporter, and an acknowledged Gore partisan, but on this matter he pretended he was not carrying a bias. "Having lost the popular vote, he took no account of the special circumstances of his election and governed as if there was a popular mandate for the whole program of the hard right." So Bush should have scuttled his own presidency and governed as a Democrat out of respect for the hurt feelings of the left.

Why then did Florida quickly fade as a journalistic issue, Kurtz asked? "The media did not want to face the idea that we had an illegitimately installed president," Hertzberg said. "That's too big a piece of bad news that shakes too many kinds of civic faith."

In the early stages of its descent into hysteria, the contradiction was not so evident to the left. Bush was both smart enough to steal the election and yet stupid enough to turn himself into a puppet on the strings of unseen forces.

Soon bland acceptance of such contradictory notions set into the collective mind of the left. Bush stole the election. Bush is plotting against the nation. Bush is stupid. No, Bush is arrogant. No, Bush is Hitlerian. The arguments went on and on, bringing public discussion to new lows.

"Mr. Bush's real problem is arrogance—he thinks we are stupid," Frank Rich fumed in a column about the selection of John Ashcroft as attorney general. In the same column Rich declared it was "unfair" to call Bush stupid. He later changed his mind.

In September 2003, as the left was gearing up for the national primaries, Jonathan Chait of the *New Republic* wrote a much discussed piece called "The Case For Hating George W. Bush."

"I hate President George W. Bush. There, I said it," Chait wrote, publicly unburdening himself. "I think his policies rank him among the worst presidents in U.S. history. And, while I'm tempted to leave it at that, the truth is that I hate him for less substantive reasons, too. "

Chait didn't like it that Bush was born into a famous and powerful family, yet seemed to think he had made his own way to the top. "I hate the way he walks—shoulders flexed, elbows splayed out from his sides like a teenage boy feigning machismo. I hate the way he talks—blustery self-assurance masked by a pseudo-populist twang. I even hate the things that everybody seems to like about him. I hate his lame nickname-bestowing—a way to establish one's social superiority beneath a veneer of chumminess (does anybody give their boss a nickname without his consent?). And, while most people who meet Bush claim to like him, I suspect that, if I got to know him personally, I would hate him even more."

Chait offered more solid reasons for hating Bush—the invasion of Iraq, the deterioration of American prestige—but these additional reasons seemed pointless. A person who hated Bush for the way he walked and talked could be counted on to hate him for taking us to war in Iraq.

A short time later, conservative columnist Charles Krauthammer noted that Chait's manifesto seemed to bring many more Bush haters out of the closet, and asked what made his opponents so angry. "Democrats are seized with a loathing for President Bush—a contempt and disdain giving way to a hatred that is near pathological—unlike any since they had Richard Nixon to kick around." Krauthammer quoted "an otherwise reasonable man," Julian Bond, who described Bush's appointees as "the Taliban wing of American politics." He noted that the *American Prospect* had called Bush "the most dangerous president in all of American history—his only rival being Jefferson Davis."

Krauthammer pronounced himself puzzled—at first. Then the problem became clear. "Bush's great crime is that he is the illegitimate president who became consequential—revolutionizing American foreign policy, reshaping economic policy and dominating the political scene ever since his emergence as the post–9/11 war president." Krauthammer, a trained psychiatrist, later became notable for his identification of a psychiatric condition he labeled "Bush Derangement Syndrome."

Meanwhile the left continued to pile up offenses. The list of charges against Bush grew to be extremely lengthy. Indeed, it read like a prayer chanted in unison, covering their basic points:

Bush stole Florida
Bush dropped the ball on 9/11
Bush let bin Laden get away
Bush took his eye off the ball after Afghanistan
Iraq was a war of conquest fought for oil
Bush lied about Saddam's role in 9/11
Bush lied about Saddam's link to bin Laden
Bush lied about WMD
Bush killed a million Iraqis
Bush spied on Americans
Bush outed a CIA agent
Bush destroyed our moral standing with torture and illegal
    imprisonment
Bush let New Orleans drown

This book will attempt to rebut this lengthy list of charges, but it's worth looking at a few of them here.

Bush could have stopped 9/11. The entire investigation by the 9/11 Commission was meant to prove Bush could have acted to stop the attack but was too lazy and indifferent to care. The left's consensus on the causes of such towering negligence seemed to settle on Bush's obvious incompetence and arrogance, and the leftover bad habits of his slothful youth.

After 9/11, Bush did too much and went too far. It infuriated the left that Bush focused on Iraq. For the left, he should have been keeping the UN inspections going. According to the left, he should have been disarming Saddam and locking Iraq in a "box." This earnest advice, of course, came after years of the left wringing its hands about Saddam. Even though they turned out endless studies of Saddam's human rights abuses, all it took was for Saddam to become a target of George W. Bush to suddenly morph into a victim of imperialist aggression. Once deposed, of course, nobody on the left would have dared to demand Saddam's release and return to power. But there was something very wrong about removing him from power.

Connections between Saddam and al Qaeda were numerous both before and after 9/11. Though some of these contacts were murky and difficult to prove, would it really have been prudent to allow him to remain in power and just see how that relationship developed? The emergence of Abu Musab al Zarqawi, the Jordanian al Qaeda operative in Iraq, should have proven that would have been a dangerous gamble. Saddam allowed Zarqawi to establish himself in Iraq after escaping Afghanistan in a losing battle with the Americans. He allowed Zarqawi to travel in and out of Baghdad for medical care. He never moved against Ansar al Islam, just inside the Kurdish zone where Zarqawi made his base. Saddam's intelligence service protested they "couldn't find" him, despite his at-will movements in and around Baghdad, but the left in the United States ignored such information, even when confirmed by the Senate Select Committee on Intelligence.

Bush let bin Laden get away. True, bin Laden escaped because the American generals—foremost among them commanding General Tommy Franks—decided to depend on our Afghan "allies" to close the back door at Tora Bora, high in the Hindu Kush. Evidently, bin Laden paid better than Franks, because the warlords of the Northern Alliance took his money and let him go. But did the left really want thousands more American troops in Afghanistan? That's what it would have taken to cut off bin Laden's escape, and the Soviet experience in Afghanistan discouraged that approach.

Bush took his eye off the ball after Afghanistan. By rushing off to Iraq, Bush left the job in Afghanistan unfinished, it was said. But people who made this complaint tended to be forgetful of the facts. Nobody ever thought—or claimed—that Afghanistan was going to become a thriving democracy. The Taliban and their strict brand of Islam were always going to be a strong and disruptive force, especially with support from tribal leaders across the border in the wilds of northwest Pakistan. The country was going to continue to be an arms bazaar and a major opium producer. Indeed, Bush's smartest move in any of his war decisions was to avoid getting sucked into Afghanistan like the Russians did. The left never acknowledged that he did well to keep the problem at arm's length.

War in Iraq—wrong and immoral. The left's lie was that the bellicose Bush wanted to continue his war making after Afghanistan, and therefore went after Iraq simply because he'd always wanted to. People said he did it because Saddam tried to kill his daddy (and Laura!) when they visited Kuwait after the first Gulf War. Bush also launched the war to help his friends in the military industrial complex, including Dick Cheney's most recent employer, Halliburton. People said he wanted a way to pay off his old buddies from the Texas oil patch. People said he did it to further his personal Christian crusade.

In reality, Bush was merely continuing a tradition of U.S. presidents defending Muslims initiated by Bill Clinton and Bush 41. People said Bush didn't understand Muslim history and culture, and that his war was a bloody blunder. Maybe so. But Bush placed his faith in the Iraqis' natural desire to govern themselves rather than remain under a dictator's boot. The right of national self-determination is enshrined in the UN Charter. Isn't that a choice the left should applaud?

Bush was accused not only of "misleading" the nation into war but of incompetence in its prosecution. The brief successful combat phase quickly gave way to a long and bloody occupation no one wanted. Did Bush expect the Sunnis would go to such lengths to resist the loss of power, or that the Shia would have so many murderous scores to settle? Apparently not. Did he expect al Qaeda to flock to Iraq to wreak havoc, targeting Sunni, Shia, and Americans alike? Evidently not as much as he got despite his tough guy challenge to "bring it on." Was Bush adequately prepared to deal with the destabilizing influence of neighboring countries like Syria and Iran? Probably not as well. Did his go-it-alone attitude in the run-up to the war come back to bite him during the occupation? Undoubtedly so.

But remember, before Bush's personality tainted the project of freeing Iraq, many voices on the left were loudly calling for Saddam's ouster. His human rights violations were legendary, his threats to regional peace and stability obvious and well founded. Saddam never lived up to his surrender agreements and wantonly crushed domestic opposition after the first Gulf War while the Americans stood by and watched—an abandonment decried by many on both left and right.

The left knew the whole sordid story of Saddam's Iraq and had spent years demanding something be done. Coups had failed. International pressure and sanctions had failed. Weapons inspections succeeded in stopping his WMD programs but failed to assure the world that he had given up all of his illegal stocks. He was slippery and ruthless and he held Iraq in an iron grip. Moreover, the awful stories about his sons didn't bode well for the future.

So what would the left have done? Would they not have taken Saddam out? Or would they simply have done a better job? Perhaps they would have supported Bush in Iraq if he hadn't made so many early blunders. This at any rate is what they want you to believe. But to me it seems highly unlikely.

Bush lied about WMD. The argument "Bush lied, people died" was ultimately about the failure to find WMD. But it was nothing more than a "gotcha" moment. Bush and his surrogates promised we would find huge stockpiles of WMD, but the search for these mythical piles of the world's worst weapons stretched from days and weeks to months and years, and none was found. Did that mean Bush lied about WMD? No. The Iraqi Perspectives Project reports—several volumes—published approximately a year after the war began, clearly revealed through documentation and interviews with former regime officials that Saddam purposely kept alive the suspicion he had WMD. He did so to protect himself from his neighbors, and to keep internal plotters in check. At a certain point early in the occupation, a reasonable person might have harbored suspicions about this highly touted justification for war, but after the Iraqi Perspectives Project reports appeared that argument should have faded away quietly. But it did not. It was a brick in the wall of lies about the war and about Bush, and the left was not taking any bricks out of their wall.

Bush lied about the Saddam–9/11 connection. This was one of the most maddening of the left's swiftboating lies. At first, it was entirely based on the conclusions of the Senate Select Committee on Intelligence (SSCI) that there was "no operational cooperation" between Saddam and bin Laden. That conclusion notably ignored the wealth of evidence detailed by both SSCI and the 9/11 Commission findings that there were many contacts between the two. It was known, for instance, that they had talked through intermediaries about offering bin Laden sanctuary in Iraq. We also saw bin Laden's emissary (Zarqawi) flee to Iraq after the American invasion of Afghanistan.

Bush and Cheney had to live with the consequences of their judgment on that information; fire-breathing Bush hater and millionaire film director Michael Moore did not. Why would the country not expect the people in charge to make the most prudent decision based on the worst possible interpretation of the facts? Didn't the left condemn Bush and Cheney for failing to imagine the worst possible scenario before 9/11? The left's lie on this point became circular. If followed logically it turned back on itself. Bush's decision to topple Saddam based on the fear of a connection with bin Laden or cooperation with other terrorist groups was entirely prudent.

One only has to imagine a world with Saddam still on his throne today to see the foolishness of the argument that he should have been left in place. Yet the left persisted in willful blindness, demanding a "smoking gun" connection of a kind that would stand up in court when no such proof was possible or necessary. Wars had been fought in the past on much flimsier pretexts.

The Plame Game: The left wallowed in the accusation that Bush and Cheney outed one of their own spies to punish a critic. Former ambassador Joseph Wilson went to Africa to investigate Saddam's attempts to acquire nuclear material on the recommendation of his wife, who worked at the CIA. His report concluded that no such transaction had occurred. Later, when Bush referred to this as an ongoing threat in a State of the Union Address, Wilson went public with his criticism, claiming he had been sent to investigate by the vice president, who ignored his information because it undercut the rationale for war. In fact his report actually *confirmed* that Saddam had sent emissaries to Niger to feel out officials there on the nuclear material in question.

The contretemps naturally led to questions about who Wilson was and who had sent him to Africa in the first place. When syndicated columnist Robert Novak broke the news that it was Wilson's wife who had suggested he be sent, her husband railed against Bush and demanded that a presidential advisor be "frog marched across the White House lawn." The law was summoned, and the vice president's chief of staff was convicted of plotting to expose an undercover operative. Media figures on the left paraded the husband around like a conquering hero.

It was all a delusion. Her husband was against the war from the beginning (read his book). His wife arranged for him to perform the investigation on behalf of the CIA, acting on a request from the vice president's office. She herself wanted the story of the nuclear material purchase knocked down. (When she described the report to her husband, she called it "this crazy idea.") As for the much-debated question, "Who outed Valerie Plame?" the answer was: nobody. Novak learned her name by looking her up in *Who's Who*. Some secret agent!

Bush wiretapped me! The left hated Bush for wiretapping and other electronic surveillance in the United States, claiming that he had declared war on civil liberties. In fact, the wiretapping and domestic surveillance lie was one of the most egregious because it took the new President Obama about ten minutes to endorse the Bush position and adopt it as his own.

I could go on but you get the idea. The rest of the sordid story is told in this book.

The orgy of left-wing Bush hatred started with Florida and the charge that an election had been stolen, but eventually it came to encompass everything, from his war to his walk.

The Florida recount actually was the opening bell in a long fight the left waged in this country to make certain no Bush action or lack of action could be seen in any but the worst possible light. But the swiftboating lies continued for two terms, and the eventual result was the rejection of anybody associated with Bush or his party. Finally an inexperienced junior senator with special skills at oratory ended the Bush era by winning the election of 2008.

The inauguration of Barack Hussein Obama as president of the United States was a day of unrivaled celebration. For the left it was both the arrival of a new president and the exit of the old.

Authoritative experts in the estimation of crowd size could not come to an agreement. But HIS Jane's, a defense analysis firm, used satellite images to place the number between 1.271 million and 1.651 million (a margin of error the size of Tulsa, Oklahoma). Suffice it to say it was a breathtaking mass of Obama idolators and Bush rejectionists. The gleaming faces stretching before Obama as he walked onto the platform that cold day must have looked as endless as an ocean.

At Washington, D.C., area airports, more than five hundred private jets had arrived for the inauguration, almost twice the number for George W. Bush's 2004 inauguration. (Evidently, carbon footprints were forgiven for the day.)

Thousands of buses rolled into the capital from all over the nation. Airports were jammed and hotels booked.

Striding to his place opposite the chief justice of the Supreme Court of the United States, Obama himself could barely suppress a grin. Both the new president and his wife were in the most fashionable of winter chic. Mrs. Obama, moments from elevation to First Lady, beamed a sunny smile in her gold Isabel Toledo dress and coat ensemble. In deference to the sensibilities of the gathered liberals, she did not wear fur.

The imminent president stood erect, chin held high, dressed in a sleek gray overcoat the Secret Service later confirmed was "bullet resistant clothing." Obama's left hand lay on the Lincoln Bible held by his wife, his right hand held high in the classic sign of oath-taking as he faced the chief justice, and in an instant became the cover of thousands of magazines worldwide.

Standing behind Obama, the *Times* of London noted, George W. Bush "didn't appear to be trying very hard to swallow a smirk" as Obama and Roberts bungled the oath of office (the next day the two enacted a hurried re-do at the White House in front of a press pool).

The world's adoring masses (2.5 billion by the estimate of the Associated Press) were focused on the transcendent and transformative inauguration of President Obama. But in complete synchronicity another narrative was coming to its final moments. For this was also the time and place of the funeral of George W. Bush.

Most in the crowd were focused on the swearing in of the new president, but a noisy group gathered up front jeered and heckled George W. Bush as he walked onto the inaugural platform. They taunted Bush and Vice President Dick Cheney with a ballyard chant—"na na na na, hey hey, good-bye"—usually reserved for a pitcher headed to the showers.

With each word of the botched oath, and each sentence of Obama's inaugural address, the left simultaneously raised him on a pedestal and lowered George W. Bush into a grave.

The funereal aspect of the event was certainly no surprise. Putting Bush on the obituary page, politically speaking, writing his epitaph, chiseling the terms of his indictment in stone, and constructing a virtual crypt for the forty-third president had become a favored passion of the media in America and Europe during the last days of the Bush administration.

While this towering edifice was quite impressive, it was also full of lies and distortions, the fruit of a long campaign to undermine a nation and grab power for the left.

Considering all that is involved, the transition of power from one chief executive to the next never fails to be executed with lightning speed. One moment George Bush is president, the next he is not. One minute Barack Obama is the hope of the world, the next he is speeding off in his presidential Escalade accompanied by a phalanx of black SUVs.

The ghost of George W. Bush flew home to Crawford, with a stop for a farewell speech in the welcoming arms of Midland, Texas. He left behind a legacy of two wars won and a country kept safe from terrorism. But in many parts of the country it was a nation that seemed not to care, the majority of citizens having been convinced that Bush and his cohorts were the worst thing ever to happen to the country, or having been simply worn down by the shouting liberals, were out of gas and could argue no more.

It was a wonder to watch the construction of Bush's tomb. The last phases of construction came in the final days of the Bush presidency, when there suddenly appeared a deluge of media commentary repeating again the well-worked themes the left had played on for Bush's two terms.

On Politico.com, a pace-setting online political news service, Matthew Dallek of the University of California's Washington Center, offered an assessment titled "History Unlikely to Be Kind to Bush." Dallek listed the failure to find WMD in Iraq, the "mission accomplished" speech, the abuses of Abu Ghraib, the post-invasion chaos in Iraq, and the deaths of more than four thousand U.S. troops and thousands of Iraqis. Despite his condemnation of the Iraq War, Dallek thought the debacle of Hurricane Katrina was going to be remembered by historians as Bush's lowest point.

Oddly, Dallek admitted the likely bias of those historians: "This president is likely to have few staunch allies at his side 20, 30, 50 years out," he cautioned. "Historians tend to be politically liberal and unsympathetic to the conservative philosophy that Bush has propounded."

The ultraliberal *Huffington Post* featured a Bush condemnation from Bob Cesca, a frequent contributor whose online bio includes credits for having "written and produced hundreds of animated shorts as well as music videos for Iron Maiden, Meat Loaf, Everclear, Yes, and Mötley Crüe": "What I recall is a litany of awful, illegal, and destructive responses to September 11 on behalf of the president. I'm thinking about extraordinary rendition, I'm thinking about Abu Ghraib and illegal invasions and interminable occupations. I'm thinking about a CIA agent tasked with tracking loose nukes [who] was outed as part of [an] effort to lie about the justifications for that invasion and occupation. I'm thinking about 35,000 American military casualties. I'm thinking about post-traumatic stress disorder. I'm thinking about a system that allowed many September 11 heroes to die of respiratory-related illnesses. I'm thinking about illegal and unconstitutional searches and seizures. I'm thinking about the USA PATRIOT Act, the Military Commission Act, and the 'terrorist surveillance program.'"

Cesca, though singularly unqualified to level such charges, was simply regurgitating the main points of the anti-Bush litany that had been drummed into the public ear for years on end. In the comments that followed, one person wrote, "As long as footage of George fleeing across country to a bunker in Nebraska exists, he'll be remembered as chicken little . . . He was hustled off to Nebraska because he was scared out of his wits."

The fact that Bob Woodward, in the first of his four bestselling books on President Bush, characterized the president's response on September 11 as informed, controlled, focused, and courageous made little difference to the Cesca types. They had a technique for dealing with information that ran counter to their theories: discredit the source, deny the information, and repeat over and over that the story had been discredited and should be dismissed.

The Nation, America's premier leftist journal, carried a piece titled "Dismantling the Imperial Presidency" by Aziz Huq of New York University. "The Bush/Cheney White House leveraged pervasive post–9/11 fears to reverse what Cheney called 'the erosion of presidential power' since Watergate. Relying on pliant Justice Department lawyers for legal cover, it put into practice a vision of executive power unconstrained by Congress or the courts. It achieved what James Madison once called the 'accumulation of all powers, legislative, executive, and judiciary, in the same hands,' which he condemned as 'the very definition of tyranny.'"

So which was it? Chicken Little or tyrant? Contradictory images at best, but the discordant note passed unnoticed.

Bush was the swaggering fool who bungled his way into a war he could not win. The scheming imperialist who drummed up an unnecessary war to dominate the Middle East and enrich his friends in the oil business. As the left proclaimed him history's first completely stupid genius, they never seemed to notice that the range of condemnations didn't always square logically, much less factually.

But it was a handy tool. Whenever President Obama had a problem, he and his captive media would just point to President Bush.

For example, in the second week of January 2009, the president-elect had to endure the humiliation of a complete 180-degree reversal on an ironclad promise. He had taken the untenable position that an African American lawyer and public servant from Illinois named Roland Burris could not carry out a lawful appointment to the United States Senate.

Quickly, Burris embarrassed Senate majority leader Harry Reid into sitting down for a meeting. Reid publicly changed his mind about whether Burris could be seated. Obama sheepishly announced he was backing off his opposition. Howard Fineman wrote in *Newsweek* that Obama was going through a "bumpy start," that the Obama operatives "look dumb and Obama looks weak."

The very same day, the leftist Salon.com ran to Obama's aid with a piece called "W. and The Damage Done." Obama hits a bad note, a chorus of voices blames Bush.

This particular piece, by Vincent Rossmeier and Gabriel Winant, set its tone in the first paragraph: "President Bush inherited a peaceful, prosperous America. As he exits, Salon consults experts in seven fields to try to assess the devastation." Sounding as jaunty and precocious as university upperclassmen, they wrote, "When George W. Bush entered the White House in January 2001, he inherited peace and prosperity. The military, the Constitution, and New Orleans were intact and the country had a budget surplus of $128 billion. Now he's about to dash out the door, leaving a large, unpaid bill for his successors to pay."

It was a familiar formulation. Bush came to office and, like the drunk he used to be, just blew all the money.

The authors also counted as "damage done" the effects of waterboarding Khalid Sheikh Mohammad, mastermind of 9/11. "One of President Obama's important early tasks will be dismantling the culture of Abu Ghraib and Guantánamo, the web of white papers and executive orders that jeopardized habeas corpus and allowed—encouraged—torture." Karen Greenberg, executive director of New York University's Center on Law and Security, was quoted as saying, "the stain on America's reputation among foreigners and, for that matter, Americans, *can never be removed*" (emphasis added) and further that it was all for "little or no gain."

Actually, the gain from waterboarding KSM was enormous. He revealed active plots against the United States, including a plan to crash a hijacked airliner into the Library Tower in Los Angeles, a near duplicate of 9/11 that could have killed thousands. But in the left's world, that was "no gain."

A Salon reader named Dick Dworkin wrote: "I'll give Bush one mitigating factor though: almost half the country is as stupid, incompetent, and malevolent as he is, so he can't take all the blame." This was a rare admission. The left despises the people who thought Bush was doing the right thing, they hated those people who voted for Bush twice, they wanted to slander and insult them as much as they had heaped abuse on Bush. Yet, at the same time, these were the very people they were trying to bring over to the anti-Bush, anti-war side. Consequently, Dworkin's revelation was to remain the left's dirty little secret: They not only didn't like America, they didn't like the American people.

The last few days of the Bush administration called for a series of "exit interviews" by George W. Bush, Dick Cheney, and Laura Bush. Each was asked how history would judge the Bush presidency. All three opined that history would laud the overall achievements of the past eight years, even while noting the mistakes. Mr. Cheney offered perhaps the most stubborn defense of all things Bush, even more than the always-loyal wife.

These interviews provided fresh energy and ammunition for hammering Bush, and any and all who thought like him, especially those who agreed that it was a major accomplishment to have kept the country safe since 9/11.

At Bush's last news conference, a week before he was to leave office, he was asked—repeatedly—to reflect on the errors, the mistakes of his administration. Wrote Dana Milbank of the *Washington Post*, "He spoke as though he were an innocent bystander, watching the mishaps rather than having any culpability for them. To Bush, they were not mistakes—just disappointments."

The reporter's knowing, rueful, headshaking attitude—condescending and mock sympathetic—was to let right-thinking readers know that he agreed with them. Bush's disasters were obvious to all but Bush. Media types like Milbank were aghast at the gall of the war criminal actually offering a not-guilty plea.

Arianna Huffington, proprietress of the far-left *Huffington Post*, headlined her article on Bush's final news conference, "Still Delusional After All These Years." "Yes, he made tough decisions," she wrote. "But what is the value in that if the decisions you make are consistently wrong? And Bush has made the wrong decisions again and again and again." Ms. Huffington was one of those who had confidently declared the surge in Iraq would never work. She gave herself a pass for being wrong about that, and so much more. Owning a Web site allows you to do that.

A big problem with the left's attempt to set its narrative in stone are the facts: The war in Iraq succeeded, and the nation had been kept safe from terrorists by the use of the very techniques the left condemned—wiretapping, renditions, detention centers, enhanced interrogation, and the aggressive use of lethal force.

This campaign of rage against success left one major question unanswered: Why? Why would the left want to deny the obvious benefits of success? As Bush exchanged places with Obama in the Oval Office, Iraqis were taking over their country; an agreement with the United States government called for American troops to be out of Baghdad within six months. Death pits like Fallujah were in the control of Iraqi authorities and so calm that the marines were already pulling up stakes and going home, or more likely headed to Afghanistan to hunt for al Qaeda.

One has to wonder what was the point of cheering for an American loss in Iraq, and when the news was unexpectedly good, arguing that a win is not a win, and success is an actual loss.

Under Bush, the left maintained that government was bad, and was unrestrained in its condemnation. But as soon as Obama became president, it was instantly patriotic to believe in the benign power of government. Neil Cavuto of Fox News interviewed young Democrat "strategist" Alicia Menendez shortly after Obama's elevation to office about why she placed so much faith in government intervention in the economy. "Of course I believe in the government," she snapped. "I'm a patriot!"

Where was this patriot during the years when Bush was struggling to win a war and keep the country safe in the teeth of fierce domestic opposition? Undoubtedly, she was at her keyboard or at a left-wing meet up condemning America for its crimes and calling for the prosecution of the arch-fiends Bush and Cheney.

All of this was done for the very worst of reasons: the politics of partisan destruction.

The takeaway from the '04 elections had not been that the left was wrong in its arguments, but that it needed a few more years to let the arguments sink in. The notion revolved around inevitability: if we keep repeating these lies the American people will eventually believe them. Revulsion against Bush and the GOP will sweep the land and we can seize political power.

Unfortunately for the rest of us, it worked.

C h a p t e r   T w o

Bush Was No Churchill. Seriously, He Can't Talk. So What?

E very president becomes the butt of jokes by late-night comics, but George W. Bush held a special place in that pantheon of greats. Cheney, Gore, and Bill Clinton were also treated as piñatas filled with laughs. Hit them and funny falls out. There were crucial thematic differences, however. Clinton jokes were about sex, Gore jokes were about losing the election, gaining weight, and growing a beard, and Cheney jokes were about the sense of threat he seemed to emanate.

But with Bush it was different. In his case, the president of the United States was characterized through national—international—humor in two phases: first as stupid, second as suffering from dementia.

No question, much of the slavering derived from Bush's own fumbling words. Jacob Weisberg of *Slate* has created a small shelf of books on Bush's gaffes, malapropisms, spoonerisms, and sentences that resist all attempts to diagram.

There are hundreds, perhaps thousands of examples, and it is near impossible to repeat even a substantial number of them. But let us take just one page of one of Weisberg's dozen "Bushisms" books (evidently a thriving subset of the publishing industry). Here is page 18 of *Bushisms: the Deluxe Post Election-Edition*, published in 2004 by Fireside Books:

"There's no question that the minute I got elected, the storm clouds on the horizon were getting nearly directly overhead."
—Washington, D.C., May 11, 2001

"One of the common denominators I have found is that expectations rise about that which is expected."
—Los Angeles, California, September 27, 2000

"Never again in the halls of Washington, D.C., do I want to have to make explanations that I can't explain."
—Portland, Oregon, October 31, 2000

"Brie and cheese."
—To reporters, on what he imagines reporters eat, Crawford, Texas, August 23, 2001

"Will the highways on the Internet become more few?"
—Concord, New Hampshire, January 29, 2000

"I hope we get to the bottom of the answer. It's what I'm interested to know."
—As quoted by the Associated Press, April 26, 2000

Admittedly, Weisberg's books are slim volumes of about a hundred pages, bulked up with jokey pictures of Bush. Nonetheless there is no credible argument that Weisberg charged Bush with an offense he did not commit multiple times.

Suffice it to say the late-night comics, with armies of talented writers, had an eight-year romp, dragging Bush around like a toy doll.

David Letterman: "Political pundits are saying President George W. Bush has made gains in two key states: dazed and confused."

The "Bush is stupid" theme was given international status six days into the first Bush term when Fidel Castro fired a rhetorical shot at the new occupant of the White House by saying he hoped the new president "is not as stupid as he seems."

"Someone very strange, with very little promise," Castro said in a speech to his impoverished nation, "has taken charge of the leadership of the great empire we have as a neighbor."

The Associated Press report datelined Havana further quoted Castro: "That gentleman has arrived there, and hopefully he is not as stupid as he seems, not as mafia-like as his background makes him appear."

Stupid—comedy writers demonstrated they could work with that.

Jokes came slowly after 9/11, and a sharp-eyed observer might have noticed a bit of comedic timidity at the time of the "Shock and Awe" invasion of Iraq. But once the war became a national irritant, dragging on months and years after it should have been over, the idea that crept into the jokes about Bush was, well, okay, if President Bush is really as stupid as people say, then his ideas, his initiatives, his strategies and tactics must be stupid, too. To put it algebraically: Stupid=Bush=War=Stupid.

During a town hall meeting in Orlando, Florida, on December 4, 2001, Bush described his first reaction to the report that a plane had hit the World Trade Center on September 11: "There's one terrible pilot."

The correct construction for authentic and true West Texas patois would have been, "There's one *sorry* pilot." Bush actually prettied the quote up for the national audience, but he might as well have not bothered.

The president spoke on Earth Day 2002, in Wilmington, N.Y.: "Some of our biggest sources of air pollution are the power plants, which send tons of admissions into our air."

Admissions for emissions? A "terrible" pilot on 9/11? The left cried, *he's a moron*!

David Letterman: "President Bush says he is looking forward to the testimony of Condoleezza Rice. Yes, he is very excited about Condoleezza Rice's testimony before Congress. Well, it makes perfect sense—he wants to know what's going on, too."

Jokes are meant to be funny, and every president finds his way into the monologues of David Letterman, Jay Leno, Conan O'Brien, Bill Maher, Craig Kilborn, and the rest. But occasionally the audience can tell that the person telling the joke really means it.

Bush didn't help himself by creating a library of fractured language, and the occasional quip that seemed to reveal the real man—a president who might not possess the attention to detail and the long-range vision he needed to function in a manner that the public would approve. The natural authority and respect for the president began to erode as over a couple of important years Bush began to appear to many Americans as a stubborn, bullheaded man who didn't seem to seek out information or give reflective thought to his decisions.

It is a quote that has become lore, but he really did say that his whole life he had been "misunderestimated."

Asked by a reporter shortly after the fall of Baghdad what his message to the Iraqi people would be: "You're free. And freedom is beautiful. And, you know, it'll take time to restore chaos and order . . ."

June 2003, the president aboard Air Force One: "I'm also not very analytical. You know, I don't spend a lot of time thinking about myself, about why I do things."

In August 2004, *New York Times* reporter Jason Zengerle surveyed the field of Bush jokes and came to a conclusion that should have been more than a little alarming. "To mangle a presidential line," Zengerle wrote, "the state of the George W. Bush joke is *mean* and *partisan*." (Emphasis added.)

Bill Maher: "Bush bragged that more Iraqis say their country is on the right track than Americans say our country is on the right track. Boy, there's a campaign slogan for you—'America: More F*cked up than Fallujah!'"

The *Times* reporter was on to something, and it played out in a big way over the next four years. According to Zengerle, jokes about G. W. Bush became much harsher than jokes about his father, or about Bill Clinton, or even about the early days of Bush's own administration, when he was played as a simple dunce who often stumbled when he spoke. "Now many Bush jokes portray the president as an irresponsible, duplicitous menace," Zengerle observed.

Why? Times change, the war had become worse, but most of all, reported Zengerle, "since Mr. Bush took office, the left has belatedly rediscovered humor as a political tool."

You can put something together with a tool or take it apart. This tool was used to take Bush apart, bolt by bolt, until there was nothing left but a pile of parts.

Proving he could gaffe more than once in the same month, in August 2004, the president was speaking in Washington, D.C., to Pentagon brass: "Our enemies are innovative and resourceful, and so are we. They never stop thinking about new ways to harm our country and our people, and neither do we."

The college-educated left was incredulous. Did he even listen to himself?

The president sat for an interview with Brit Hume of the Fox News Channel: "I appreciate people's opinions, but I'm more interested in news. And the best way to get the news is from objective sources. And the most objective sources I have are people on my staff who tell me what's happening in the world."

After his reelection victory in November 2004: "With the campaign over, Americans are expecting a bipartisan effort and results. I'll reach out to everyone who shares our goals."

To the left and the media—growing closer by the moment—the president had brought his "with-us-or-against-us" approach to the war on terror home to domestic politics. If you agree with me, we can work together; if not . . . we won't.

Best of all for his opponents, the president could gaffe himself on almost any subject. Appearing before a crowd of nearly twenty thousand in Poplar Bluff, Missouri, he said: "We've got an issue in America. Too many good docs are getting out of business. Too many OB/GYNs aren't able to practice their love with women all across this country."

As the 2004 election approached, the left was sure that John Kerry would win. After all, he was so thoughtful, so articulate, so smart. How could the idiot Bush defeat this charming and athletic war hero with the Kennedy good looks?

John Vinocur, a veteran of the *International Herald Tribune* (a *New York Times*–owned paper), went to Florida just before the election and concluded the Redneck Riviera was fairly typical of a Bush-supporting area. Could Kerry win without these people? Could Kerry get the "stupid" vote?

Apparently not. Bush was reelected with a handy margin, and the left and the media went into a spasm of outrage and grief. Many spoke of moving to Canada or Europe. Others set out to analyze and interpret the election results, leading many to conclude that America itself was a foreign country.

Neal Starkman of the *Seattle Post-Intelligencer*, writing just after Bush's second inauguration, said that a mysterious S factor explained Bush's popularity.

Bush's voters had confounded the writer. "What can account for so many people being so supportive of the president?"

It was not so much that Bush was stupid, Starkman said, but that Bush *voters* were stupid. "It's the 'Stupid Factor,' the S factor: Some people—sometimes through no fault of their own—are just not very bright.

"The people I'm referring to cannot understand the phenomenon of cause and effect. They're perplexed by issues comprising more than two sides. They don't have the wherewithal to expand the sources of their information. And above all—far above all—they don't think." He suggested an intelligence test to earn the right to vote.

The University of Connecticut's *Daily Campus* newspaper published a letter from an alumnus responding to another reader, whose own letter had objected to calling George W. Bush "an idiot."

The writer, Peter Carney, quoted "the immortal Forrest Gump, to wit: 'Stupid is as stupid does.' Following this logic, Bush definitely qualifies as 'stupid.'"

An online business was selling bumper stickers that declared "Bush is stupid spelled backwards."

The Web site eHow.com offered five easy lessons on how to talk like George W. Bush. One through four involved adopting a southern drawl, using phrases like "y'all," making certain to mix metaphors and scramble idioms, and forgetting every rule of grammar. The last was the most important: "Speak with confidence. If there is one positive aspect about George W. Bush's speech it is that he speaks naturally and with confidence."

Confidence was, indeed, the very essence of Bush's linguistic troubles. He never mumbled a mistake; they were always full throated and confident. "We cannot let terrorists and rogue nations," he said in Des Moines, Iowa, "hold this nation hostile or hold our allies hostile."

A sense of the degree to which saying "Bush is stupid" had become the norm occurred early and often, as well as very late in the game. On February 13, 2008, the NBC Network News president, and the president of its sister network, MSNBC, allowed Keith Olbermann to go on the air and say the following under the aegis of the NBC peacock:

"This, Mr. Bush, is simple enough even for you to understand. . . . You're a fascist—get them to print you a T-shirt with 'fascist' on it!"

Olbermann not only called the president an extremely derogatory name, but also assumed he was too stupid to know what it meant.

Olbermann spoke those words on network television in prime time and it might as well have been the official position of the parent company of NBC, General Electric. The pulse of the nation had evidently been taken in the highest offices at NBC and GE, and their executives saw nothing remarkable about the statement. This was the same network that at one time in its history had taken a major star off the air for saying the words "water closet." In fifty years the network had traveled from not being able to say the name of the thing one pisses in, to letting its anchors piss on the president of the United States.

In January 2005, while aboard Air Force One, Bush was asked why the United States hadn't yet captured Osama bin Laden. "Because he's hiding," Bush replied.

The way the left and the media played it, the president's grasp of the weighty issues before him and his commanders seemed so tenuous as to constitute no grasp at all.

In May 2005, while pushing for Social Security reform: "See, in my line of work, you got to keep repeating things over and over and over again for the truth to sink in, to kind of catapult the propaganda."

If he had been speaking of his political opponents, it would have been an incisive observation; but as he was speaking of himself, it was yet another foot in the same mouth.

Was that botched line really a slip of the tongue that revealed that the president was trying to pull one over on the public? Doubtful, but the left took every opportunity to interpret each mangled sentence in the worst possible light.

In fact, almost all the jokes and the intellectual criticism about Bush were taken from something he actually said. "More and more of our imports are coming from overseas," and, "After all, religion has been around a lot longer than Darwinism," and, "Rarely is the question asked: Is our children learning?" and, "It's clearly a budget. It's got a lot of numbers in it."

On occasion Bush mangled a sentence, provoking laughter or derision from the left over a thought that was perfectly normal and rational. In April 2006, he was asked about the criticism coming at him over the conduct of the war, which seemed to be stuck in a ditch. "I hear the voices, and I read the front page, and I know the speculation. But I'm the decider, and I decide what's best."

Explaining "the buck stops here," like many presidents before him, Bush invented yet another new word, and managed to make himself sound like a simpleton with dictatorial aspirations.

The president sat for a series of interviews with Bob Woodward, which were published in four bestselling books on the Iraq War: "I'm the commander—see, I don't need to explain—I do not need to explain why I say things. That's the interesting thing about being the president. Maybe somebody needs to explain to me why they say something, but I don't feel like I owe anybody an explanation."

Horror! He thinks he's king!

When it came to hashing his own words, backfiring himself into odd linguistic corners, Bush was The Natural. His syntax seemed to spring from the authentic sound, cadence, and colorful vocabulary of West Texas, but richly out of place when forced into the tight shoes of international diplomatic and political messages.

"First, we would not accept a treaty that would not have been ratified, nor a treaty that I thought made sense for the country," he remarked about the Kyoto accord in an interview with the *Washington Post*.

There were occasions when the garble was 100 percent complete, total, wall-to-wall: "Redefining the role of the United States from enablers to keep the peace to enablers to keep the peace from peacekeepers is going to be an assignment." There is a way to read that sentence to shake out the meaning, but most people wouldn't even try.

It became a case of stupid is as stupid does. Bush was stupid, therefore the war was stupid; but wars can't be merely stupid, so instead such a war must be wrong, and a tragic blunder, perhaps even a war crime. On the eve of the Obama inauguration Keith Olbermann was imploring the new president on national television to prosecute George W. Bush.

To the ever growing number of Bush haters, the original sin was always his abuse of language. If a president can't communicate his meaning clearly, how can he lead a nation to war, maintain public support through difficult times, and persuade our allies to stay the course?

. . . .

TO BE SURE, the "Bush is stupid" narrative arose out of the president's unusual gift for shredding language. But it also served a higher purpose when the left needed to hammer down a rationale for opposing the war: the president is stupid, he made a stupid mistake going to war, he is too stupid to see how bad it is, he is too stupid to notice he's losing, and he's too stupid (and stubborn) to get us out.

The president's fractured tongue thus became a handy weapon in the left's war against the war. Whatever else might be said about why the war was good and right, one only had to point to the "stupid" president who ordered it to prove that it was, on its face, wrong, a blunder, a bungle, a mistake, an error, and as the years and the casualties piled up, a catastrophic disaster.

And the cancer spread to whatever President Bush said. In 2007, Keith Olbermann felt free to take to the airwaves of MSNBC and rail about a recent warning from Bush on Iran's drive to build nuclear weapons, coupled with an obscure government report that Iran would need years to accomplish the nuke bomb project.

"We have either a president who is too dishonest to restrain himself from invoking World War III about Iran at least six weeks after he had to have known that the analogy would be fantastic, irresponsible hyperbole, or we have a president too transcendently stupid not to have asked, at what now appears to have been a series of opportunities to do so, whether the fairy tales he either created or was fed were still even remotely plausible.

"A pathological presidential liar, or an idiot in chief. It is the nightmare scenario of political science fiction."

Olbermann's manner of delivery was to thunder the words, rattling the lightbulbs. A tone of absolute certainty contributed mightily to his denunciations. Of course, sixteen months later when President Obama's intelligence services reported it would be difficult if not impossible to stop Iran's drive for a nuclear weapon, Olbermann remained silent. There was no point. The damage was done, and Olbermann and NBC operated on a hit-and-run philosophy anyway.

The left had been *en fuego* about Bush's deficiencies for years. Just before the 2006 elections the comments pages on the Dailykos Web site were raging with anger. "Idiot, sociopath, lying asshole, all of the above. We're stuck with this monster for two more years plus five months, and I agree there's nothing funny about that," said *Lyingeyes*, a nom de blog flame, Daily Kos, August 25, 2006.

"Angry toy robot, meat puppet. That says it all. Bush is that, and he is tired of being Rove's meat puppet . . . but a helpless sack of bolts nonetheless. My theory is that, like all men above their heads, he knows that he is out of his depth and really doesn't want the job anymore. It is hard to wake up and face your incompetence every day . . ." said *vivdarkbloom*, the same day.

The rage on the left about George W. Bush was a bubbling font that seemed to gurgle up from angry depths without end. To that end, Bush's uncomfortable relationship with his own native language became a useful political strategy, or as Bush once put it, *strategery*. It was not just that Bush mangled the language, it was that the mangled language exposed something deeper and more important about Bush. There was a great deal of argument about precisely what that was, but in the end the explanation always returned to the war. Bush's stupidity, paraded before us every time he spoke, was the real reason why the country had been dragged into a mistaken and disastrous war.

People who spoke well were intelligent and made good, unassailable decisions. People who did not speak well were stupid and made idiotic decisions. This was the conclusion the left wanted the public to draw from listening to George W. Bush hack away at a sentence, while watching his war go badly wrong.

It was a free-floating observation, apropos of nothing. But in the aftermath of 9/11, when the Bush administration launched an invasion to remove Saddam Hussein from power, the left adopted Castro's criticism of Bush, and honed it to a razor's edge. Nowhere were the attacks sharper than overseas.

The chairman of the Arab Psychiatrists Association, Dr. Adel Sadek, who was also head of the Department of Psychiatry at Ein Shams University in Cairo, wrote an open letter to President Bush in the Egyptian newspaper *Hadith al-Madina*, and repeated his charges in subsequent Arabic language television interviews.

"Although you invest a lot of effort in proving yourself, you are not successful in doing so because you are stupid and understand nothing about what is happening in the world. 'Stupidity' and 'idiocy' are synonyms and if you don't like the word 'stupid,' you are an evil person with an ugly soul," Dr. Sadek wrote. "I equate your stupidity with mercilessness and inhumanity, and swear that I knew you were stupid long before it became known to the entire world," he continued. "Your stupidity is reflected in your facial features. Your face reminds me of the face of those who frequent a clinic for the mentally retarded. Your gaze is mindless and unfocused. Your eyes are misleading. Your facial expressions are incompatible with the matter (being discussed), and your tone of voice is completely disconnected from the content of your words—a salient characteristic of the mentally retarded."

Interviewed later on the Saudi-Egyptian satellite channel Iqraa, Dr. Sadek repeated these slurs against Bush, and discussed his more favorable view of *suicide bombers*. "When the martyr dies a martyr's death, he attains the height of bliss. As a professional psychiatrist, I say that the height of bliss comes with the end of the countdown: ten, nine, eight, seven, six, five, four, three, two, one. And then, you press the button to blow yourself up. When the martyr reaches 'one,' and then 'boom,' he explodes and senses himself flying, because he knows for certain that he is not dead."

Dr. Sadek may have lost some of his following in the West by illuminating his thinking on suicide bombers, but the theme that Bush was unforgivably dumb was nonetheless quite popular overseas.

In Britain, the *Independent* newspaper published an opinion piece by Joan Smith in which she declared: "The man is stupid.

"He is nowhere near as stupid as he seems, I have been told, a proposition that has some force solely because it is hard to imagine any world leader being afflicted with quite the degree of bovine incomprehension that the president habitually displays," Ms. Smith wrote.

His defenders, Ms. Smith thought, were ignoring his "bovine incomprehension." He was as stupid as a cow, and anybody could, or should, see it. Bush didn't know what was happening in his own presidency. Bush can't speak English. Bush reveals himself as insensitive or thoughtless. Bush reveals himself as arrogant, power addicted. Bush tells the world it is dealing with a shallow thinker.

The worst of the "stupid" insults stood in a category by itself. Shortly after the Bush victory in 2000, contested immediately of course, and a source of endless bitterness on the left for years, a site called "Bush or Chimp?" popped up on the Web. By 2004 the propri-etor of the site boasted "Bushorchimp?" had been featured on CNN, MSNBC, the UK's Channel 4, BBC Radio, in magazines such as *Es-quire, Maxim, TV Guide, Der Spiegel,* and newspapers such as the *Village Voice,* the *San Francisco Chronicle,* and the UK's *Guardian.* The chimp theme proved extremely popular. Google amassed over 5 million hits on the words "Bush chimp." Entrepreneurial types quickly began to spread and monetize the concept.

An anti-Bush Web site popped up called "The Smirking Chimp—Chronicles of the Bush Administration," criticizing the president for any number of his alleged offenses. Calling Bush a chimp, or just renaming him "Chimpy," became standard left jargon.

A person calling him/herself "Radicallyrightsradicallywrong" posted a question on the leftist Web site ThinkProgress in March 2008 that demonstrated how the "Chimp" idiom had become part of the normal vocabulary of the left: "Didn't Chimpy say, 'We listen to the commanders in the field . . .'? Yep, he listens to them and fires the ones that disagree with his asinine policies."

In September 2007, the *Huffington Post* ran a column by Philip Slater, a professor of sociology, called "New Scientific Study Reveals Bush is a Chimp." Professor Slater was a little late to the game, as Bush had been called a chimp, and pictured side by side with chimps to prove he was really, honestly a chimp for the past seven years; but slow-footedness in the thinking department was not about to stop him. "A new study reported in *Science* found that while chimps and orangs could count and add as well as human children, only humans were able to learn by watching others and seeing how they do things," Slater wrote. "Prior to reading this new study I was under the mistaken impression that Bush was a parrot, because of his ap-parent inability to say anything about Iraq except 'progress is being made,' which he repeats mechanically every time the topic is raised. But now the scales have fallen from my eyes. Bush is a chimp. It seems so obvious now, watching him speak."

Professor Slater was writing at a moment when, in fact, Bush was being proved right in his oft-repeated statements: progress *was* being made in Iraq, and it was beginning to be obvious. His Bush-as-chimp claim came at the precise moment that people who actually watched what was happening in Iraq saw the turn against al Qaeda, and the growing success of the strategy that ended the Sunni uprising, and the Shia sectarian killings. But no matter. Bush was still a chimp.

As a later contretemps over a *New York Post* editorial cartoon amply demonstrated, call Bush's successor a chimp and the case against you as an outright racist is open and shut. But with Bush it was just fine.

The chimp theme seemed downright masturbatory in its popularity: a great deal of pleasure seemed to be derived from stroking the same metaphor over and over. A Web site called "Totallylookslike" posted a split screen picture of Bush and a chimpanzee (there are literally thousands of such posts on various Web sites), and a commenter who called himself Lethal Larry said, "Thank god I live in Canada—we've never yet elected an *evil retard* as our national leader. . . ."

Somehow Lethal Larry let Jean Chretien slip his mind. But chalk it up to seething hatred for the American president.

That particular occasion in which Bush was called an "evil retard" was only one of many. A scruffy British music video host named Russell Brand called President Bush a "retarded cowboy" at the 2008 Grammy Awards, shown on national television, and after an initial round of shock, Brand was hailed by the left media as a hero and truth teller.

Portraying Bush as a chimpanzee was fairly common in editorial cartoons, in newspapers as varied as the *Guardian* in Britain, and the *Hartford Courant* in the United States. People who were fond of the "Bush equals chimp" narrative could buy a "Hail to the Chimp" T-shirt, and Bush depictions as a chimpanzee could be purchased as bumper stickers, lapel buttons, and frame-ready art.

What was the purpose of portraying Bush as a chimpanzee? Of course, it was to convince more and more people that not only didn't he think, he couldn't think. Worse, you Americans elected a chimp! Repent! Change your ways! Abandon the path of doom!

In the second Bush term, the "Bush is Stupid" or "Bush is a Chimp" narrative in both criticism and humor changed to a much darker hue, revealing a much more vibrant and serious criticism. Bush was now morphing into a seriously ill man in the onset of a degenerating mind.

Bush was portrayed in other articles as a man with early onset dementia; debates were held online and in newsprint about whether Bush was stupid or evil. Evil often edged out stupid, though there wasn't much argument against the proposition he was stupid; it's just that evil seemed to fit him so much better.

It was getting to be quite a long indictment. But the left was not done.

Bush was attacked for comparing his situation in Iraq to that of Lincoln in the American Civil War. The same leftists who spent weeks babbling on about how "Lincolnesque" Obama was practically spit fire when Bush made a light and passing comparison of his situation to that of Lincoln.

By the way, Bush was not at all off base in making this comparison. Not only did Lincoln, like Bush, hold firm to his goal of defeating the South in the face of fierce political resistance at home and abroad, but he, too, was compared to an ape and subjected to withering scorn and condemnation in the opposition press.

ALSO ON THE Bush-hating radar were those who diagnosed Bush from afar and detected signs of an actual medical condition that would account for his difficulty with words. Both dyslexia and dementia were thrown around as diagnoses by experts and clinicians who examined the president from a great distance.

Bush Hatred, which Dr. Charles Krauthammer aptly named "Bush Derangement Syndrome," was a river with four main tributaries.

At first, as shown previously, was the simple narrative that somehow or other the country had elected a dunce, somebody with low-wattage brain power, who was comically but irrefutably stupid.

The second was the notion propounded by Bush's self-appointed language cop, Jacob Weisberg. This notion was unique to Weisberg and it held that Bush was not stupid at all, but in fact fairly intelligent. The evidence was his success at Harvard Business School, which was not as tough as many academic institutions, but wasn't easy either. Instead, Weisberg posited, Bush *chose* to be ignorant. It was Bush's choice to ignore information that would inform his decisions, to not seek out difficult contradictions and wrestle with weighty decisions. Bush was lazy about being smart, and he rejected as elitist any outward show of intelligence. This theory, which uncharitably cast Bush as the nation's most slothful president, might have gained some currency on the left. Ultimately it did not, and the most likely reason was it was just not nasty enough.

A third theory held that Bush's self-professed Christian faith explained why he seemed high-handed and dictatorial (though it would not, admittedly, explain his broken sentences). In this scenario, Bush saw himself as the hand of God, intuitively confident his decisions were correct and not open to the slightest questioning from himself or anyone else.

The final and most troubling theory held that Bush's destruction of the language was a sign of a diagnosable degenerative medical condition, most likely pre-senile dementia.

People only had to search "Bush Can't Talk" and the videos of Bush mangling sentences popped up for endless amateur diagnosticians.

The president is on video saying; "I know how hard it is for you to put food on your family." And, "I know that the human being and fish can coexist peacefully." And, "Rarely is the question asked, are . . ." pause, "is our children learning?" Years of such wildly off-the-mark sentences began to suggest something ominously wrong with the president.

As far back as the 2000 campaign, best-selling author Gail Sheehy had written in a *Vanity Fair* article that all signs pointed toward a diagnosis of dyslexia. She quoted a dyslexia expert from Houston, Texas, named Nancy LaFevers as saying, "The errors you've heard Governor Bush make are consistent with dyslexia."

Governor Bush's campaign denied the charge. The experts pointed out that such disorders are genetic, and there is a history in the Bush family. (George W.'s brother Neil is dyslexic.)

In 2004, in advance of the presidential campaign, *BusinessWeek* published an article reporting the analysis of learning-disability experts who had examined the war the president seemed to have been conducting with the English language. Their conclusion: He might need to come in for an appointment. "Ample signs indicate that something unusual is going on in the left side of his brain, where language and hearing are processed."

Clinicians thought there was at least the possibility that he suffered from some dysfunction in the way he hears words, the way he processes what he hears, or the way he retrieves words when he tries to speak. When a patient uses the wrong word, commits malapropisms, and has difficulty with grammatical sentences, neuropsychologist William Stixrud said, "Typically [we] suspect at least a subtle language disorder."

The author of the *BusinessWeek* article, Stan Crock, said he suspected another condition, called central auditory processing disorder (CAPD), which he'd heard about from the family of a sufferer.

CAPD was not a recognized formal diagnosis, but the article asserted that the telltale signs pointed to George W. Bush: confusion of similar sounding words, terse communications, better hearing when watching the speaker, and trouble hearing when it's noisy.

The article reported that what experts seemed to agree on is that "Bush exhibits 'phonological' problems, which is difficulty breaking apart and putting together the discrete sounds that make up words." Crock concluded, "[Bush's] professed distaste for nuance could stem from an inability to process *the complex sides of an issue.*"

The dyslexia theory actually made a reappearance in book form, *The Dyslexicon of George W. Bush*, by Mark Crispin Miller. In it, the author examined the many language problems of the president and asked the question: How did someone like George W. Bush get to be president of the United States?

Miller's answer was off script, straying from the diagnosis of medical problems. He blamed television, a medium that he said creates a "corporate version of dyslexia . . . by showing us one thing and telling us another. Those who just can't buy it feel as if they must be going crazy, what with all those smooth authoritative voices claiming that this man should be our president—when we can see, and have seen all along, that this is simply not the case."

Long-distance psychiatry was practiced on George W. Bush repeatedly, by anybody who could connect a computer to the Internet.

On a Web site devoted to issues relating to Vietnam veterans and assorted fringe political causes, a review was published of two books: *Bush on the Couch* by Justin A. Frank, M.D., clinical professor, Department of Psychiatry, George Washington University, and *The Superpower Syndrome* by Robert Jay Lifton, M.D., distinguished visiting professor of psychology and psychiatry, Harvard University.

The reviewer was Jack Dresser, Ph.D., who claimed many years' experience as a military psychologist. Upon reviewing the work of the two authors, Dresser diagnosed Bush with adult attention deficit hyperactivity disorder (ADHD). "Easily mistaken for resoluteness, Mr. Bush's impulsiveness, snap decisions, and disinterest in abstractions or complexities are all suggestive of adult ADHD."

Dr. Dresser also noticed "continuing indications of dyslexia" and quoted a colleague who observed, "He may seem decisive, but his behavior represents the fallback position of someone trying to manage the anxiety of not being able to think clearly."

Dresser identified a variant in Bush's form of the language disorder, which he called defensive dyslexia: "Mr. Bush has learned to use his legendary difficulties with language to avoid meaningful communication, to obfuscate meanings for tactical concealment. Unable to think and communicate with language in normal ways, he has learned to use it manipulatively—to attack, dismiss, distract and intimidate, to control rather than communicate with others. Most alarming is his genuine inability to think clearly and to develop cognitive models that even remotely match the complex realities for which he is responsible."

For this long-distance clinician (Dr. Dresser never claimed to have met or examined President Bush), the ultimate sign of a mental disorder was "the smirk."

Dresser asserted Bush's reactive smile, "the smirk," which he called one of Mr. Bush's characteristic expressions, "is a telltale indication of sadism. It reveals pleasure in inflicting or observing pain, defeat, or discomfort in others while attempting to suppress more overt and unbecoming expressions of his pleasure. He is a profoundly angry, destructive man who, in Dr. Frank's words, 'needs to break things.'"

CAPD, dyslexia, ADHD, sadism—it was heavy stuff. Nonetheless others upped the ante to a pathological condition.

At the time of one of the Bush-Kerry debates in the fall of 2004, the author James Fallows had written in the *Atlantic Monthly* that he had noticed a deterioration in Bush's ability to string a sentence together over the past decade, and wondered about some undiagnosed organic condition.

In response to the Fallows article, Dr. Joseph M. Price of Michigan wrote a letter to the *Atlantic* editor suggesting, "pre-senile dementia runs about the same course as typical senile dementias, such as classical Alzheimer's—to incapacitation and, eventually, death, as with President Ronald Reagan, but at a relatively earlier age."

Dr. Price elaborated: "Bush's 'mangled' words are a demonstration of what physicians call 'confabulation,' and are almost specific to diagnosis of a true dementia."

Price helpfully offered some advice: "Bush should immediately be given the advantage of a considered professional diagnosis and started on drugs that offer the possibility of retarding the slow but inexorable course of the disease."

Others picked up the theme, which was batted around in the press in a lively debate that centered on the notion that the president of the United States was going mad from wormholes in the brain.

What could be worse than that? It might seem that the president of the United States, afflicted as though he had mad cow disease, would be, well, out there. But there was actually an even more serious accusation arising out of Bush's marble-mouthed English.

Author Ron Suskind published a long piece in the *New York Times Magazine* in October 2004, with a completely different theory of what was wrong with George W. Bush. The president, Suskind concluded, believed he was on a mission from God.

Suskind quoted Bruce Bartlett, a former Reagan advisor, who said Bush was convinced that God had told him to do certain things, and that was why Bush was so indifferent to the ideas of others, or additional information that might bolster his judgment when making decisions.

"This is why George W. Bush is so clear-eyed about al Qaeda and the Islamic fundamentalist enemy. He believes you have to kill them all. They can't be persuaded, they're extremists, driven by a dark vision. He understands them, because he's just like them," Bartlett said.

Suskind said of Bush, "He has created the faith-based presidency."

"This is the one key feature of the faith-based presidency," Suskind wrote. "Open dialogue, based on facts, is not seen as something of inherent value. It may, in fact, create doubt, which undercuts faith. It could result in a loss of confidence in the decisions-maker and, just as important, by the decision-maker. Nothing could be more vital, whether staying on message with the voters or the terrorists."

Bush, said Suskind, has insisted others have the same faith in his decisions that he has. "Once he makes a decision—often swiftly, based on a creed or moral position—he expects complete faith in its rightness." Worse, "Bush's intolerance of doubters has, if anything, increased and few dare to question him now. A writ of infallibility—a premise beneath the powerful Bushian certainty that has, in many ways, moved mountains—is not just for public consumption: It has guided the inner life of the White House."

Bill Moyers sounded the same alarm in 2002, a few days after the Republicans emphatically took control of Congress: "If you like God in government get ready for the rapture. These folks don't even mind you referring to the GOP as the party of God."

Bush speechwriter Michael Gerson, a respected White House figure, and a fellow man of faith, wrote in 2005, "The danger for America is not theocracy." Gerson, as the head White House speech-writer, insisted that the Bush White House's interest in faith was not the Taliban constrictive, but very consistently old-fashioned Ameri-can do-gooder. "We've consistently called attention to the good works of people motivated by faith."

He might as well have saved his breath. The Bush era was re-morselessly characterized as theocratic and close-minded. Bush's faith became another weapon for the left to attack him.

As Bill Maher, the comedian whose antipathy to religion and re-ligious faith is his calling card, remarked: "What scares me about a guy like George Bush—and I say this many times, I know people get sick of it—but it's the certitude that people get when they are people of faith," Maher said. "I know he's a person of faith, so no matter how low his approval rating goes, he doesn't care because he sees himself as a messianic figure that history will judge."

The deconstruction of George W. Bush was all encompassing. But the purpose behind it was more than the thrill and exhilaration of a lynch mob storming the county jail. It was more than just getting a sick man professional help. It was more than just warning the coun-try that a religious zealot was standing watch at the helm, and pitch-ing the ship of state into a gale.

The totality of the condemnation of George W. Bush was clearly more than its outrageous tiny bits. The big picture was put up for all to see in order to once again demonstrate for a now worried public that whatever Bush had done was for naught because he didn't have the intelligence to think through a decision. Additionally, it could be chalked up to the megalomania of a despot who took direction from

God, or even worse, it was all the mad calculations of evil incarnate, that Bush was the reincarnation of the Mad King George, the British monarch who toyed with the American colonies until he incited rebellion. Most of all, it was to cement in the minds of persuadable Americans that they had made a grievous error in electing him and allowing him to lead a nation.

From 2004 forward, the left's mission was to create doubt about the president and the war. If those two ideas could be drilled into the American consciousness, the left could seize power and enact an agenda that could be instituted no other way.

It was the opportunity of a political lifetime, and the left grabbed it with both hands. And as we have seen, it worked to perfection.

Lies repeated over and over and over become close enough to the truth to win. It mattered not that the lies would be found out. By that time, the victory would be chalked up, and the vast powers of the United States government would be in the hands of people whose only concern with telling untruth lay in the question, "Will it work?"

The answer was yes.

The real question should have been, "So what?"

Whatever his failings of language, whatever his inability to sell the worthiness of the war, and to inform the American people that he was not stuck on stupid, that he was not blithely allowing the gargantuan effort to needlessly go down the drain, in fact he did persevere, he did find the right general eventually, and he did prevail. The Iraq War has proved to be the long-sought success that the left predicted it would never be.

Bush was not a good wartime speaker, but he turned out to be a good wartime leader. He did not allow America to lose, despite the best efforts of the left to convince America it had already lost.

The country owed him a debt of gratitude. The left owed him an apology.

Chapter Three

The Swiftboat Twins: How Jon Stewart and Frank Rich Teamed Up to Mock and Discredit Bush

Ridicule and repetition: these were the primary weapons of the swiftboating left, and they were wielded with devastating effect by two New Yorkers with an outsized influence in American media.

Washington, D.C., is the nation's capital, but it is New York City where opinions are formed, developed, and disseminated to the rest of the country. New York City is the media capital of the nation, where television news—still the nation's most important media product—is made. New York is also the center of the publishing world, both periodicals and books. The opinions of a few New Yorkers therefore have wide reverberations across the country. If a pebble in a pond forms wide ripples, the opinions of New York's media elite make waves that eventually slosh around the globe. Even if the rest of the country is distrustful of New York and New Yorkers, in subtle ways the country is deeply influenced by the radiation emanating from the island of Manhattan.

During the eight years of the liberal media's war against the Bush administration, two of the most important figures turned out to be New Yorkers whose Upper West Side sensibilities came to dominate public opinion. One is a wildly successful comedian who has managed to obscure his left-wing politics behind a translucent gauze of humor. The other is a longtime theater critic who boasts of treating politics, political figures, and public policy on serious matters like war and national elections as nothing more than a show to be dissected, flayed, laid open with a knowing smirk.

These two men are Jon Stewart, the former comic turned liberal pundit, and Frank Rich, the former drama critic turned mouthpiece and file keeper for the anti-Bush left.

Their styles differed significantly. Stewart came after Bush with a modicum of information, and even less that was correct, but armed with all the weapons of the joker: the smirk, the funny faces, the comic glare, a shockingly fluent use of obscenities, an award-winning deadpan, and brilliant timing. For a man who doesn't know much, he certainly made much of the little he did know. Stewart and his staff of sullen young comedy writers could take a cupful of information and a thimble of truth, and squeeze out joke after joke about Bush the dimwitted, Bush the frightening, Bush the world wrecker. Even when he was operating on bad information, old information, erroneous information, he could be devastatingly funny.

As the *New York Times*' theater critic, Frank Rich had earned the name "Butcher of Broadway" for his devastating reviews and his special skill at overnight destruction on deadline. He applied those same skills to eviscerating the Bush administration.

While a political thinker writing on a blog or in a magazine column must have at least a semblance of fact on which to base his or her opinion, it is a much simpler matter for a comedian to twist or misstate a fact—as long as the punch line is funny. Stewart has mastered the art of creating laughs out of his personal political biases and prejudices. Other comedians do the same—Bill Maher is an example—but while most comedian philosophers (like Maher) take themselves extremely seriously, Stewart is the only one whose self-seriousness has been rewarded by the validation of his audience.

Stewart's viewers think he really is a newsman and that he really is delivering the news they need to know. (The number of people who identify Stewart's *The Daily Show* as their primary news source is shocking—more men between 18 and 34 than any other newcast.)

As for Rich, his primary urge is to review politics as if it were nothing more than a drama with a cast and a director and someone writing lines. He takes apart what people say, projects onto them motives and thoughts and a narrative that seem to fit but are not necessarily true, and creates in the minds of the audience a simple, devastating thought: This show is a stinker, don't buy tickets . . . er . . . excuse me . . . don't vote for these people.

Stewart and Rich together actually functioned as a Bush-hating tag team. Rich put together the contradictions and missteps of the administration, especially on the war in Iraq, almost as a wholesaler, while Stewart repackaged and retailed the material for laughs to entertain his many young viewers.

Each nominally goes after "both sides," but only for the sake of appearances. Both are transparently liberal, both feel revulsion for conservatives and Republicans, both openly root and sometimes campaign for the left to prevail. Both have also become quite open about admitting their own political biases. Stewart has even gone so far as to allow that, yes, he is a Democrat, even "a bit of a socialist" (whatever that means). Rich has been more circumspect about his political biases, but there can be little confusion about where both men stand.

Both are routinely declared smart—super smart—in an Upper West Side of Manhattan way. Byron Curtis wrote of Rich's influence in his *Slate* magazine column in 2005: "The critical voice Rich honed on the theater beat . . . is perfectly tuned to the voice of Manhattan liberalism."

As for Stewart, as the country careened into the 2008 election, the *New York Times* published a profile with the headline, "Is Jon Stewart the Most Trusted Man in America?" The answer was an emphatic "yes."

But if Stewart is so smart, why does he say such stupid things?

April 28, 2009, for example. Stewart's guest was Cliff May, who runs an organization called the Foundation for the Defense of Democracies. May had been invited to debate the use of "enhanced interrogation techniques" or "EITs," which Stewart opposes as torture. Stewart's position is that these techniques are not only bad things to do, but that we Americans are a people who don't and shouldn't do such things. The debate went on excessively long, nearly twenty minutes, and Stewart's producers aired only a portion. Whether by accident, or in the interests of full disclosure, the short part that did air was perhaps the most devastating for Stewart. In fact, two days later he went on the air to apologize, and take back the most egregious things he said.

Late in the argument, Stewart asserted that the United States had tried and executed enemy soldiers for doing things that we were now doing in our war against al Qaeda.

"You think in World War II we did not inflict pain and suffering on suspects?" May asked.

"I hope we didn't waterboard people," Stewart replied.

May pounced. "We did do Hiroshima. You think Truman is a war criminal for that?"

Stewart didn't hesitate. "Yeah."

May was startled. "You do?"

Again, Stewart didn't hesitate. "Yeah. Yeah."

"Ok," May said, shrugging his shoulders. He seemed to know how far out on a limb Stewart had put himself. This point has been debated for years, and Stewart seemed to take a college sophomore's approach: Dropping the atom bomb on civilians was horrible, therefore the president who ordered it was wrong, therefore he had committed a war crime.

But Stewart wasn't done. He had more advice for President Harry Truman. "Here's what I think about the atom bomb. I think if you drop the atom bomb fifty miles offshore and you say the next one is coming to hit you, then I think its ok. But to drop one on a city and kill a hundred thousand people, I think that's criminal."

May tried to be kind. "Ok, that's your opinion," he said, shrugging, but clearly not agreeing. After all, he was a guest on Stewart's show, and it's bad form to show up the host.

But Stewart wasn't through digging himself into a hole. "Here's my point that I want you to listen to as well. I understand temporary insanity as well. And what I understand about what we did in this country, I don't say . . ."

Startled, May jumped in: "You think Truman was temporarily insane when he dropped the bomb?"

"Yes," Stewart replied, again without hesitation.

May leaned forward into his argument. Speaking of Truman, he asked, "He didn't think, 'If I send troops into Japan we're going to lose a million lives'? Because that's what he thought, a million

American lives, and at least a million Japanese lives because they'll fight to the last man . . ."

Stewart interrupted. "I'm saying is that war is temporary insanity, and so the things that happen there have to be looked at in the context of that . . ."

"We're in a war, we're in a war!" May objected, his hands and arms chopping the air.

Stewart retorted, "But you can't have it both ways. You can't say we're in a war but the Geneva Conventions don't apply."

"The Geneva Conventions apply where they apply," May said.

Stewart was smirking, "They apply where you want them to . . ."

"No," May interrupted, "they apply to those who signed the treaty. It doesn't apply to al Qaeda."

Stewart looked cornered. "But we did, they apply to us . . ."

May was shaking his head furiously. "No . . . no . . . that's not right. And not according to me. Eric Holder, the attorney general under Obama, said that's not true."

Two days later, Stewart appeared on his own program, chastened and chagrined. He said he shouldn't have called Harry Truman a war criminal, that it was stupid, and as soon as he said the words he had the feeling he should reach out and take them back.

But he didn't take back the idea that waging war, even defensively, is temporary insanity, and he didn't take back the idea that Americans should obey rules that our enemies don't, even if doing so is to the enemies' advantage.

Stewart shouldn't have apologized. It was a stupid thing to say, but it was honest and it was revealing. It showed the audience that his careful dance around the toughest of issues hides and obscures his real feelings, which he knows are at odds with those of the American public. Despite his apology, he does think Harry Truman was a war criminal, and he does think that in a war with an enemy like al Qaeda we must take civilian casualties to maintain our pristine moral status.

Stewart's empty-headed commentary is not exclusive to the war, however.

For example, in an interview with the youth-oriented Web site eye .com in 2002, Stewart said, "This is a real moment when leadership counts. Our country should be engaged right now in a space race—style search for renewable energy. You can create a baby in a dish, but you can't recalculate the formula for oil?"

The interviewer let this pass, but honestly: recalculate the formula for oil? There is no such thing as a formula for oil, but it was precisely the kind of airy unrealistic thing that young comedy club-goers would reflexively applaud. To actual grown-ups, it made Stewart look vapid and empty-headed.

The questionable—ok, stupid—things both Rich and Stewart said or printed were often witty, and clever, and seemed thoughtful. But stupid can often seem smart, while failing an intelligence test by missing key concepts. Both Rich and Stewart heaped criticism on Bush and his policies for keeping the country safe, but neither had an alternative plan that would have passed a laugh or smell test. They fixated on criticism and left the reader or viewer to assume, to take it for granted, that almost any other approach would have been an improvement. Both seemed to think the choices a president makes are always between "bad" and "good," while in reality the choice is often between "bad" and "worse."

Never once did either argue that Saddam Hussein would have been no long-term threat to the United States, only that he did not have the capabilities Bush said he had when Bush said he had them. Never once did either acknowledge that other methods were attempted to extract information from hardened terrorists that did not prove effective, only that "torture" offended their delicate moral sensibilities. Both seemed offended by the president's religious beliefs, and both made too much of the quite reasonable suspicion that English was not George W. Bush's native language. Shooting fish in a barrel should not have won the accolades of the crowd, but in the cases of Stewart and Rich it more than sufficed.

From the moment George Bush was elected, Stewart and Rich pushed multiple story lines: Bush was illegitimate, never elected; Bush was stupid and over his head in the job; Bush was a cowboy who embarrassed America in the eyes of the world; Bush allowed the evil Dick Cheney to seize control of the government; Bush brought the country to moral, political, and economic ruin.

Swiftboating George W. Bush on the island of Manhattan was never a difficult task. The trick was making the hatred spread from the Upper West Side, and the echo chamber of the West Coast, to the great middle of the country. New York and Hollywood have a long history of pushing soap and stars into the great middle of America, but this was new territory. Unsurprisingly, they managed just fine.

STEWART TOOK OVER *The Daily Show* in 1999. It was a program that focused on Hollywood stars and other celebrities, and Stewart set out to change the focus to bigger targets in Washington, D.C.

The next year, in December 2000, Larry King had Stewart on his program for an hour, and took questions from callers.

"I was wondering," one caller asked, "is it hard to make political jokes and not be on, like, either side?"

King turned to Stewart and said, "You can't be for either side," and Stewart interrupted to correct King. "No, that's not true, I mean, I think you—most people can't hide their political [views]."

Which moved King to say, "I think you're a Democrat, Jon."

Stewart nodded. "I think that's probably correct. I think I would say I'm more of a socialist or an independent but, yes, I mean, no one would ever, watching our show, think, 'Boy, that guy is just leaning so far right.' "

In 2000, Stewart told *George* magazine that in high school he was "very into Eugene Debs"—the American socialist—"and a bit of a leftist." Take him at his word, but he is also a rich socialist. He earns $14 million a year and lives in a $5.8 million, six thousand square foot apartment in New York City.

During the 2000, recount, Stewart deadpanned, "All we can really tell you is the electoral count stays the same. Bush has taken twenty states. Gore has taken thirteen. The interesting thing is Bush has swept the South: Alabama, Georgia, Kentucky, Louisiana, Mississippi, North Carolina, South Carolina, Texas, Oklahoma, Tennessee, Virginia." Pause, thoughtful pulling on the chin. "I seem to remember these states getting together once before. I can't remember when . . ."

Republicans as the new Confederacy, fighting to reinstate slavery. During the great Democrat beat down of Republicans following the Obama election, that same theme reappeared. Republicans as slaveholders, Republicans as Confederate soldiers, Republicans as those who would break up the Union. What Stewart left out, of course, was the historical fact that the opposite was true. Republicans held the Union together, Republicans freed the slaves, and Democrats resisted basic change. But no matter. His audience didn't know, and probably would never discover the facts. He could jab, joke, and lie with impunity.

Shortly after the 2000 Florida recount, Stewart was interviewed again by Larry King. The comedian offhandedly referred to the president-elect as "Chuck E. Cheese," a forewarning of how the next few years were going to unfold on *The Daily Show*. The Clinton years had been the subject of constant hammering by the Bush team during the election; Gore tried to pretend he hardly knew the former president. Stewart predicted that the country would one day look back fondly on the Clinton years, scandals and all.

"You know what, two years from now we're going to want [Clinton]," Stewart declared to King. "Two years from now, we're going to show up on Bill Clinton's doorstep in Chappaqua, naked with a box of cigars, going, stick it wherever you want, just come back. Whatever you got to do."

But Stewart has punctuated his career with attacks on "straight" news media. Thus, he explained his thoughts about the inadequacies of television news to Connie Chung in 2002: "Dirty bomb. That was a great example of [television] excess," he said. "When the dirty bomb was announced," he said—referring to the arrest of José Padilla, who was accused of plotting to set off a so-called 'dirty bomb' in the United States—"everybody went into dirty-bomb mode."

"What is a dirty bomb?" he asked. "Well . . . they would show a nuclear explosion. It's not that." He explained to Chung that the news media would "jazz everybody up" and "at the very end of it, they'd go, 'and in conclusion this is not a very dangerous thing at all.' It's like the old method [the news uses to promote upcoming stories], 'You won't believe what's in your washing machine that could kill you.' Those old scare tactics to get you to watch."

For Stewart, warnings about terrorism were to be taken no more seriously than the on-air promotions television stations used to draw people to their news programs.

In dozens of interviews (Comedy Central's PR people evidently work very hard), Stewart repeated this same analogy, referring to local news programs that hype overblown "investigations" of house-hold or common dangers in order to attract people who, in Stewart's words, "are just living their lives" and not paying attention to the big issues of politics and international relations.

"You know that one video shot of the World Trade Center coming down and that huge cloud of white smoke and people running for their lives?" Stewart asked Ms. Chung. Television news—and here he seemed to mean the cable news channels, Fox, MSNBC, and CNN, but particularly Fox—used that image over and over to scare people. "These are tragic images and they're using them as bumpers in and out of commercials." His point seemed to be that television news was desensitizing viewers. "You're not supposed to watch [these channels] all day long because the aggregate weight of what comes at you is devastating, diminishing."

The Stewart swiftboating—undermining the credibility and legiti-macy of the president—continued unabated through the 2004 election cycle. On November 3, 2004, the day after the election that returned George W. Bush to office for a second term, Stewart's show opened with worldwide "reaction" to the re-election of President Bush.

"[British Prime Minister Tony] Blair's decision to support Bush during the Iraqi war was very unpopular in his own country," Stew-art deadpanned, anchorman style, "and judging from the reaction of the British press to Tuesday's results . . . uhhh . . . " and here he paused for comic effect as an image of the front page of the *London Daily Mirror* rolled onto the screen, revealing a picture of George W. Bush, emblazoned with the headline "How Can 59,054,087 People Be So Dumb?"

Stewart let the image sink in; the audience cheered wildly, and Stewart let the applause roll over him. "Reaction in other parts of the world ranged from angry, to violently angry," he said, ignoring the fact that the 59 million Americans who voted for Bush were obvi-ously not angry. They simply did not count in his thinking.

Jon Stewart's show was an eight-year attack on George W. Bush, for which there was never any effective defense. How would the presi-dent—any president, for that matter—defend himself against jokes? In the humor-impaired Bush administration, no one ever came up with a good answer, other than trying to ignore the constant jabs and hope for the best. It was not a strategy that seemed terribly promising, but there seemed few real alternatives. Complaints about jokes—or trying to answer a joke—tended to make the subject of the punch line look even more foolish.

The problem was exquisitely illustrated by Stewart's show of December 4, 2008, when he handed the president an exploding cigar over his series of exit interviews with star journalists.

"The most fun of these 'exit interviews' with the president," Stewart began, "is watching the news anchors try to delicately assess whether the president realizes just how bad he's fucked things up." Cutting to video, the audience saw ABC News anchor Charles Gibson asking President Bush, "Was there an 'uh-oh' moment?" Stewart popped back on the screen, his face puckered. "An 'Uh-oh moment'? Why do we have to talk to this jackass like he's four?"

Bush "fucked things up." Bush is a "jackass." Stewart used obscenities and insults to underscore his political points. And he did so with the elbow-to-the-jaw technique he learned as a stand-up comic putting down a heckler.

If Stewart felt free to call the president a "jackass," if he felt free to tell GOP vice presidential candidate Sarah Palin "fuck you" on national television (reacting to her statement that she loved "small-town America" home of "real American values"), why wouldn't his audience of angry young voters feel equally free to speak and think of Bush and Palin and other Republicans in similarly harsh and uncivil terms?

Shockingly, humor aimed at nineteen-year-olds delivered by a superbly cynical and manipulative forty-seven-year-old seemed not only to be driving the election of 2008, but formed general public opinion of the soon-to-be ex-president. It was the hallmark—and the shame—of the transition from Bush to Obama that the Bush critics could not quietly accept victory, but wallowed in their anger, compelled to continue to bash the former president. The rule held firm that whenever President Obama ran into difficulties, the immediate reaction of the White House and the media was to disinter Bush and give his bones a few more whacks.

Stewart's house audience of college students and young professionals whooped wildly at the daring of calling the president names and the crude message that anything goes when it comes to Bush. An expression of extreme self-satisfaction crossed Stewart's face whenever he called the president a gutter name: another slash across the back in Stewart's long campaign to inflict death by a thousand cuts on George W. Bush.

By the end of the Bush administration, Stewart had been at his fake anchor desk, on his fake news program, playing the fake newsman for a full decade. With ten years' experience at this weird game, he had honed his persona to a razor sharp and (for his occasional conservative guests) dangerous edge. While denying that he was a real journalist, thereby escaping the responsibility that goes with the job, he simultaneously embraced the role of principal news source for millions of informationally challenged young people. A 2004 poll by Pew Research found that one in four people between eighteen and twenty-nine got their news from either *The Daily Show* or *Saturday Night Live*. Stewart clung to his status as the Cronkite of the beer-bong and hackey-sack set, while constantly denying any interest in so lofty a position.

Making fun of the news while acting as the sole source of news for a large national audience empowered Stewart to run roughshod over the rules that bind journalists, and to effectively manipulate young voters without serious challenge. Under the rules of comedy as news, as long as the punch line was funny, the set up to the joke could be misstated, or stated with a decidedly partisan bent. Stewart's own politics drove his comedy, and he was insistently anti-Bush, relentlessly opposed to the Iraq War, and a merciless critic of the legitimate news business, which he blamed for allowing Bush to gather support for a war that Stewart and his fellow lefties thought was wrong and should never have been waged.

Republicans—particularly neo-cons—got us into the war in Iraq, according to Stewart, and these were precisely the people whose views should be rejected, people he defamed at every opportunity.

Stewart's criticism of television has been relentless, if not obsessive. The aggregate weight of stupid things that happen in television news seemed to be the central point of his program. But he never seems to have considered the aggregate weight of his own pointed, vicious jokes about the president of the United States, the funny lines that caused young people to lose faith in their government or to withhold their support of the war. That particular "aggregate weight" was perfectly acceptable because it served the purpose of undermining a president and a war he did not like.

Stewart famously went on the CNN program *Crossfire* on October 15, 2004, and confronted hosts Tucker Carlson and Paul Begala about their show, which had been on the air for two decades and was known for its shouting and loud confrontations between proponents of right and left. Stewart confessed that he came on the program because he had criticized it in private with friends, and thought it only "fair" that he come on the show to scold them in public before their own audience. Begala and Carlson were under the impression he had come to be funny, but they were sadly mistaken. His first words were, "Why do you guys fight?" When the hosts replied that they were a debate program in which sharp distinctions between right and left were aired, Stewart replied, "Stop, stop, stop, stop hurting America." The discussion grew increasingly uncomfortable and it soon became obvious that Stewart had set up an ambush of the hosts on their own show, an unexpectedly nervy tactic.

Who was hurting America more? The bow-tie wearing conservative whom Stewart went after because Carlson challenged him ("You're not being funny, Jon!") and chided Stewart about his softball questions to Democratic presidential nominee John Kerry? Or Begala, whom Stewart did not attack because as a liberal Stewart agrees with him? Or Stewart himself, by misinforming the nation's young voters, and setting in their minds certain false anti-Bush talking points of the left?

Stewart was especially dangerous for Carlson ("You're as big a dick on your show as you are on any show!" he snapped) because he was the lone conservative voice on CNN, a network that evidently realized the wind was changing in a decidedly liberal direction and desperately wanted the audience that Jon Stewart had clapping like seals each night, clamoring for another anti-Bush treat.

So Stewart complains that the divisive partisan name-calling on *Crossfire* hurts America, and then responds to a polite challenge by calling one of the hosts a "dick." No one called him out on this glaring inconsistency. Nor did anyone suggest to Stewart's face that frequent recourse to obscenity and schoolyard taunts lowers the tone of national debate.

Within a short time Jon Klein, president of CNN, cancelled *Crossfire*, putting Carlson out of work. (Begala returned to his Democratic campaign consultancy and was back on the air on CNN as a paid "analyst" in short order.) "Basically, I come down in the Stewart camp on this one," Klein explained, a few days before dumping the show. Stewart later bragged that all he had to do to get a show cancelled was say it should be cancelled.

For a decade, Stewart has hidden his partisanship behind the notion that he plays a journalist on television—for comic effect—but in fact is only an entertainer whose main interest is getting the audience to laugh. Yet he basks in an additional status: the one person in the media who is more of a journalist than the real journalists.

In April 2007, Stewart sat for an interview with Bill Moyers, another fake journalist who makes scant effort to hide his partisanship.

> Moyers: You've said many times, "I don't want to be a journalist, I'm not a journalist."
> Stewart: And we're not.
> Moyers: But you're acting like one. You've assumed that role. The young people that work with me now, think they get better journalism from you than they do from the Sunday morning talk shows.
> Stewart: I can assure them they're not getting any journalism from us.

If he had stopped there, people would have had to give Stewart credit for honestly presenting himself as a satirist, a comedian, an entertainer. But his denials soon gave way to the truth. Stewart's "journalism" is as phony as that of any other partisan posing as a newsperson. And Stewart consistently commits the phony journalist's crime of pushing a line that was wrong, and in some instances had been proved wrong while he blithely insisted on ignoring inconvenient facts.

Stewart interviewed John McCain on April 27, 2007. He had a list of Iraq War talking points that he wanted to go over and the two got into a spirited argument about whether the surge strategy—then less than four months old—was the correct course. Stewart's position on the surge boiled down to a sentence: "What I believe is less supportive to the good people who believe they're fighting a great cause is to not give them a strategy that makes their success possible." This is a direct quote, and consequently sounds incoherent, but Stewart's point was coherent enough—that support for the troops demanded a strategy for success, and that he judged the surge as falling short.

McCain began, "We now have a strategy," referring to the plans of General David Petraeus.

Stewart interrupted: "Adding ten thousand people to Baghdad? Add three hundred fifty thousand, then we might have a shot." The audience cheered. No one questioned Stewart's qualifications to make this military judgment.

McCain tried to explain that he understood why people disapproved of the way the war had been managed—he flatly stated that it was mismanaged—but said that he approved of the new strategy and thought it was a much better option than declaring a date at which U.S. troops would leave, which in his view would amount to surrender and defeat.

Stewart took exception, saying it was unfair to characterize the desire of the American people for a timetable for withdrawal as defeatist. This of course was not what McCain had said, but that didn't matter to Stewart or his audience.

That was just a few months into the surge. It was not clear what was going to happen, and perhaps Stewart's skepticism could be considered reasonable. A year later, when McCain made his thirteenth visit to *The Daily Show* ("the guest with the most appearances on this show," crowed Stewart, conveying that he was "fair" to Republicans), Stewart strangely did not mention the surge or the Iraq War. By May 2008, of course, it was abundantly clear that the surge had worked, and that the strategy Stewart derided had succeeded. It was time for Stewart to apologize to McCain for the beating he had administered to the old war hero when in fact Stewart himself was just plain wrong.

No apology was forthcoming. Instead Stewart talked to McCain about his campaign, about the Democrats bashing each other in the primary, about anything but revisiting the scene of his error. McCain graciously did not bring it up. This would have been the moment for Stewart, if he were honest, if he were really the evenhanded "fake" newsman he claimed to be, to say to McCain, "I was wrong, you were right." But he did not. It was a cowardly moment, papered over by Stewart's usual skill at generating laughs.

He also passed up the opportunity to correct the record when he appeared on the Bill Moyers show a few days after McCain's earlier appearance. Moyers, of course, delighted in talking down McCain— or any other Republican—and tried to get Stewart to agree that McCain had looked "shriveled" as he felt the argument slipping away from him. Stewart replied, "It's just that, it appears that this is not the smart way to fight this threat," he said.

So in the space of three days, Stewart had said twice on national television that McCain and Bush were wrong and that he, Stewart, knew better how to prosecute a war than either the war hero he professed to admire, the "jackass" president he took pains to insult, or the superb commanding general whose strategy snatched victory from the jaws of defeat.

IN THE ELECTION of 2008, Stewart got his way. Republicans were finally expunged from power in the nation's capital.

A cartoon plastered on newspaper boxes all around San Francisco following the election of Barack Obama illustrated the power of what might be called the Jon Stewart effect: over a caricature drawing of Bush waving good-bye, the cartoon screamed, "Adios, Douchebag!" Who empowered young people in America to speak of the president in such terms? The guy who felt justified in calling the president a "jackass" and worse on nightly television.

Stewart's display of bias against conservatives showed itself again with his brutal smack down of CNBC stock hustler Jim Cramer, who was absolutely dismantled by Stewart in an angry and unfunny attack on Stewart's show in early 2009.

Cramer found himself blamed for the collapse of the economy, while Stewart ignored the depredations of prominent Democrats in the debacle. Barney Frank and Chris Dodd, Democratic chairmen of the House and Senate banking committees, were not mentioned in Stewart's angry diatribe, though both had sheltered Democrat-run Fannie Mae and Freddie Mac from regulation and oversight during the period both were ordering banks across the nation to issue loans to the credit unworthy.

Despite the systematic and relentless use of the hammer, Stewart's television persona was that of the sly, irony laden "anchorman" for America's youth. His view of the White House and of national and global events was the prism through which millions of young Americans saw the news and the politics of the Bush years. But there was no denying where Stewart's own politics lay.

It has been a theme of Stewart's since he started at *The Daily Show* that he and his staff view the absurdities of government as a source of humor. But there was an illuminating note in the introduction to a Stewart interview in *Rolling Stone* magazine, in which the interviewer tells of visiting *The Daily Show* prep meeting early in the day, before show time. "The comedic tone of *The Daily Show* is all deadpan irony, but the mood behind the scenes is one of intense youthful passion, and even fury," the interviewer wrote. Stewart's deadpan skills hide that fury from the audience when the program comes on the air, but fury—and partisanship—drive the show.

"I'm stunned to see Karl Rove on a news network as an analyst," Stewart told Howard Kurtz of the *Washington Post* after the Obama election victory. Of course, he didn't think CNN's use of Paul Begala and James Carville—who were employed as actual advisors to the campaigns of Hillary Clinton and Barack Obama while appearing on CNN as "independent" analysts—was a problem at all. "I don't think [Carville] was being passed off as any kind of sage," Stewart told Kurtz, strangely ignoring the obvious.

Stewart thus demonstrated that he is a man who is very comfortable with his own hypocrisy.

In a moment of honesty, Stewart admitted to Kurtz that poking fun at Barack Obama was dangerous because the candidate was so loved by the very audience the jokes are meant to entertain. Yet slipping back into blatant dishonesty, he said to Kurtz, "An age joke about McCain is at this point somewhat meaningless—because it's already trite."

This was disingenuous. It's not that a McCain joke would be "trite." It's that the joke had outlived its political usefulness. McCain had already lost, so what would be the point?

Stewart is clearly a smart man, with a dangerously quick wit. People who sit down with him to be interviewed had better be on the edge of their seat, and never assume he is a fan. He brings people on to destroy them, and the punch line is usually an uppercut to the guest's jaw that seems to come out of nowhere.

Stewart was well trained by the comedy circuit in the brutal art of the devastating putdown that stops a heckler in his tracks and shuts him up. In the face of any challenge, he goes for the kick to the testicles. He chops the legs out from under them, calls them names, and will deal in shocking profanity to set a challenger back on his heels.

Stewart viciously kills his opponents, not so much simply to have another scalp on his belt as to establish credibility with his core audience—ensuring that they will half-wittedly and without thinking accept the underlying premise of his next joke. The premise of a brutal political joke doesn't have to be correct; it only has to make sense in the context of the laugh line. Stewart is a master of that sleight of hand.

Stewart says he is interested in the absurdities of government and the media. That is essentially what his jokes are all about. He evidently believes that creating in his young and barely educated audience the kind of skepticism that requires them to reject literally anything their government does—at least if it is a conservative government—is an important public service.

Politicians are faced with a disastrous choice: stay away from Stewart's show and hope the deadeye and devastating jokester-ism doesn't do too much damage, or go on the show, accept the ridicule face-to-face, and hope a display of courage and good humor limits the damage. Did it help John McCain to go on Stewart's show a record thirteen times? Probably not, but McCain had to figure it was better than letting Stewart fire his salvos from a distance.

Remember: Stewart is a television performer whose favorite trick of late is to go on television programs hosted by others and lambaste them with the charge they are hurting America. Considering his own modus operandi, who is hurting America more?

LIKE STEWART, FRANK Rich is a highly paid Manhattan-dwelling liberal who was appalled by the presidency of George W. Bush. He got a slow start, but steadily ramped up his attacks, and since just before the 2006 elections hammered the Bush administration incessantly. Rich's problem—unrecognized or acknowledged—was that, as his columns piled fact upon fact and report on report, he still managed to come to the wrong conclusions time after time. Where Stewart had the decency and courage to go on the air and take back his charge that Harry Truman was a war criminal, Rich has seldom taken anything back, no matter how erroneous or irresponsible.

A professional critic by nature and training, Rich began the Bush years with a pox-on-both-your-houses attitude, rejecting the worthiness of either former Vice President Al Gore or Governor George W. Bush. Soon he had morphed into one of the most aggressive and dynamic of left-wing swiftboaters, ceaselessly railing against Bush and the entire White House crew.

Unlike bloggers who raged against the war to audiences of the zealous and already decided, Rich operated using the megaphone of the *New York Times*, giving him enormous influence on opinion makers in the muddled middle, as well every other leftist trying to paint the war in the darkest and most hopeless terms. As the war began he was skeptical, quickly criticizing what seemed to him an abandonment of the war against al Qaeda, and foretelling disaster in the hurry-up war.

There were several ideas behind the war that he never accepted, even when the truth emerged and should have convinced him to reconsider his objections. For one, he never acknowledged what eventually became obvious: that al Qaeda was in Iraq, that it was both the spark and the fuse of the explosive insurgency, and that it was as good a place as any to fight the war on terror.

Eventually, of course, American troops and Iraqis either killed most of the al Qaeda who came to Iraq or chased them into Pakistan, where a devastating killing campaign using Predator drones firing Hellfire missiles began to decimate them in the last six months of the Bush administration. Even the new president embraced this campaign and continued it after Bush returned to Texas. But by the time the story became public—and obvious—Rich was in concrete-encased denial. By 2008 he had devolved into a reflexive Bush opponent, railing against anything and anyone connected to the Bush regime, and the war. It was a change that came over him quickly; but it wasn't always so.

At the moment Bush won the presidency, Rich was disgusted with Al Gore and was hilariously unkind to him: "Mr. Gore's public protestation that what he is 'focused on' is 'not the contest, but our democracy' offers yet further confirmation of his unctuous disingenuousness," he wrote during the recount in Florida. In fact, Rich was so put off by Gore, he didn't much lament the coming Bush years.

On the eve of the 2000 election, Rich wrote of Bush: "For every other civic problem, Mr. Bush offers cheery bromides like 'leadership' and 'vision' and a laissez-faire, let-the-other-guy-do-it solution. Let our 'friends' shoulder problems abroad. Let a tax cut and 'faith-based charities' lift up the poor. Let industry regulate its own pollution. Declare a new era of 'personal responsibility' that requires no national sacrifice." Rich resented Bush's promised tax cuts, and as the wars later heated up, his mantra about a lack of national "sacrifice" expanded to include both tax cuts and the all-volunteer military. Compulsory military service has been the left's last ditch gambit to stop an unpopular war: young men and women (and their parents) who are subject to a draft can be a powerful antiwar constituency.

Nonetheless, Rich was relatively sanguine about the arrival of the Bush administration. He even seemed to relish the prospect of a few years of an easy target in the White House.

To demonstrate how things quickly changed, roll ahead to a Rich column five years later, in November 2005, summing up the Bush administration to that point, including 9/11, the Afghanistan War, the Iraq War, and everything President Bush and Vice President Cheney were doing to protect the country from further attacks. Headlined "Dishonest, Reprehensible, Corrupt," Rich added "shameless" in the body of his column. "The more we learn about the road to Iraq, the more we realize that it's a losing game to ask what lies the White House told along the way. A simpler question might be: What was *not* a lie?" (emphasis added).

Writing once a week in his signature double-length column, Rich was brutally quick with his judgments. But what could anyone expect from a theater critic who is accustomed to having heard the entire story when the curtain comes down? A play doesn't update itself the next day, and Rich seemed to think the world worked the same way. Every day he could condemn the performance of the president, he felt free to do so. After all, tomorrow was another day, another curtain-raising at the White House. A reader of Rich's column could fairly conclude that for him, history was not a thing that unfolded day by day, month by month, year by year, but something that began at eight in the evening, and was over in time for the reviewer to get to his desk, bang out a review, and still be home at a decent hour.

Despite his evident ambition to be taken more seriously as

a commentator on national events, at heart Rich has remained a drama critic. Widely hailed for his brilliant reviews, after thirteen years of sitting in the dark, judging the play or musical before him, he decided he'd done enough, and the *Times* gave him a column and the freedom to "review" anything that caught his interest.

One of his first forays into American political life was his coverage of the Clinton inaugural, which he panned as "a K-Mart inaugural," to the enormous displeasure of the Clintons themselves. His colleague at the *New York Times*, Maureen Dowd, said of Rich's "review," "His theatrical assessment was correct, as always."

Six months after the Bush inauguration, Rich was focusing on George W. Bush the person, the actor on the world stage, and he didn't think much of his performance. "The real ideology that drives Mr. Bush remains less that of the hard right than that of his soft character, which is a product of a biography full of easy landings." Rich resented Bush's pedigree, his education at a prestigious East Coast boarding school, and his degrees from Yale and Harvard, which Rich judged to be yet another exercise in skating through. He demeaned Bush's business experience as a résumé of taking advantage of his friends and family connections.

The importance of Rich's theater orientation cannot be overstated. His observations about politics, war, terrorism, and the world always revolve around cultural references. He delights in comparing political figures he has come to dislike with hapless or evil characters from screen or stage. Thus in attacking what he labeled the Bush administration's transparent lies, he called the president "Mr. Cellophane," a character from the Broadway musical *Chicago*.

Rich even questioned Bush's motives for buying a ranch in Texas. "Right before George W. Bush runs for president, he buys a ranch—one that isn't really a ranch—to establish the image that he is a red-state shit-kicker rather than the scion of one of the most aristocratic families in the United States, a graduate of Andover, Yale, and Harvard," Rich wrote. "All of us need to question this level of cultural manipulation." Bush's ranch in Crawford comprised seventeen hundred acres, which amounts to almost three square miles. If a real estate agent were to list Bush's property for sale, it would certainly be described as a ranch. So why would Rich quibble about it other than to diminish him, to suggest he is a fraud?

But what we really need to question is whether Frank Rich could understand why *anybody* would want a ranch in Texas. A reasonable conclusion is that Rich himself would not. But does Frank Rich's taste for city life, with its theaters and restaurants and efficiently productive newsrooms, make that life desirable for everyone? He somehow failed to notice that Bush had grown up in Midland, Texas, went to high school there, and returned to Texas as soon as he was out of college and business school. Rich could understand running away from Texas, but not returning to it.

Rich himself grew up in Washington, D.C., and yearned to be in the theaters of New York from an early age. He went to Harvard and launched his career in a series of newspaper and magazine jobs in New York. If Frank Rich had bought a ranch before running for president, the "cultural manipulation" would be obvious. Rich was admitting his own cultural blind spot, a complete ignorance of the enormous country outside the Boston-New York-Washington cultural corridor. But the remark was typical Rich: a low blow wrapped in faux sociology and the presumption of urban sophistication.

A friend from college, *Boston Globe* writer John Powers, said of Rich's writing style, "Some critics work with cleavers and hacksaws, but Frank always operated with a stiletto." His aim was for the soft spot between the ribs.

Four days after 9/11, Rich's column was, of course, all about this enormous event. It covered everything you might expect, but buried deep in the body of the column was a stiletto line about President Bush. "In all this we've been blessed, for there were 48 hours during which the president was scarcely visible or articulate." Was this really the appropriate moment for a snarky jab at President Bush? Rich went on in a similar vein: "Mr. Bush will have to prepare the nation for something many living Americans, him included, have never had to muster—sacrifice."

Rich of course had a ready audience for his skeptical view of the president, his administration, and his many supporters spread across the country. The Florida recount and the Supreme Court decision that ushered in the second Bush era was still a raw issue for many on the left, who refused to accept Bush as legitimate.

Approaching the first anniversary of 9/11, Rich's tone was even more jaundiced. "Our history still repeats itself first as tragedy and then as farce, but most of all as entertainment, with a full line of merchandise and an undertow of nostalgia," he wrote of the anticipated day of coast-to-coast memorials, which included something "tasteful" on the cable television Food Network.

In the same article, he began gearing up his criticism of President Bush's anticipated pivot from Afghanistan to Iraq and the growing population of "enemy combatants" at Guantanamo Bay, Cuba. "By keeping the names and court proceedings of his detainees under wraps, John Ashcroft could for months cover up his law enforcement minions' inability to apprehend a single terrorist connected to 9/11." The failure of the Bush administration to capture Osama bin Laden would become a consistent fall-back criticism over the next seven years. If fresher arguments seemed insufficiently appealing, there was always the al-Qaeda-got-away canard. Perhaps it was reasonable to be anxious for the 9/11 culprits to be clapped into irons, but it was also a case—one of many to come—of Rich jumping the gun. Within seven months, 9/11 logistics planner Abu Zubaydah would be captured in Pakistan. A year later, 9/11 mastermind, Khalid Sheikh Mohammad would also be taken into custody.

No Bush critic was properly kitted out unless he or she had an anti-Bush book to hawk on MSNBC, PBS, and other left-wing redoubts. Rich was no different. As he was preparing for publication, his anti-Bush fever began to noticeably rise. Titled *The Greatest Story Ever Sold*, his book was a withering attack on Bush, accusing him not just of negligence, or even the occasional lie to cover up a bad decision, but a systematic campaign of lies, distortions, intentional mischaracterizations, and wholly invented fictions, orchestrated by his minions in the White House to sell the country on an immoral and unnecessary war.

On one Sunday, for example, three administration officials repeated a line the president had used the previous week that particularly bothered Rich: The country has to act preemptively before the next attack, because "the smoking gun could be a mushroom cloud." The inference that Saddam might supply terrorists with a nuclear weapon was obvious to Rich, and to others, and they wanted the Bush administration held to account for its warning. If Saddam didn't turn out to have nuclear weapons, the call to war would be manifestly based on a lie.

Of course, as it turned out, Saddam did not have nuclear weapons, and Rich would not allow the substitution of an "active nuclear program" as a suitable justification. On the other hand, Libya did have a nuclear program that was on the eve of producing the first Arab nuclear bomb, and Muammar Qaddafi volunteered to give it up after seeing American troops roll into Baghdad. But Rich never allowed that fact to enter the debate. A mushroom cloud *was* prevented by the Iraq invasion—which also led to the exposure of the previously unknown A. Q. Khan proliferation network—but Rich stood over the Bush people holding transcripts of their Sunday morning statements as though they were binding contracts, demanding they be followed to the letter, and declaring any breach to be a criminal violation.

Rich's book—researched and written six months to a year before its publication in the fall of 2006—set the course for coming years. Engaging in the first rule of the Bush-hating left—relentless repetition—Rich was at the beginning of a five-year stretch of weekly beatings of the Bush administration—angry, passionate, devastating, and unforgiving. He was also trigger happy, slipshod, too quick to condemn, and shockingly error prone.

"Like the Japanese soldier marooned on an island for years after V-J Day, President Bush may be the last person in the country to learn that for Americans, if not Iraqis, the war in Iraq is over. 'We will stay the course,' he insistently tells us from his Texas ranch. What do you mean we, white man?" he wrote in August 2005, in one of his more fevered and injudicious moments.

It is certainly true that in 2005 the war in Iraq was not going well. The president was searching for a way to stem what had become a horrifying bloodbath of sectarian violence. But it was also true that al Qaeda in Iraq was on the offensive, purposely trying to ignite a sectarian war. This was a fact proclaimed by the leader of al Qaeda in Iraq, Abu Musab al Zarqawi, but Rich willfully ignored it. "Nothing that happens on the ground in Iraq can turn around the fate of this war in America . . . There will be neither the volunteers nor the money required to field the wholesale additional American troops that might bolster the security situation in Iraq," Rich wrote, all but writing the war off as a loss. "The country has already made the decision for Mr. Bush. We're outta there." With a few keystrokes Rich brought America home, and promptly moved on to electing new people to carry out his will. "Now comes the hard task of identifying the leaders who can pick up the pieces of the fiasco that has made us more vulnerable, not less, to the terrorists who struck us four years ago next month."

Rich thus began his campaign for a change of regime—not in Iraq, but in America.

"The tragic bottom line of the Bush catastrophe: the administration has at once increased the ranks of jihadists by turning Iraq into a new training ground and recruitment magnet while at the same time exhausting America's will and resources to confront that expanded threat," Rich wrote in November 2005. Catastrophe, creating more jihadists, a terrorist training ground, America out of gas and without resolve. The more Americans believed all that, the sooner the hated Republicans and their leader would be gone, perhaps forever. "The public knows progress is not being made, no matter how many times it is told that Iraqis will soon stand up so we can stand down."

With an eye to the elections for the control of Congress a year away, Rich was deep into his narrative of inevitable defeat.

But a year is a long time in the column writing business. At least fifty columns, and much to be done. Rich was fond of cherry-picking the intelligence, just as he accused Bush of doing. Thus he pushed the line that Saddam's relationship with al Qaeda had been hostile. "Saddam, who 'issued a general order that Iraq should not deal with Al Qaeda,' saw both bin Laden and Abu Musab al Zarqawi as threats and tried to hunt down Zarqawi when he passed through Baghdad in 2002."

Rich certainly knew, or should have known, of a number of pieces of information that ran counter to his claim. The same Senate Intelligence Committee report that he relied on for his charge also reported that there had been dozens of contacts and discussions over the years between agents of Saddam and emissaries of bin Laden. Rich knew or should have known that a foreign intelligence service (presumably the French) had told Saddam where to find Zarqawi as he "passed through Baghdad." (The SSCI actually reported that Zarqawi was in Baghdad for two months recovering from wounds inflicted by the Americans in Afghanistan, which renders laughable the notion he was just "passing through.") Yet Saddam's otherwise deadly efficient internal security apparatus claimed it could not find him. Rich wanted so badly to believe that Saddam was innocent of involvement with al Qaeda that he would seize on any fragment of fact to support his belief.

In this he resembled no one so much as George W. Bush—at least the paranoid, scheming, manipulative Bush that he had conjured in his own imagination.

AS THE NEXT national election approached, Rich went into overdrive to attack and discredit Bush. Thus he chose the fifth anniversary of 9/11 to retail the enduring myth that White House press secretary Ari Fleischer had issued a threatening call to Americans to "watch what they say" in the immediate aftermath of the attacks. It is worth recalling the circumstances that gave birth to this seemingly unkillable swiftboating lie.

A few days after 9/11, a Republican congressman from Louisiana named John Cooksey made the following ill-judged remark: "If I see someone come in and he's got a diaper on his head and a fan belt around that diaper on his head, that guy needs to be pulled over and checked." The left and liberal media went to town, making Cooksey out to be a spokesman for racial profiling. The White House press corps clamored for a reaction from the president. The mild-mannered Fleischer would only say that the president was "very disturbed" by Cooksey's inflammatory comment.

Shortly after this, the comedian Bill Maher flippantly remarked on his late-night talk show that American pilots shooting missiles from miles away were "cowards" compared to the terrorists who gave up their own lives flying airplanes into buildings. Now it was the right's turn to be outraged. It *was* an outrageous thing to say, and it eventually led the ABC network to drop Maher's show. The left, of course, cried censorship and made Maher out to be a hero of free speech sacrificed on the altar of right-wing political correctness.

Pressed for comment at a White House briefing, Fleischer replied—obviously speaking only for himself:

> I'm aware of the press reports about what he's said. I have not seen the actual transcript of the show itself. But assuming the press reports are right, it's a terrible thing to say, and

it's unfortunate. And that's why—there was an earlier question about has the president said anything to people in his own party—they're reminders to all Americans that they need to watch what they say, watch what they do. This is not a time for remarks like that; there never is.

The outrage on the right against Maher was now dwarfed by the outrage from the left directed at Fleischer. Freedom of speech was now out of bounds! Self-censorship was the new order from the White House! Bush wanted to impose a fascist dictatorship!

Fleischer apologized and explained that he had meant no such thing, but the charge that he was some kind of agent of totalitarian repression took hold on the left and wouldn't let go. Three years later *New York Times* columnist Paul Krugman repeated the myth that Fleischer had "ominously warned" Americans to "watch what they say," and said that this amounted to telling them "to accept the administration's version of events, not ask awkward questions."

Fleischer responded in a letter to the *Times* but Krugman issued no retraction or apology and the swiftboating of Fleischer as a stand-in for Bush continued unabated. The left-wing blogosphere echoed the charge endlessly, and proved impervious to all efforts at correction.

Thus Frank Rich could write with a straight face on September 10, 2006:

> The presidential press secretary, Ari Fleischer, condemned Bill Maher's irreverent comic response to 9/11 by reminding "all Americans that they need to watch what they say, watch what they do." Fear itself—the fear that "paralyzes needed efforts to convert retreat into advance," as FDR had it—was already being wielded as a weapon against Americans by their own government.

Christopher Hitchens responded to this "pathetic canard" with a sober and judicious column in *Slate* that carefully reconstructed the original context of Fleischer's remarks and exonerated him of any such intention. (The article was titled "Fear Factor: How Did We Survive Ari Fleischer's Reign of Terror?") But of course it made no difference to the left. It was the meme that would not die. Even today,

Fleischer's name can hardly be mentioned in the left blogosphere without noting that he was the Bush official who ominously warned Americans to "watch what they say." (No such outrage ensued when Obama spokesman Robert Gibbs warned people to "watch what they say" about Obama's Supreme Court nominee Sonia Sotomayor and her racially tinged comments and written opinions.)

ON THE SUNDAY before election day 2006—a crucial turning point for the left—Rich urged voters to "Throw The Truthiness Bums Out." He'd borrowed the word "truthiness" from comedian Stephen Colbert, who along with Jon Stewart, Rich admired and referenced frequently in his column. "The overwhelming majority of Americans now know that we were conned into this mess in the first place by two fake story lines manufactured by the White House, a connection between 9/11 and Saddam and an imminent threat of nuclear Armageddon."

These essentially baseless charges had been carefully nurtured by the left over a period of years. It had taken a long time to move them from the fever swamps of the left where they were initially hatched to the *New York Times* editorial page, where they could be confidently declared common knowledge, something that "everyone knew."

Rich seized on both issues because at least from a superficial point of view it was hard to refute them. The Senate Select Committee on Intelligence had "concluded" that there were no "operational" ties between Saddam and al Qaeda, meaning that there could not have been collusion on the operation that came to be known as September 11. But even if true, the committee—and Rich—missed the point: Iraq was certainly the next entity on the list after al Qaeda that could have mustered the operational strength and harbored the animus to pull off another 9/11. The Iraq War was never so much revenge for 9/11 as it was preemption of another or the next 9/11. Rich was smart enough to know that. He ignored that fact because it didn't help his argument.

As for the nuclear weapons issue, while the Bush administration was careful not to issue warnings that an Iraqi nuke was headed our way in the next few days or weeks, their warnings of a nuclear Iraq were taken as such. Rich also knew better, but took care to regard the

Bush administration warnings as if they were predicting an imminent attack. The fact that no one thought there was an imminent attack coming was doubled up with the fact that no significant amount of WMD of any kind were found to make a potent argument for Rich that Bush and his people had lied on two counts.

The fact that the Bush people sought a link between Iraq and 9/11 and didn't find one was taken by Rich as confirmation that there wasn't any. But there is a difference between not finding a link and there not being a link, in fact.

The fact that Bush later said that he never found proof of Iraqi involvement in 9/11 could be regarded by Rich as an admission by the guilty party, Bush, that Frank Rich had been right. In fact, Rich was not right. Iraq was involved with al Qaeda, but evidently not involved in 9/11. Iraq was a good suspect as a perpetrator of the next 9/11 not the past one. Iraq had WMD at one time, and wanted WMD again. The fact that it didn't have much in the way of WMD at the time we invaded should have been judged by Rich as an interesting fact, but not terribly relevant. Instead, both issues for him became a two-phrase, bumper-sticker shout down, like the drunk at the end of the bar who insists on continuing an argument he has obviously lost.

It is true that Vice President Cheney continued to believe there was a meeting between Mohammed Atta and an Iraqi security service officer in Prague. Cheney's belief arose from the facts of Atta's itinerary and he held to his belief despite the SSCI's conclusion that Atta's cell phone was actually in the United States and in use on the dates in question. Rich chose to believe that Atta was not in Prague meeting with the Iraqis, and Cheney chose to believe he did. They disagreed, and Rich's facts did not trump Cheney's, nor was the source of his opinion necessarily more authoritative. Intelligence experts and rival agencies disagree with one another all the time.

What Rich refused to acknowledge was that the leaders charged to protect the United States from further terrorism would have been foolish to ignore the festering international wound called Iraq. If Frank Rich had been president would he have ignored Iraq and left Saddam in place? If the answer is yes, we can say with reasonable certainty that it would have been a major failure of the Rich administration.

The Senate Select Committee reported its findings after a long investigation culminating in 2004. The WMD issue was fairly straightforward: Saddam Hussein had convinced everyone, even his own generals, that he had WMD. His actions toward the UN weapons inspectors strongly suggested he was hiding something. Moreover, his capabilities of restarting a bio weapons program quickly and easily had not been diminished by the years of weapons inspections and sanctions. Rich never wanted to confront those inconvenient facts.

As for a connection to 9/11, Rich conflated the notion that America had reason to be wary of Iraq-sponsored terrorism with the notion that there was a direct connection between Iraqi officials and the people who planned and executed the 9/11 attack. The truth was that after 9/11 any responsible government official would have been urgently asking the question: Who do we worry about next?

It certainly would have been difficult to pick a country other than Iraq. There could be no serious argument that Iran did not pose a mortal danger, but no one would have proposed invading a country of 60 million people with a much stronger military than Saddam's. One could make a case that Saudi Arabia's Wahabbist clerics and radicalized youth were a danger that rivaled Iraq. But could any president rationally attempt a takeover of the country that controlled the world's economy with its daily exports of millions of barrels of oil? Not likely.

The Senate Select Committee on Intelligence—the controlling authority on Iraq pre-war intelligence—issued a report on pre-war intelligence that was dense, circuitous, and drew conclusions that seemed to be at odds with its own reporting. In its ambiguous pages, Rich could ignore contradictory evidence and rely selectively on the SSCI's "factual" conclusion, which said: "There was no operational relationship between Iraq and al Qaeda."

This is what the report also said: "Regarding the Iraq–al-Qaeda relationship, reporting from sources of varying reliability points to a number of contacts, incidents of training, and discussions of Iraqi safe haven for Osama bin Laden and his organization dating from the early 1990s."

These were inconvenient facts. So Rich suppressed them in his own reporting.

In September 2006, six weeks from the crucial congressional elections, Rich was beating the electoral war drums. "The untruths are flying so fast that untangling them can be a full-time job," he wrote about Bush and Cheney, though he might as well have been speaking of himself.

Rich attacked the president for saying that a future stable Iraq would be "a strong ally in the war on terror." Watch out! Here comes the stiletto! "As is often the case, the president was technically truthful. Iraq will be a strong ally in the war on terror—just not necessarily our ally. As Mr. Bush spoke, the Iraqi prime minister, Nouri al-Maliki , was leaving for Iran to jolly up Mahmoud Ahmadinejad." Jolly up? What would Rich know of the content of the meetings between the leaders of Iran and Iraq? Would he prefer they returned to the days of the million-man slaughter when tanks advanced through the marshes over the bodies of dead enemies?

" 'Even the most sanguine optimist cannot yet conclude we are winning,' John Lehman, the former Reagan navy secretary, wrote of the Iraq war last month," Rich began. "So what do we do next? Given that the current course is a fiasco, and that the White House demonizes any plan or timetable for eventual withdrawal as 'cut and run,' there's only one immediate alternative: add more manpower, and fast." This turned out to be especially hilarious given Rich's abject opposition to the "surge" Bush would announce three months later. Then his own proposal of sending more men to Iraq would become a subject for scorn and ridicule—because it was endorsed by the president.

The election came out exactly as Rich would have wanted. Antiwar Democrats were swept into power. But somehow the war did not go away. Somehow the antiwar Democrats were not the miracle workers Rich expected them to be.

By early December 2006, Rich was announcing that the war in Iraq was over, even as Bush prepared to send more troops. "The actual reality is that we have lost in Iraq . . . The longer we pretend that we have not lost there, the more we risk losing other wars we still may salvage, starting with Afghanistan."

Amazingly, Rich knew more about the progress of the war than the men who were fighting and directing it. Somehow his years of training as a military historian and strategist had inadvertently dropped off his résumé. Or maybe it was just one of a series of roles he adopted like so many Halloween costumes, to be put on as required by his starring role as the *Times'* universal authority.

Christmas Eve 2006 brought another dour assessment, calling the war a "needless catastrophe" whose architects were, to his mind, escaping "scot-free." He despaired as "our country sinks deeper into a quagmire" and lamented the fact that "even a conclusive Election Day repudiation of the war proves powerless to stop it." He recalled better wars: "Nostalgia for the Cold War, which America won unambiguously, was visible everywhere this year as we lost a war that has divided the country."

The start of 2007 brought the horror of horrors to Rich and his fellow swiftboaters: the surge. For Rich it was almost a gift, laden with possibilities for ridicule and condemnation: we have been telling you to leave Iraq, how dare you send more troops?

"President Bush always had one asset he could fall back on: the self-confidence of a born salesman. Like Harold Hill in *The Music Man*, he knew how to roll out a new product, however deceptive or useless, with conviction and stagecraft." He went on to describe Bush—in theatrical terms, of course—as a "defeated Willy Loman who looked as broken as his war" while speaking to the nation about the surge of troops he had ordered.

He went on to attack neo-conservatives Frederick Kagan and William Kristol and "the retired Gen. Jack Keane" as the architects of the surge and concluded, "Given that these unelected hawks are some of the same great thinkers who promoted the Iraq fiasco in the first place, it is hard to imagine why this White House continues to listen to them." Kagan and Kristol are, perhaps, fair game because as academics and commentators their opinions carried no more weight than Rich's own. But to attack General Keane was the height of journalistic arrogance. Keane was widely credited as the man who convinced Bush there had to be a new way forward in Iraq and persuaded him to give a free rein to one of his own protégés, the man who shortly saved the American bacon in Iraq, General David Petraeus.

But ignorance of the facts never stopped Frank Rich. He attacked the surge as not only too much, but too little—too few troops. "By any of these neo-cons' standards, the Bush escalation of some 20,000 is too little, not to mention way too late."

A week later, Rich had worked himself into a frenzy. In a column titled "Lying Like It's 2003," he wrote, "This time we must do what too few did the first time: call the White House on its lies." What lies were those? "In reality we're learning piece by piece that it is the White House that has no plan. Ms. Rice has now downsized the surge/escalation into an 'augmentation,' inadvertently divulging how the Pentagon is improvising, juggling small deployments in fits and starts. No one can plausibly explain how a parallel chain of command sending American and Iraqi troops into urban street combat side by side will work with Iraqis in the lead."

A week after that, Rich declared, "The latest plan for victory is doomed."

In retrospect, these hysterical charges are laughable. Rich had no standing to make such confident judgments and predictions in the first place. When you think about it, it really is amazing that the reporters, editors, and readers of the *New York Times* took anything he wrote seriously, as though the Butcher of Broadway had suddenly become a great strategic thinker with deep sources in the Pentagon and foreign intelligence services.

In the end, of course, the surge did work, Iraq was pacified, Rich was proved wrong. But following his usual pattern, he never doubled back to say, "Oops, I was wrong about that." Instead he pressed forward with more generous helpings of outrage and condemnation.

Rich's next target was General Petraeus himself. The first few months of the surge, as has been explained many times, were hard, brutal, and deadly. But by mid-summer 2007 the effects of Petraeus' counterinsurgency techniques were being felt—at least in Iraq, if not in Frank Rich's office.

"The Petraeus phenomenon is not about protecting the troops or American interests but about protecting the president," Rich declared. "For all Mr. Bush's claims of seeking 'candid' advice, he wants nothing of the kind. He sent that message before the war, with the shunting aside of Eric Shinseki, the general who dared tell Congress the simple truth that hundreds of thousands of American troops would be needed to secure Iraq. The message was sent again when John Abizaid and George Casey were supplanted after they disagreed with the surge."

Abizaid and Casey were generals whose plans to subdue violence in

Iraq did not work and whose failures had previously been condemned by Rich in his campaign against Bush. Now he held them up as victims, run out of Baghdad on a rail for opposing a strategy designed to cure the very ills they had helped cause. One day Rich declares the war is "lost," the next he's holding up the generals responsible for that loss as sympathetic victims. Meanwhile, Rich himself was revealed as a man who would shamelessly push any argument, no matter how untrue or contradictory, as long as the result was to tar Bush.

By August 2007, Rich's denial of reality went off the charts. He actually wrote that Khalid Sheikh Mohammad, the killer of Danny Pearl, the mastermind of 9/11 and self-declared leader of the "Sura Council" of detainees at Guantanamo Bay prison, had been railroaded by agents of George W. Bush with a false confession. "The confession was suspect; another terrorist had been convicted in the Pearl case in Pakistan in 2002. There is no known corroborating evidence that Mohammed, the 9/11 ringleader who has taken credit for many horrific crimes while in American custody, was responsible for this particular murder. None of his claims, particularly those possibly coerced by torture, can be taken as gospel solely on our truth-challenged attorney general's say-so."

KSM, of course, had bragged about beheading Pearl "with my blessed right hand." But Rich, now suddenly a distinguished international lawyer in addition to his other amazing accomplishments—was there nothing this guy didn't know?—confidently declared that the case would not hold water. Who were you going to trust anyway: one of the worst mass murderers in history, or the "truth-challenged" attorney general of the United States?

Rewriting history on a terrorist in U.S. custody was not enough for Rich. So potent was his rage and indignation that he felt moved to publish a theory of the insurgency in Iraq that not only ran counter to the president's, but that of every person whose expertise on Iraq came from months and years on the ground.

In announcing his surge strategy the president had referred to the February 22, 2006, bombing of the holiest of Shiite shrines in Iraq, the gold-domed mosque in Samarra, as the moment when Shiite-Sunni sectarian violence exploded. In this, Bush was by no means alone. Iraqis have said much the same, and any number of Americans with experience in Iraq, including the *Times*' own long-time bureau chief John Burns, have agreed that the Golden Dome Mosque bombing was a watershed provocation. None of that was good enough for Frank Rich, who claimed to know better than everybody else.

"This narrative was false," he flatly declared, reverting to his constant theatrical framework. "Shiite death squads had been attacking Sunnis for more than a year before the Samarra bombing. The mosque attack was not a turning point." Rich, an experienced drama critic, knew a turning point when he saw one, and this wasn't it. Instead, the bombing was "merely a confirmation of the Iraqi civil war" and that "with no proof, Mr. Bush directly attributed the newly all-important Samarra bombing to 'Al Qaeda terrorists and Sunni insurgents.'" This howler was never revisited by Rich, as it should have been. In fact the bombing was carried out by agents of Zarqawi for the express purpose of stirring up more trouble between Sunnis and Shiites. In fact, Zarqawi pledged in a letter to bin Laden that one of his principal targets in Iraq would be Shiites, owing to their apostate beliefs.

In the same column, Rich dug himself deeper in a rhetorical and factual hole. He argued that when the president blamed an al Qaeda agent for the bombing plot, "Bush had the last synthetic piece he needed to complete his newest work of fiction: 1) All was hunky-dory with his plan for victory until the mosque was bombed. 2) 'Al Qaeda in Iraq' bombed the mosque. 3) Ipso facto, America must escalate the war to defeat 'Al Qaeda in Iraq,' those 'very same folks that attacked us on September the 11th.' True, true, and true—unless you are in the foxhole of denial along with Frank Rich.

"'Al Qaeda in Iraq' is not those very same folks," Rich went on, hastily donning his intelligence expert's costume. "It did not exist on 9/11 but was a product of the Iraq war and accounts for only a small fraction of the Sunni insurgency. It is not to be confused with the resurgent bin Laden network we've been warned about in the latest National Intelligence Estimate." Wrong, wrong, and wrong. Al Qaeda in Iraq existed as a result of the Afghan War, and had arrived in Iraq before America invaded. To call it a "small faction" of the Sunni insurgency was to ignore its outsized influence, owing to the effects of its brutality and violence directed at Shiites and Sunnis alike who did not go along. It was also the al Qaeda of the "resurgent bin Laden network we've been warned about." But bending facts to his will (in apparent imitation of the president he hated) was becoming a specialty of his.

Where were the *Times*' editors in all this? Evidently, completely cowed.

"But this factual issue hasn't deterred Mr. Bush. He has merely stepped up his bogus conflation of the two Qaedas by emphasizing all the 'foreign leaders' of 'Al Qaeda in Iraq,' because that might allow him to imply they are bin Laden emissaries." Well, would several long letters from Zarqawi (a Jordanian national) to bin Laden pledging his loyalty and obedience count in Frank Rich's world? Apparently not.

"The enemy that did attack us six years ago, sad to say, is likely to persist in its nasty habit of operating in the reality-based world that our president disdains," Rich concluded. Considering the facts known at the time, the facts that would emerge later, and the result of the much-despised surge, one has to wonder exactly who was and who wasn't "reality based."

We now know that General David Petraeus, a sharp critic of the management of the Iraq War before he assumed command, did in fact have the secret to how the war could be won, or if that is too strong, how it could "succeed." But the mere fact that Petraeus had committed the crime of associating himself with President Bush made him the enemy, so nothing he said could be trusted. Referring to Sunday morning talk show appearances by both General Petraeus and Ambassador Ryan Crocker, Rich dismissed the architects of the surge as presidential boot lickers.

"General Petraeus and Mr. Crocker wouldn't be sounding like the Bobsey Twins . . . were they not already anticipating the surge's failure," he wrote, as though he were some kind of mentalist who knew what these men were "really" thinking. "Both spoke on Sunday of how (in General Petraeus's variation on the theme) they had to 'show that the Baghdad clock can indeed move a bit faster, so that you can put a bit of time back on the Washington clock.' The very premise is nonsense. Yes, there is a Washington clock, tied to Republicans' desire to avoid another Democratic surge on Election Day 2008. But there is no Baghdad clock. It was blown up long ago and is being no more successfully reconstructed than anything else in Iraq."

Here Rich demonstrated that his only real concern was "Election

Day 2008" rather than taking even a passing interest in a successful outcome in Iraq. He turned out to be wrong, of course, though he has yet to admit any such thing. Bush must admit his mistakes. Even Jon Stewart has done so on occasion. But seldom Frank Rich.

Of course, Stewart was caught in a mistake that Rich would not have made and had to walk back his error. Generally, however, they both give themselves exemptions from the rules they apply to the president, and they did so for a single-minded purpose: to present lies as the truth, to drive voters away from supporting a war we had to win, and to poison the minds of Americans about the president who kept them safe and who eventually won the war precisely by ignoring the clamor of know-nothing media critics like Stewart and Rich.

Rich's denial of what he described as "the reality-based world" actually stepped up as the 2008 election approached. At the end of March, the prime minister of Iraq, Nouri al-Maliki, a Shiite, decided to move against the Shiite gangs and militias that had taken over Basra. Maliki personally directed the Basra "invasion" of 40,000 Iraqi troops. It did not go well at first, but with American help, it eventually turned out to be a very successful operation. It forced Muqtada al-Sadr's Mahdi Army out of Basra, it was a defeat for the Iranians who were directing the lawlessness in Basra, and it proved to Sunni Iraqis that their Shiite prime minister would use deadly force against his co-religionists.

But for Rich it was just another chance to declare a Bush defeat. His April 6, 2008, column headlined, "Tet Happened, No One Cared," was a stunningly slipshod piece of work for the *New York Times*' most prominent columnist. "It's no surprise that so few stopped to absorb the disastrous six-day battle of Basra that ended last week—a mini-Tet that belied the 'success' of the surge," Rich wrote, showing his hand early in the column. "It was a defining moment all right. Mr. Maliki's impulsive and ill-planned attempt to vanquish the militias in southern Iraq loyal to his Shiite rival, the cleric Muqtada al-Sadr, was a failure that left Mr. Sadr more secure than before."

Huh? This was simply not true. Sadr remained in Iran during the entire episode, hiding. He called off the battle when his ragtag Mahdi Army was cornered and running low on ammunition. His

Iranian enablers in Basra had either been killed or chased back across the border into Iran.

Rich took each report of a Maliki setback as though it were another Vietnam. "Though some Iraqi armed forces were briefly in the lead, others mutinied." True, but insignificant to the outcome. "Eventually American and British forces and air power had to ride to the rescue in both Basra and Baghdad." True again, but so what? The Iraqis depend on the Americans for airpower. "Even then, the result was at best a standoff, with huge casualties." Flat out wrong. "The battle ended only when Mr. Maliki's own political minions sought a cease-fire." True, but it was a ceasefire with Maliki on top, having won. "None of the objectives have been met." Flat wrong again.

It was less than a month later that the *Times*' own Iraqi reporter, Ammar Karim, went to Basra for a first-hand look and inadvertently refuted Rich's version of events.

"There was a new feeling. I had never seen before the Iraq Army, without hesitation, accusing the Mahdi Army of being involved in all the disorder there," Karim wrote. "One of the soldiers told me: 'The Mahdi Army are a group of criminals, they will destroy everything if we don't stop them.' In the past, I have never seen soldiers dare to say anything about them. I felt the reign of fear is broken, and that is it. Exactly the same feeling as when the Baathist regime fell."

You had to wonder from what disgruntled low-level military source Frank Rich was getting this bad information. Yet instead of the retraction he ought to have published, Rich doubled down. On April 13, 2008, at a point when the surge had long been recognized as successful by those experts and reporters who had bothered to look into the matter, Rich—apparently watching last season's reruns—was still declaring it a failure and blaming General Petraeus, who was now back in Washington, D.C., testifying before Congress, along with the U.S. ambassador to Iraq, Ryan Crocker.

Once again he viewed this critically important testimony as nothing more than a piece of bad theater to be eviscerated. "The prevailing verdict on the Petraeus-Crocker show is that it accomplished little beyond certifying President Bush's intention to kick the can to January 2009 so that the helicopters will vacate the Green Zone on the next president's watch. . . . Unable to even look at the fiasco anymore, the nation is now just waiting for someone to administer the last rites," he wrote.

The reference here to helicopters in the Green Zone offers a key to Rich's whole mentality and outlook. He and other liberals of his generation who cut their teeth protesting the war in Vietnam were determined to see Iraq as a replay of that disastrous intervention, which had ended ignominiously with the last Americans being air-lifted from the embassy roof in Saigon. So attached were Rich and his fellow liberals to that old familiar script that they insisted on im-posing it frame by frame on the very different situation in Iraq. As a result they were unable to perceive the truth until it hit them in the nose—and for many, not even then.

The trick for Rich and the other liberal swiftboaters was to be able to deny that the war had turned a corner and that the presi-dent had found, whether by luck or design, a winning strategy. The election was coming, and not anticipating the precipitous economic disaster that swept Barack Obama to victory, the left was still wedded to the narrative of a lost war as the principal argument to reject John McCain and choose Obama.

In a column called "Last Call for Change We Can Believe In," published at the end of August 2008, two months before the presi-dential election, Rich demanded that the Obama strategy "that van-quished Hillary Clinton must be rebooted to take out John McCain."

"Take out" John McCain? In the *New York Times*? Once again, are the editors so cowed by one columnist that all the old rules were to be ignored?

And what editor let Rich publish this howler? "What Obama also should have learned by now is that the press is not his friend." This patent absurdity was given a free pass. Rich cited a source for the assertion ("George Mason University's Center for Media and Public Affairs documented in its study of six weeks of TV news reports this summer, Obama's coverage was 28 percent positive, 72 percent nega-tive") but it flew so directly in the face of reality and common sense that this particular study had to be regarded as a project by the blind.

Rich was evidently in a panic that Obama would somehow— with only six weeks to election day—manage to lose, though no credible polling, public or private, showed that was even a possibility. He even said this: "Obama is never going to be a John Edwards–style populist barnburner."

What? Nobody but John Edwards himself placed John Edwards in the same league as Barack Obama. But that didn't stop Rich from interjecting himself in what he saw as a flailing Obama campaign.

Rich should not have panicked. His man won.

He should have worried more that a war he had condemned and declared lost had in fact been won before the election. But the public somehow did not discover this fact, any more than Rich himself, and went to the polls in large majorities believing that the war was both wrong and irretrievably lost—a disaster, a catastrophe, the worst foreign policy blunder in American history. Anybody who said otherwise was a liar or a madman or both.

In a word, Frank Rich and Jon Stewart had done a much better job of lying to the public than even they imagined.

Chapter Four

Who Let Keith Olbermann Go off His Meds? A Look behind the Curtain of Left-Wing Cable News

When Lyndon Johnson lost Walter Cronkite he knew it was over. What George W. Bush and his people evidently never saw coming was a media onslaught led by a sports anchor, a comedian, and a theater reviewer: Keith Olbermann, Jon Stewart, and Frank Rich. They said for the Washington, D.C., media what those potentates of capital opinion couldn't say for themselves. They said for members of Congress things the members might say, but to whom no one would be listening.

Stewart, with his *Daily Show* on the Comedy Central cable channel, influenced a lot of young people, particularly college-age new voters, who came to view the president as a clown and the war as a joke. The theater critic, Rich at the *New York Times*, led the thinking of smart-set urbanites who liked to read lively and blood-boiling treatises on the depredations of George W. Bush.

But it was Olbermann, the sports anchor at cable channel MSNBC, who set the pace for everyone in the Bush-hating media with his baroque ravings and eye-bulging condemnations and spittle-spewing venom. He was omnivorous in selecting from the anti-Bush buffet. He railed about the war, he bellowed about the beautiful blond spy, he roared about the government listening to phone calls

and scanning email, he got in the president's face about his sometimes fractured language, and he demanded the president be tried
and imprisoned for torture.

The left loved Stewart because he openly mocked the president.
The left loved Rich because he made them feel smart and fully informed, even if it was mainly sleight of hand.

But they loved, loved, loved Keith Olbermann because he viciously
attacked their favorite targets, George W. Bush and Bill O'Reilly,
and he did it every night, no matter what, on the thinnest of excuses.
If you wanted to hate on O'Reilly, Olbermann's *Countdown* show was
the place to go. If you wanted your daily rave about Bush—let's say
you fancied yourself a debater at the office—Olbermann was tailor
made for you.

(It should be noted that I worked at MSNBC from the moment it
first went on the air until just before the 2000 election, when NBC
notified me—for the second time—that it would not be renewing my
contract. I spent the next eight years as an anchor for Fox News, but
during the formative years of MSNBC I observed the workings of the
network from the inside.)

How did Keith Olbermann become king of left-wing cable news?
The answer is not his obvious skill at fang and claw attacks, his passion for venom, or his special talent for reading a teleprompter, which
may even surpass Barack Obama's much praised skills. Olbermann's
dominance of the left cable niche owes little to his volcanic outbursts
or his long, faux-literate rants. His rise and dominance arose from
MSNBC's long and tortured history of failure.

In normal circumstances, if a news executive were faced with an
on-air talent who wanted to say the things Olbermann said about
George W. Bush or any president, the answer would have been no.
But at the point when key NBC executives were faced with Olbermann's breaking of many of the hallowed rules and traditions of
broadcast journalism, MSNBC was a decade-long failure. And Olbermann was the first thing that had worked.

It no longer mattered if an NBC brand operation went headfirst
into the deep end of partisan politics. Apparently, all that mattered
was whether it worked, or appeared to work. And the first thing
that shined the dimmest light in a slightly promising direction jolted
NBC executives into action. With the first glint of Olbermann's

angry success, MSNBC would be allowed to let him range far to the left, and the mothership, NBC News—its august anchors, its war-hardened correspondents and producers who suffered hardships and danger (and sometimes gave their lives) for the network and its reputation—would just have to accommodate itself to a partisan and endlessly embarrassing sister network shouting itself red in the face from under the wing of the NBC peacock.

"Mr. Bush, you are a fascist. Get them to print you a t-shirt that says 'FASCIST'!" Olbermann bellowed into the camera.

"Mr. Bush, you are not America," he sternly warned the president.

"You, Mr. Bush, are a bald-faced liar," he hissed, working himself into a lather about the "surge" on the same night he called Bush the "idiot in chief."

This was a man who could not have said those words on any NBC property anytime in the company's long history, if it had not been for the DNA of failure at MSNBC. As the tenth anniversary of the network's launch approached, MSNBC seized this one glimmer of hope amid its enormously expensive record of failure, no matter what the cost to the reputation of the parent network. Better to be brazenly partisan than a continuous flop.

MSNBC debuted in June 1996. For year after tortured year, the network seemed to operate under a curse. Nothing succeeded, no matter how much star power, no matter how much money spent on sets or graphics or overloaded staffs. At first, dismal results didn't seem to matter, because CNN wasn't getting much in the way of audience (ratings) either. Still, whatever MSNBC tried seemed doomed to failure.

These were the early days of cable news competition, a new thing in 1996. CNN had the field to itself for more than a decade, and had plodded along with a somber low-key style that begged for a challenge. Viewers came to CNN when they heard of a big news event, and when it was over they went away in droves. A sustained story like the Gulf War produced big audiences, but after a big story dribbled out into day after day of "follow-ups" the audience quickly faded into the woodwork. Feast and famine were a way of life at CNN, and many people believed it would always be that way.

With the advent of MSNBC and Fox, the cable news business became competitive. Early on, the talk around the industry was whether the market (people who watched television) would support three cable news networks. It was generally assumed that three were at least one too many.

The weak sister was thought to be Fox. After all, MSNBC had the money of Microsoft and the know-how of big-time network people from NBC, and it was thought to be the one most likely to one day overtake CNN.

When MSNBC went on the air one of the key people sent to its Secaucus, New Jersey, studios was an energetic producer named Phil Griffin. He'd had long experience with some of the biggest stars at NBC—Tom Brokaw, Katie Couric, Ann Curry, Bob Costas—and he always seemed to be in the center of things. Along with him came another well-thought-of young producer from the NBC system, Steve Capus. By the time Olbermann blossomed into a carnivorous flower at MSNBC a decade later, Griffin and Capus were running MSNBC and NBC respectively.

It was Griffin and Capus who let Olbermann loose to go hard left at MSNBC. They had been partners in cable crime for a decade without winning, and the story of Olbermann's rise from the obscurity of sportscasting to become the king of left-wing cable was in large part a backstage drama of two executives who simply had to get the monkey off their backs.

NBC entered the cable news game thinking it would be easy to power over CNN and the long-shot rival that Rupert Murdoch and Roger Ailes were starting at Fox.

Media journalist and author Ken Auletta later reported that the deal for a partnership with Microsoft and NBC came when Bill Gates visited NBC President Bob Wright's office in New York to talk about working together. Gates wanted NBC content for his Internet businesses and NBC wanted a partner with deep pockets. In Wright's office, a live shot of Tom Brokaw had been piped in from Washington, D.C., where Brokaw was anchoring *Nightly News* on the occasion of the Million Man March.

Brokaw pointed out all the technology NBC was using to cover the story, all the reporters on the air, all the producers supplying information, the live coverage of marchers, speeches, politicians, and he told Gates, "We can put all of this on television, on cable, and on the Internet and it won't cost us one dime more."

Gates was impressed and agreed to the partnership. Microsoft would have access to NBC archives, but even better it would have access to current NBC material for a news Web site, and it would have its name front and center on a revolutionary new cable news channel, MSNBC.

After a decade and at least a billion dollars, Microsoft finally allowed itself to be bought out. Multibillionaire Gates might have never missed the money, but it was an open secret among executives at other networks that the reason NBC News seemed to be able to field more crews, more satellite trucks, and more producers was that the other networks didn't have Bill Gates' money.

One of the first shows that MSNBC announced was called *Internight*, after Microsoft's desire to have the network sound *Internetty*. An afternoon program was called *Newschat*, because Internet people were in "chat" rooms. A show called *The Site* starred Soledad O'Brien, a smart young woman who had been science correspondent Robert Bazell's producer at NBC. She hosted from a Silicon Valley–type set in San Francisco. It featured her speaking to a character created by a person offstage wearing a suit of electronic sensors that would translate his movements into an on-screen image.

Phil Griffin's first assignment was to produce *Internight*, an hour-long interview program with a revolving cast of big-name NBC stars. This program aired just before the 9 PM news hour anchored by Brian Williams, a fast-rising young reporter from the New York station WCBS, who had been personally recruited by Brokaw. Brokaw would do one night, Katie Couric the next, then Matt Lauer, Bob Costas, and finally Bill Moyers. How could it miss?

NBC was going to bring network-quality stars to cable and it expected network results. Griffin faced a difficult task. He was producing a highly touted program featuring big stars who got 10, 12, even 18 full points of ratings on the network shows; but in cable news there was almost no chance that they would gather audiences that big. Griffin was going to have to soften the blow when his big stars learned that they would measure their new cable audience in thousands, not millions.

MSNBC launched in June 1996 and within a few months moved to expensive new headquarters in Secaucus, New Jersey. For a while, everything was calm. The network was new, the stars didn't expect to be an overnight success, and luckily ratings weren't available for a few months. Here and there a major story blew up and MSNBC executives would be encouraged by decent-looking audience numbers, but viewership immediately fell off to near zero as soon as the crisis passed. In terms of ratings, which is how television earns a profit, it was hills and valleys. Feast and famine. One day signs of life, the next day back to Death Valley.

MSNBC liked to boast about its flashy studios in Secaucus, but the location made life difficult. Bringing guests into the studio was essential, but guests tended not to want to leave Manhattan and the bill for car services was soon way over budget. MSNBC was a non-union shop, and to avoid union problems at NBC headquarters, executives not only moved the start-up network off the island of Manhattan, a union stronghold, but put it over the first ridge in New Jersey, where it couldn't even be seen from New York. MSNBC soon became known as "The Swamp," because it was located out in the Jersey marshes where the mob used to dump bodies.

Fox went on the air a few months after MSNBC. Roger Ailes, the longtime television producer and political strategist who joined forces with Rupert Murdoch to launch the new network, picked strong personalities and was building programs around people, not simply the news. Bill O'Reilly was doing something no one in the business understood, and Sean Hannity seemed to have brought his conservative radio program to television.

MSNBC, on the other hand, thought of itself as a junior varsity version of its much more polished sibling at NBC. It was steady and dignified, as close as it could come to old-style network news done on twenty-four-hour, fly-by-the-seat-of-your-pants cable. Meanwhile, Fox was already distinguishing itself as something different, while CNN had twenty years of brand loyalty with the audience. MSNBC was a me-too network nobody wanted.

The little-noticed problem was that the people who produced and anchored shows for MSNBC regarded themselves as a farm team for the mother network. Consequently, nobody wanted to do anything that wasn't acceptable to their betters at 30 Rock. The reporting was network news style, the anchoring was network news style, the shooting and editing all designed to please the network news types who sat in judgment at NBC headquarters, and whose expertise was making television that was watched by large numbers of people.

Except those large numbers of people didn't watch cable news. Or didn't watch much. Brian Williams' big newscast struggled. The *Internight* cast of big stars started to look like high-gloss cable access, and it was sometimes hard to get NBC correspondents to come on the air. A kindly overseas correspondent who didn't know how badly MSNBC was doing would show up on the air occasionally, and then disappear for months at a time.

Then two things happened that defined MSNBC in the pre-leftist years.

First, on August 31, 1997, Princess Diana died in a car crash in Paris. Soledad O'Brien's computer show passed the word that they didn't really do royalty or car crashes, so why didn't they take the night off so MSNBC could continue its special coverage? The show never came back on the air.

Princess Diana scored big numbers, and MSNBC milked it for a year. Coverage and rehash of the Princess Diana story not only ate the Soledad O'Brien show, but the big stars who had been roped into *Internight* took the opportunity to quietly bow out. With the exception of Brian Williams, the Brokaw heir-apparent, the network had no big stars. It also had no big numbers.

The second transformative event was the Clinton-Lewinsky scandal, which broke on January 17, 1998. This was a story that had it all, and it seemed it could be ridden for a long time. A president having sex with an intern in the White House, under the nose of the First Lady, the staff, and the press corps was obviously huge. And like OJ, the story featured new players and new developments day after day after day. MSNBC scored big by going after Clinton, and whatever the politics of the network figures involved, the story was too juicy and sensational not to go after in a big way.

It was just before this period that Keith Olbermann showed up at MSNBC. The network lacked an 8 PM star for the hour before Williams, and Griffin was trying to talk Olbermann into taking the job. Olbermann had left ESPN after a public falling-out with the executives there. He was one of a class of sportscasters who came to the job not as former players—jocks—but as a spectator and fan, and in his case, a baseball card collector. He had been living unhappily in Bristol, Connecticut—ESPN's studios and headquarters—and wanted out.

In October 1997, *The Big Show with Keith Olbermann* went on the air at 8 PM, just before the big Brian Williams newscast. He was a big star and got big star treatment. *Newsweek* ballyhooed his move to MSNBC with a feature story that called him "the nation's smartest, sassiest sportscaster" and described his relief at escaping farm country in Bristol, Connecticut. "Today the 38-year-old Olbermann sits high above midtown Manhattan in his new million-dollar apartment, content amid his 35,000 baseball trading cards and seats from such relics as the Montreal Forum and Ebbets Field," wrote *Newsweek*'s David Kaplan. "To the south there's a view of the Statue of Liberty, to the north a view all the way up the Hudson, in the elevator Al Pacino and Goldie Hawn! On the street are restaurants galore and always a cab. Olbermann is single, doesn't drive and dislikes farm animals—life is good. Plus his $350,000 salary is doubling."

Olbermann did well, but after the first year, trouble began. When the Lewinsky story broke, MSNBC execs knew it was a story to grab and they went after it in a big way, mostly following their betters as NBC's producers and correspondents folded in all the related permutations involving Paula Jones, Linda Tripp, Lucianne Goldberg, Susan McDougal, and a wider cast of characters. It had the crucial ingredient that cable needed: namely, the tabloid obsession factor. If the details kept coming, the audience would keep showing up. By and large MSNBC did well with it, though still losing to CNN, and not paying enough attention to what Ailes was doing at Fox.

This was when Olbermann went crazy, leading the author to later observe that he's the only guy in TV who takes off a straitjacket to put on a suit jacket and go to the studio to do his show. The problem was that he hated the Clinton-Lewinsky story so much he began to refuse to come in to do his show if that's what they were going to cover. More and more often a fill-in host was required to stay late and do Olbermann's show. The impeachment hearings were getting ginned up, and Olbermann's broadcast had been renamed *White House in Crisis*. Olbermann was increasingly angry over MSNBC's brutal Clinton coverage, and started staying away more and more often.

NBC executives were starting to worry, and the pressure was coming down on Phil Griffin. It was not uncommon for Griffin to be on the phone while people waited in his office, and it became more and more common to hear him in endless conversations with his biggest problem child, Keith Olbermann. People would leave and come back, hoping for it to end. Keith would be at home—lounging in his bathtub smoking a cigar—refusing to come in to work. Phil would beg him to just get out of the tub and go downstairs to a waiting car, which had been there for hours. The conversation would go on most of the day, and finally Phil would give up and tell the fill-in host he was doing Keith's show again.

This behavior led to friction with NBC News president Andy Lack, and by this time it was clear that Olbermann was on his way out. A combination of things pushed him to try to get out of his contract: first the Clinton business, which he hated, and later said would "make me ashamed, make me depressed, make me cry." Another factor was money. Fox Sports was offering him double what he was making at MSNBC, to over a million dollars a year. Eventually Andy Lack made Fox buy Olbermann out, paying NBC to extract him from his contract.

Olbermann left MSNBC to its ratings miseries and went to Los Angeles to work for Fox Sports. A visitor later found him living in a hotel even after he'd taken a beach house in Malibu. It turned out there were two sounds Olbermann can't stand while trying to sleep, surf and traffic. One side of the house had cars whizzing by on the Pacific Coast Highway, the other was bathed in the soothing sound of waves lapping the beach. Somehow he hadn't seemed to notice when he took the house.

At Fox Sports, Olbermann insisted on breaking a story that Fox was going to sell its controlling interest in the Los Angeles Dodgers, when Fox owner Rupert Murdoch did not want the story out. "He was crazy—I fired him," Murdoch later said in an interview at the *Wall Street Journal*'s All Digital Conference.

In the summer of 2000, NBC News president Andy Lack was pondering a new direction for MSNBC. He'd grown tired of the cable news wars over very small ratings and thought he had come up with a way to outflank CNN and Fox. It was a plan to turn MSNBC into a combination Discovery Channel and news channel. "Let's say there's a plane crash," an NBC executive said, describing Lack's plan. "Andy wants to pick up the phone and say, 'Give me an hour documentary tonight—Why Do Planes Crash?'" Lack had ramped up the documentary unit, let some anchors go, and was taking MSNBC in a new direction.

It might have been a good plan. But no one ever found out. A month before the Bush-Gore election, Lack realized that it was a close race with high drama and ordered MSNBC to turn on a dime—again—and ramp up election coverage.

Election Day 2000 turned into a monthlong recount of compelling national interest. It had all the elements of what has become signature cable news coverage: suspense and the unexpected. Absurd images of elections workers examining dangling, hanging, and dimpled chads filled television screens around the world. OJ-style helicopter chases of government vehicles ferrying impounded ballot boxes to the state capitol competed for screen time with lawyers holding news conferences outlining strategies. And ultimately, an election decided by justices of the Supreme Court of the United States. Nobody could have asked for a better cable news story.

But Fox spurted ahead in the ratings, sometimes passing CNN, and leaving MSNBC far behind.

A year later, on September 11, 2001, Fox surged again, and with the invasion of Iraq in early 2003 Fox became a dominant force. During this period, Olbermann did a sports segment in national radio syndication. He was out of the action.

Anybody who knew him had to know that he wanted back in, but it was still a big surprise to see him turn up again on MSNBC in 2003 as a substitute host for Gerald Nachmʌn, and a general anchor for war coverage as the Iraq War got underway. Griffin had saved him. Eleven days after the launch of the Iraq War he began a new program for MSNBC called *Countdown*.

During the period he had been away Fox News had taken the lead, and there was no question MSNBC was in third place behind CNN. This was especially painful for its long suffering executives because at launch, MSNBC had been the golden child of cable, loaded with money, run by the best and the brightest in network news . . . and still a failure.

When a cable news program goes really low, it scores "hash marks," meaning that the number of people watching is smaller than the number that would qualify as even a fraction of a ratings point. Today Fox News has programs that score two and three full points. Before the Iraq War, half a point was a solid show, and three quarters of a point was a big success. If any car chase or celebrity death scored over a full point, it was time to break out the champagne. MSNBC had come tantalizingly close for a long time, but when the car chase was over, so was MSNBC's audience.

CNN had its brand-name following. Fox had its unique position as the one network that actively engaged a conservative point of view. MSNBC didn't have anything to make it distinctive. Phil Griffin briefly toyed with doing right-wing opinion lite, but it was another half measure and did not work.

By the time Olbermann came back in 2003 the network was hopelessly mired in third place, Fox having stormed ahead and pushed CNN into second place.

Griffin and Capus had spent years swimming upstream with MSNBC, and had finally made their escape. Capus, longtime producer and confidante of Brian Williams, had ascended to president of NBC News. Williams would not be far behind, as Brokaw was getting ready to retire as the anchor of NBC *Nightly News*. Griffin too had abandoned the Lincoln Tunnel commute to Secaucus, and settled into a comfy office at 30 Rock, where he took over as senior vice president overseeing the *Today* show. He left Rick Kaplan behind at MSNBC to run the place. Kaplan was a three-decade veteran of the top levels of the network news business. He'd been at ABC for many years, and later ran CNN.

Still, Capus and Griffin were the last men standing among the MSNBC founders and had a certain responsibility to see the thing through. Olbermann's *Countdown* program went on the air in October 2003, going up against Bill O'Reilly. No matter how Olbermann did, the time slot meant almost certain third place, possibly rising to second if CNN stumbled. A sports guy, Olbermann's tendency was to attack someone—a hapless pitcher who can't find the strike zone, a running back who drops the ball, a manager whose team is losing—and the strategy quickly developed that he would swing up at O'Reilly whenever he possibly could. He went after O'Reilly with gusto, inventing the "Worst Person in the World" segment in order to have a place to attack O'Reilly every day.

But there had to be more than just making O'Reilly a bad guy. That's when Olbermann discovered he was against the war in Iraq, against the "fear mongering" of 9/11, against the president who pushed the war, and he started his march toward leading the American left as it frog marched George W. Bush out of office.

Olbermann himself picks up the story in his 2007 book *Truth and Consequences*. In the prologue he writes about his anger over the death of NBC News correspondent David Bloom. In trying to convey his all-encompassing grief, he writes that he decided to go to a ballgame. As he walked to the press box, where he could pour out his heart to his sportswriter confreres, two drunks recognized him and called out, but then thought better of it. One said to the other, Olbermann reports, "Nah, forget him. He's a liberal."

"I had been back at MSNBC less than two months," Olbermann wrote of his fuming anger.

"We had launched *Countdown* six days earlier.

"We had put virtually nothing on the newscast except reports from Iraq and Washington. . . .

"We had sent David Bloom into harm's way and he wasn't coming back.

"And I was not to be talked to because somehow I was a liberal."

Keith Olbermann got mad.

He wasn't going to take it.

He began to look askance at the war. "Then the plotline in Iraq turned out to be not just phony, but also ridiculous. Not only were there no weapons of mass destruction, but the chemical warfare the generals and ex-generals nightly told us to expect also never materialized. Saddam Hussein not only had no offensive weapons, he didn't have any defensive ones."

He also discovered that the military seemed to have created the heroic narrative about Pvt. Jessica Lynch—captured by Iraqis, then released in a daring "rescue" operation—out of something less than the whole truth, and claimed to have been the first news outlet in the country to repeat a Canadian newspaper report that the story didn't add up. He was causing trouble telling the "truth." "The right-wing water carriers buffeted our management, and our management buffeted me."

But he says, to management's credit, the truth meant something to them. "They smelled the rats as surely as did I. Management only wanted to make sure I clarified that I wasn't attacking the heroism of the troops who broke into the hospital. *Of course I wasn't*, I thought to myself, *they were just as sincere as I had been.* Just as patriotic. Just as much—what was the other word beginning with 'pat'?—oh, patsies."

"Management" had to mean Rick Kaplan, then president of MSNBC, and his superiors at 30 Rock, Olbermann's old friend Phil Griffin and network president Steve Capus. In Olbermann's cranky objections to the war, they surely had seen an opportunity—go left, young man!—and they were trying to manage the cyclonic personality who might bring MSNBC out of its long and burdensome failure.

Olbermann went on to describe how Saddam Hussein had been tarred in *guilt by association* with the 9/11 hijackers "for the vast majority of people who couldn't tell al Qaeda from Al Jarreau," the popular singer. He wrote that the president and his administration used the confusion to "grab all kinds of un-American powers over the American legal system the way President Adams tried to, or President Nixon, or Joe McCarthy or anybody else who ever recognized inchoate fear in the public, who was ever eager to protect freedoms by surrendering them."

He wrote, "But amid all the tumult and threatening and name calling"—he evidently got some angry email from viewers, and put-downs by bloggers—"I have yet to see serious refutations of either the facts or the conclusions in these comments."

Well, he must not have looked. The Senate Select Committee on Intelligence refutes his "conclusions," as does the Iraqi Perspectives Project Report, and many of the dozens of books written by war-wearied authors and investigative reporters, even those who were against the war and the way it was prosecuted. Even President Barack Obama—who Olbermann worked strenuously to see elected—would later reconfirm Bush decisions, which Olbermann had condemned in the strongest possible terms, such as the National Security Agency's program to monitor phone calls and electronic communications, and the Bush decision that some detainees were too dangerous either to put on trial or release, but would have to be indefinitely incarcerated.

The first year of his new television program, things didn't change much for MSNBC or its beleaguered executives. Olbermann was hired for the second time in the seventh year of failure. He had returned after a long hiatus, contrite and polite. Insiders at NBC reported, "He's been really nice." But those who remembered him storming off five years earlier in a Tasmanian-devil hissy fit didn't think it would last long.

The executives at MSNBC had now tried everything, but the audience ignored them and Fox just surged ahead. Capus and Griffin knew they were coming up on the expiration of Microsoft's ten-year contract that had been supporting MSNBC (and NBC News) for years. The entire enterprise was threatened if they did not get some traction with the audience.

Olbermann himself identified a moment when he saw the landscape changing for his program. He described it in his book as the day he invited former ambassador Joe Wilson on his show to talk about the outing of Wilson's CIA operative wife, Valerie Plame. Olbermann complained he'd been receiving faxes all day from the White House on talking points to hit Wilson with, and he showed the emails on the air. "And he laughed and I laughed and the audience ratings grew a little bit, and I had an odd feeling that the show and the country would turn out all right after all."

In the four years of nonstop denunciation beginning at the start of Bush's second term the left fell behind three leaders who spearheaded the charge with enormous gusto, indefatigable energy, and polished skills at rhetorical warfare. Gone were the days when a half-embalmed mandarin of the Senate or House would pronounce a few words of condemnation and expect the country to shudder at the force of the blast. In this great project to take down a president, the deep stentorian voices under the Capitol dome were largely ignored, and the gray eminences of the newspapers and television produced nothing but bleating in the wind. It was left to an odd troika to lead the charge against the president—Stewart, Rich, and Olbermann.

In September 2005, 182 people were killed in attacks in Baghdad. A month earlier, a car bomb had killed 114 in the Iraqi city of Hila. In January 2004, a letter from Abu Musab al Zarqawi to Osama bin

Laden had been intercepted, which outlined how Zarqawi was going to ignite a civil war by attacking the "heretics" (the Shia) and catching the "unbelievers" (the Americans) in the cross fire. The American military had been after Zarqawi since well before the capture of the letter, but at least with its publication one had to know there was a fight underway with al Qaeda in Iraq.

Yet at this precise point in September 2005, Olbermann decided it was time to initiate open warfare with the president. He began his first of dozens of "Special Comment" pieces on that day, attacking President Bush over Hurricane Katrina, because New Orleans was under water. It was the perfect "bash Bush" story. Nobody could be accused of being unpatriotic or not sufficiently in support of troops in the field by attacking the president over a hurricane. "As I would later tell an interviewer, this was one of those moments when it felt like the words were just coming out of my fingers—when my indignation, more as a citizen than as a journalist, made it necessary to address a topic and at length."

The September 5, 2005, "Special Comment" launched an anti-Bush campaign that did not let up even after he had disappeared into retirement in Texas.

Olbermann was not certain how far to go in attacking Bush directly. "(N)ationally, these are leaders who won re-election last year largely by portraying their opponents as incapable of keeping the country safe. These are leaders who regularly pressure the news media in this country to report the reopening of a school or a power station in Iraq, and defy its citizens not to stand up and cheer. Yet they couldn't even keep one school or power station from being devastated by infrastructure collapse in New Orleans . . . ," he read from the teleprompter in his Germanic *I-give-the-orders-here* style. "This is the Law and Order and Terror government. It promised protection—or at least amelioration—against all threats, conventional, radiological or biological," he thundered. "It has just proved that it cannot save its citizens from a biological weapon called standing water."

Olbermann reads the prompter flawlessly, and he has learned over the years to pepper his script with words that make people reach for the dictionary, with a knife-to-the-ribs punch line. Phil Griffin or Rick Kaplan or Steve Capus evidently liked it. "The Katrina comment apparently struck a chord," Olbermann wrote. "My boss pulled me aside to encourage me to make similar remarks whenever the spirit moved me."

Olbermann's denunciations became a sensation of the left-wing blogs, and of YouTube. Olbermann curried favor with the Internet community, blogging on the far left Daily Kos, and gathering fans among the angry Berkeley High School types who frequented the site. It began to work. The show's numbers began to come up. Not really challenging Bill O'Reilly's total domination of the time slot, but enough to encourage two NBC News executives who had literally tried everything else. Something was starting to work and it soon became evident to outside observers that Griffin and Capus had given Olbermann free rein. If he was going to go left and get an audience, they were going along for the ride.

Jeff Zucker—the onetime boy wonder producer of the *Today* show and a close friend of Griffin—had risen to CEO of NBC Universal Television and Films, but owing to his close relationship with both Griffin and Capus it was difficult to imagine he was not involved in the decision they were about to make. It would be, after all, NBC News' most perilous—and ultimately shameful—moment, when it allowed people on its own air to tarnish its brand by morphing the once-respected network into a partisan arm of a political party. They made the decision in 2006, as Olbermann was warming up for the fall campaign, which would see Democrats take over the Congress, because they needed something that resembled success after a decade of frustrating failure.

Olbermann's first "Special Comment" was September 5, 2005—by his account—but the first one in which he came roaring out of the closet was a little over a year later, on September 11, 2006. He did the show remote from Ground Zero, which at that point was still a hole in the ground with stacks of blueprints scattered around New York in various offices. The project had been held up by the Port Authority, the governor, the mayor, the chief of police, and by insurance companies suing to avoid paying off billions of dollars in policies.

But Olbermann found a way to pin it all on George W. Bush.

"Five years later this country's mass grave is still unmarked. Five years later this is still just a background for a photo op."

He blamed the politicians without naming them, but then went on to give a description anyone would recognize. "[The politicians] bicker and buck pass. They thwart private efforts, and jostle to claim credit for initiatives that go nowhere. They spend money on irrelevant wars" (here he was clearly talking about Bush, conflating him with the local and state politicians whose squabbling had held up rebuilding at Ground Zero). "Five years later, Mr. Bush, we are still fighting the terrorists on these streets. And look carefully, sir, on these sixteen empty acres. The terrorists are clearly still winning."

What an absurdity to blame George W. Bush for the fact that New York City had not rebuilt the towers in time for the fifth anniversary of 9/11! It was a dishonest conflation, but one with a silver lining that must have warmed the hearts of Capus and Griffin: If Olbermann could turn a solemn national observance into an occasion to attack Bush, and the result was a pleasing boost in the ratings, then they were on to something at long last.

A week later Olbermann opened a "Special Comment" with the announcement that "the president of the United States owes this country an apology." The reason was even flimsier than the week before. Bush had answered a reporter's question with a figure of speech that displeased Herr Olbermann: "It's unacceptable to think that there's any kind of comparison between the behavior of the United States of America and the action of Islamic extremists who kill innocent women and children to achieve an objective."

" 'It's unacceptable to think,' he said." Olbermann railed, throwing the president's words back in his face. "It is never unacceptable to think," he thundered, as if Bush had actually said any such thing. He concluded a few long minutes later, "Apologize, sir, for even hinting at an America where a few have that privilege to think and the rest of us get yelled at by the president."

This eruption arose out of a question from a reporter: Since former Secretary of State Colin Powell said the world was beginning to doubt the moral basis of our fight against terrorism, didn't he, Bush, think that Americans and the rest of the world could be wondering whether he was following a flawed strategy? It was an innocent question, and an innocent enough response, but it proved that Olbermann could fashion a red-faced attack on Bush out of the smallest of crumbs.

This kind of unprecedented attack on the president of the United States by the anchor of an NBC network show was breathtaking in its audacity. But Capus and Griffin were happy, and evidently encouraged him to do more. And it had a wider effect. The tone around the rest of NBC turned sharper, too. Anchor Chris Matthews joined the fray, as did lesser lights like David Shuster, a reporter who had left Fox news in an anti-conservative huff a few years earlier.

A week later, Olbermann called Mr. Bush "un-American" and demanded, as though he were confronting Senator McCarthy himself, "Have you no sense of decency, Sir?"

The next week Olbermann peeled off another long one in which he defended the performance of former President Bill Clinton in an interview with Fox's Chris Wallace, describing Wallace as "a monkey posing as a newscaster."

Wallace had asked Clinton what he did in his administration to capture or kill Osama bin Laden. The truth was that Clinton had fired some cruise missiles at an al Qaeda camp after the attack on the USS *Cole*, but his people had refused to pull the trigger when they had bin Laden in the crosshairs, afraid that others present would also be killed. "At least I tried," Clinton replied, blaming Bush for not acting against bin Laden for the first eight months of his presidency. It was a little much that the former president was equating his eight years of inaction with eight months of Bush's "inaction," but a detail such as that goes unnoticed in Olbermann's world. Instead he blamed Bush for 9/11.

"You did not try," Olbermann scolded.

"You ignored the evidence gathered by your predecessor.

"You ignored the evidence gathered by your own people.

"Then, you blamed your predecessor.

"That would be a textbook definition, Mr. Bush, of cowardice."

Any NBC producer charged with script approval would have stopped that in an instant. But Keith Olbermann didn't worry about people approving his scripts.

The truth is that Bill Clinton refused to accept a personal briefing from the CIA, never had a private meeting with his own CIA chief, and evidently barely read the CIA briefing papers he got every morning. By comparison, on the first morning he was president, George W. Bush took the CIA briefing in person and told the briefer that he better get used to going wherever the president went because he wanted a briefing every day, no matter where he was. The briefer thought to himself, "This guy gets it."

The book containing that information was published three years before Olbermann tried to shift the blame for 9/11 from Clinton to Bush, but Olbermann didn't mind being wrong. Who was going to call him on it?

A week later, Olbermann attacked the president for a campaign appearance in which Bush had said that Democrats wanted to take a law enforcement approach to terrorism—as Clinton did, locking up the '93 World Trade Center bombers—and "that means America will wait until we're attacked again before we respond."

It was an absolutely routine comment. The Democrats had always opposed Bush's doctrine of preemption, and therefore had all but agreed that their approach would be to wait until the country was attacked before striking the attackers.

Yet Olbermann objected: "No Democrat, sir, has ever said anything approaching the suggestion that the best means of self-defense is to 'wait until we're attacked again.'"

Well, yes, that was precisely the Democrat position. They rejected preemptive strikes, therefore objectively they preferred to be hit before responding. Perhaps no Democrat had said as much—it would certainly be foolish—but as a matter of deduction it was obvious.

"You have dishonored your party, sir; you have dishonored your supporters; you have dishonored yourself.

"Why have you chosen to go down in history as the president who made things up?"

Setting aside for a moment the effrontery of a sportscaster turned partisan news anchor actually chewing out the president of the United States, not on some obscure cable sports show nobody watches but on the leading cable outlet of one of America's oldest and most respected broadcasts, NBC *Nightly News*, he flung out this bell ringer: "The premise of a president who comes across as a compulsive liar is nothing less than terrifying."

October 19, 2006—it was getting close to election day, and Democrats were feeling victory yips—and Olbermann was laying it on thick. On this day, addressing the president of the United States again, he said, "Sadly . . . the distance of history will recognize that the threat this generation of Americans needed to take seriously was you."

The issue was military commissions—trials by military judges— for detainees at Guantanamo Bay, Cuba. Olbermann felt his personal liberties were at stake because an al Qaeda fighter imprisoned by the United States or a 9/11 planner under lock and key might have fewer legal rights than the average American. In the swirling mass of gray matter behind his wildly bulging eyes, hysteria reigned.

Four days later, he unloaded on Bush and the Republican Party over a campaign advertisement that suggested al Qaeda wanted to attack America again, a statement one might consider fairly ordinary during a political campaign. Olbermann accused the Republicans of joining with al Qaeda to terrorize America by broadcasting their threats.

"The leading terrorist group in this world right now is al Qaeda. But the leading terrorist group in this country right now is the Republican Party," Keith intoned, mock serious and self-righteous.

In the same piece he brought up the news that after five years a few more bone fragments had been found under a manhole cover near Ground Zero. "The victims had been lying, literally in the gutter, for five years and five weeks," he said, turning to Bush. "You can't even recover our dead from the battlefield—the battlefield in an American city—when we've given you five years and unlimited funds to do so!" Yet once again, he was blaming George W. Bush for the responsibilities of New York City and state officials.

Griffin and Capus must have been rolling their eyes—but smiling. The fragments in question could hardly be compared to corpses left to molder in some foreign battlefield. Yet, the guy found a way to blame Bush. Who else in the entire NBC News system could do that and keep a straight face? "You do not know what you are doing," Olbermann hissed at Bush.

Over the next few outings, Olbermann told Bush, "You are far more stupid than the worst of your critics have suggested," and reminded the president, "Mr. Bush, you are not the United States of America."

He attacked Bush's reasons for going to war in Iraq: "You, sir, have been making it up as you go along." A previous administration at NBC might have asked a reporter or anchor who wanted to say such a thing to please come to the boss' office with the proof that backed up the statement. Not Capus and Griffin. Ten years of losing the ratings war seemed to be over, and they were not going to be put off by little things like broadcast standards.

After the 2006 congressional elections, the Democrats were in charge, and Olbermann was apparently under the impression the president would simply turn over the reins of government to whatever Democrat first showed up at the White House.

Consequently, when in early January 2007, word began to leak that President Bush was going to set aside the most important recommendations of the Iraq Study Group, and instead was going to "surge" troops in Iraq, Olbermann reacted with horror. Apparently Bush was determined to win the war, and was not going to take bipartisan recommendations to just get out and accept defeat.

Olbermann was outraged that the president hadn't been listening to him and following his instructions: "More American servicemen and women will have their lives risked. More American servicemen and women will have their lives ended." It was a nice way to give the troops a big send-off.

Actually, he was beside himself. He called the plan "palpable nonsense" and said, "the additional men and women you have sentenced to go there, sir, will serve only as targets." He said we had shown the enemy "that we will let our own people be killed for no good reason." He wailed that Bush's judgment on Iraq was at "variance with your people's to the point of delusion." He insisted the president fire himself if he could not carry out the orders being delivered at the very moment: "This country does not want more troops in Iraq. It wants fewer. Go and make it happen, or go and look for other work."

An NBC News anchor was firing the president as if he were nothing more than the manager of a losing baseball team.

This was a hallmark of the Olbermann screed. He liked to fire people, demand they quit or resign, insist they move on to another line of work. Theatrical bullying from a man so weak he wouldn't dare say it to your face, from someone whose opinions are so fragile in the face of fact he never allows a rebuttal or a debate.

"This country has already lost in Iraq, sir," he declared, punctuating his sentences with a transparently disrespectful use of the honorific. "First we sent Americans to their deaths for your lie, Mr. Bush. Now we are sending them to their deaths for your ego."

There's no question the surge was a matter of considerable controversy, but watching these deranged howlings it would have been fair to wonder, Where is Tom Brokaw? Where is Tim Russert? Where is the vice president of Standards and Practices, who enforced the rules of the news gathering organization? Where were the grown-ups?

It's hard to believe that NBC News' military correspondents were completely unaware of who General David Petraeus was, or the fact that he would be coming in to take over and execute the surge. It was well known among those who followed such developments that Petraeus was widely regarded as one of the smartest generals in the military and that he'd been in Fort Leavenworth, Kansas, for a year writing the army's new Counterinsurgency Manual. NBC producers and correspondents were doubtless updating the computer every day with new information on the arrival of Petraeus and his plans for the surge, putting to use the newly refined counterinsurgency doctrine. It wasn't a secret to anybody but Keith Olbermann. He couldn't be bothered to find out what the plans were or how they might be carried out.

The attack on the surge turned out to be a consistent theme with Olbermann, principally because there was a leftist audience, mouth agape, demanding that more of this be shoveled down their throats. The blogs were alive with wild-eyed denunciations of Bush, thoughtful columnists lambasted the plan, public opinion was running heavily against it. No question, Bush had made a decision that cut against the grain.

A few days later, on January 11, 2007, General Olbermann spoke these words:

"The plan fails militarily.

"The plan fails symbolically.

"The plan fails politically.

"Most importantly, perhaps, Mr. Bush, the plan fails because it still depends on your credibility."

FROM THE PERSPECTIVE of late 2009 that diatribe seems especially silly and vacuous because in fact the plan did work militarily, symbolically, and politically. The war was won on Bush's personal determination and the gutsy hard work of Petraeus and 150,000 U.S. troops. Olbermann had said it couldn't be done. He was wrong.

In fact, Olbermann has been consistently wrong in his pronouncements about the reasons for going to war, the success of the war, the techniques used to capture and interrogate terrorists, and anything else done by George W. Bush. NBC turned its airwaves over to a man with a political agenda and a swollen ego. But NBC didn't care. Olbermann could play the fool; they had the numbers to make it worthwhile.

"Mr. Bush, this is madness.

"You have lost the military. You have lost the Congress to the Democrats. You have lost most of the Iraqis. You have lost many of the Republicans. You have lost our allies.

"You are guaranteeing that more American troops will be losing their lives, and more families their loved ones. You are guaranteeing it!

"This becomes your legacy, sir: How many of those you addressed last night as your 'fellow citizens' did you just send to their deaths?"

Would Keith Olbermann have gone to Iraq to say those things to Saddam Hussein, a true despot, who actually murdered people himself, had people thrown off buildings, and turned his sons loose to rape and pillage? Would he have been so brave in a country with a true dictator, instead of one he simply made up and trotted around on television so his bosses could escape the embarrassment of a permanent loser cable network?

Was any of this working? Yes. Though Olbermann challenged Bill O'Reilly only in his delusional dreams, his ratings did rise throughout the summer of 2007 and rolling into the election campaign of 2008 he was riding along on a very comfortable cushion with a reliable audience who showed up to see him rant nearly every night.

Looking back, Olbermann might squirm at his disputations of late 2007 and 2008, because it is in that eighteen-month period that the war in Iraq was clearly being won, and the surge Olbermann so condemned was not failing, but was working very well.

But Olbermann wouldn't have noticed. He obviously failed to read—or purposely ignored—some of the reports coming from the (shrinking) American press corps in Iraq. The counterinsurgency operations of General Petraeus and General Ray Odierno were having results that could be seen in the monthly tallies of deaths and attacks. The Anbar Awakening was underway, and Sunni tribesmen were being recruited as local constabulary to protect villages from al Qaeda.

Olbermann's lockstep condemnation of the surge and related matters showed that he was not, in fact, paying attention to the war. He was paying attention to the war critics and trying to stay ahead of the pack.

In mid-July 2007, Olbermann demanded President Bush himself go fight. "This, sir, is your war," he thundered. "Then take it in your own hands, Mr. Bush. Go to Baghdad now, and fulfill, finally, your military service obligations. Go there and fight your war. Yourself."

By September 2007, reporters talking to General Petraeus in Iraq and some of his advisors, including David Kilcullen, the Australian army officer he recruited to help run counterinsurgency operations, were finding that the combination of extra troops and a new counterinsurgency strategy were actually working, and there really wasn't any denying it. Even though he keeps an office inside NBC News headquarters at 30 Rockefeller Plaza in New York City, and all the newspapers and news sources come in to that building and are circulated around, very little of it seemed to reach the cavelike office of Keith Olbermann. He was the man saving MSNBC. A Do Not Disturb rule enveloped his doorway. Staffers wanting to talk to him could leave a note in a box affixed to the door. What he didn't know kept him sharp and ready to fight another day.

"Mr. Bush, our presence in Iraq must end," he told the nation in early September. "Even if it means your resignation. Even if it means your impeachment. Even if it means a different Republican to serve out your term. Even if it means a Democratic Congress, and those true patriots among the Republicans standing up and denying you another penny for Iraq, other than for the safety and the safe conduct home for our troops. This country cannot run the risk of what you can still do to this country in the next five hundred days."

General Petraeus came to Congress to report on his progress in September 2007. He was greeted with a blast furnace of popular opinion against the war. It was an ugly scene, which even Democrats in Congress felt required to distance themselves from, but Olbermann didn't even break his stride. "Mr. Bush, you had no right to order General Petraeus to become your front man. And he obviously should have refused that order and resigned rather than ruin his military career." This is ridiculous, of course. Petraeus has emerged as the great hero of the Iraq War. His counterinsurgency techniques will be studied at West Point for generations. Olbermann was living in a dream world.

Within four weeks, Thomas Ricks would report in the *Washington Post* that the Iraq war against al Qaeda was essentially won. The terrorists had been beaten, the organization was crippled. It was over.

And yet, NBC News allowed Olbermann to go on the air and say, "And in pimping General David Petraeus and in the violation of everything this country has been assiduously and vigilantly against for two hundred and twenty years, you have tried to blur the gleaming radioactive demarcation between the military and the political, and to portray your party as the one associated with the military, and your opponents as the ones somehow antithetical to it."

Uh, yes? That was the truth, as a matter of fact. And the problem with saying so would be what, exactly?

"It is a line which history shows is always the first one crossed when a democratic government in some other country has started down the long, slippery, suicidal slope toward a military junta," he said, with gusto and confidence.

So Olbermann was now predicting a Bush military coup?

But this nonsense was getting ratings for the long-suffering cable network that was supposed to be a triumph ten years earlier, but had always disappointed. What did it matter that this blithering fool was so consistently and insistently wrong?

In November 2007, Olbermann debuted what would become a theme, a trademark, an emblem of his anti-Bush diatribes, one that continues to this day: Bush committed torture, torture is a crime, Bush should be in jail.

In the spirit of the holiday season, early December found Olbermann declaring President Bush either a pathological liar or idiot in chief, and "manifestly unfit to serve."

In the same piece he said, "You, Mr. Bush, are a bald-faced liar."

He concluded "Tonight, hanged by your own words, convicted by your own deliberate lies . . . You, sir, have no business being president."

His Valentine's Day present to the man who kept him in his job earning top dollar was yet another denunciation, this time over the FISA court bill—the Foreign Intelligence Secrecy Act—of which Keith Olbermann disapproved (it was later a great disappointment when his chosen candidate, Barack Obama, assumed the Bush position on the FISA bill) and which caused him to call the president a fascist.

Instead of objecting, Griffin and Capus began placating Olbermann's wild ego with raises, and even put up with him spreading the word that he was the one who actually ran the network. "Phil (Griffin) only thinks he's my boss," Olbermann remarked.

For those who had been around NBC during the year network producers blew up GM trucks for a fake test in a consumer protection segment, this was dizzying. An enormous investigation had ensued, the network was flogged mercilessly in public and in the courts, and new rules were promulgated over the precise issue of rigging the debate (in the GM case, rigging a test) in order to condemn a commercial product. Yet here was Olbermann doing the same thing with impunity—though it wasn't about a product, but a presidency—and he evidently had permission from the highest precincts of the NBC television network.

In this thorough and relentless condemnation of the president and the war, Olbermann was by no means alone. Plenty of people were writing hateful and erroneous things on the Internet, many columnists from brand-name news organizations were taking Bush apart every day; but Olbermann earned a special place in the hearts of Bush-hating liberals because he was so confident, so authoritative, and seemingly so correct. It helps to keep the people who want to debate you or rebut your points waiting outside on Rockefeller Plaza. In all the hundreds of interviews Olbermann has done on his show, he has always booked guests who agree with him.

Howard Dean came closest to disagreement in early 2009, when he went on *Countdown* and mentioned that it was always wrong to call the sitting president a fascist. The subject had come up in relation to some right wingers calling Obama a fascist, but still, Olbermann was slightly taken aback, because he had, after all, famously called Bush a fascist.

He offered that it perhaps would be okay if the person using that epithet "put some meat on the bones" and explained *why* the president was a fascist. Dean deadpanned, "No, it's wrong to call the president of the United States a fascist. I've said I think George Bush was wrong, but I don't believe it is right to use that kind of language directed at the president."

You could almost hear Olbermann gulp. We'll move on now. . .

During the 2008 primary and general election campaigns,

Olbermann and NBC dropped all pretense of supporting anyone but Barack Obama. Hillary Clinton was savaged by both Olbermann and Chris Matthews for the effrontery of challenging Obama. Olbermann was heard on an open mike, groaning at colleague Joe Scarborough to "get a shovel" when Scarborough was relating something the McCain campaign had told him. He could be heard in another open mike moment telling the producers that a certain Republican guest should be dumped immediately: "Get him off!" Olbermann ordered.

Eventually, he and Matthews both had to be replaced as an anchor team covering the Democratic convention because they could not control their partisan impulses. But it didn't last long. Phil Griffin and Steve Capus knew who was boss. Olbermann was back in the anchor chair within a week or two as if his earlier, partisan anti-McCain offenses had never happened.

He got his way: Obama won. Olbermann enthusiastically sang fulsome praises of the one man in America who could read the teleprompter almost as well as he. He also had a new four-year, 30 million dollar contract, and free rein to "run" a network he officially only worked at.

As for Capus and Griffin, it was back to square one. As soon as Obama was elected, the ratings they'd been chasing for over a decade faded back into the woodwork. Within a couple months, Fox News' ratings were doubling the combined CNN and MSNBC audience levels. For watering down the traditions of NBC News, Griffin and Capus had to be satisfied with a second place spot that was far, far behind the leader. They also had to be worried that hapless CNN might figure out how to crawl out of fourth place (CNN was being beat by its own sister network, Headline News), and shove MSNBC back into his usual third-place spot.

Just after the inauguration, a former MSNBC anchor was having dinner at Rao's, an Italian restaurant in New York renowned for the difficulties in getting a table. The former anchor was enjoying the conversation with his wife and another couple. Suddenly, he heard "Buddy!" and looked up to see Griffin. He and his wife were just leaving, having finished dinner. The former anchor said, "You guys are doing well, congratulations."

"Going left was the right thing to do," he said, with a big smile.

At that moment, he was still in his victory lap. MSNBC and NBC had gotten a president elected, his numbers were up, and GE, NBC's parent company, was about to be rewarded with a $139 billion dollar bailout from the Obama administration. What he didn't know was that the Obama crowd who flocked to his network to watch history being made was about to go back to what they normally did in life, which did not include watching MSNBC every night. Meanwhile, conservatives who were stunned and angry at the outcome of the election would be lining up to watch Fox.

Steve Capus and Phil Griffin had proved they could make something happen with MSNBC. It wasn't a cursed loser, entirely. True, they didn't get into first place, and the air went out of the balloon pretty fast. But still . . . It took more than a decade of ignominious losses, it took putting up with a man who on many days appeared to have misplaced his meds, but it was something of a victory. MSNBC finally did something.

On April 7, 2009, Olbermann took the last few minutes of his program to give tribute to his mother, Marie, who had died a few days earlier. Olbermann ran some home movies of his boyhood, the flickering 8mm images showing a boy and his mother going to the ball game, the mother's passion passed on to the son. You saw the nine- or ten-year-old boy, baby fatted and running like a girl, waving at the camera as he crossed the street to the stadium. Later pictures show the boy growing up at the ballpark with his mother. Still later, when he was an anchor for Fox Sports, he interviewed his mother about an incident that day in which she was struck by a ball thrown over first base and into the stands by errant-armed Chuck Knobloch.

From these pictures one can see the budding sports anchor. The images make plain, and he admits, that he was not an athletic kid. He watched sports. He talked about sports. He collected baseball cards and memorized the agate type that recorded the timeless statistics of the players.

Olbermann's expertise came purely from the point of view of a spectator sitting in seats at the stadium or arena, feeling the joy of spouting off, as fans do, about how much more he knew about playing and managing a game than the other fans sitting nearby, or even the players on the field.

He brought that same attitude to the news anchor chair. This was the same smartass sitting behind you, loudly complaining about a missed fly ball, or a bad pitch or a swing and a miss. Sure of himself, and entirely unable to do the thing he so confidently criticizes, he's the guy—or the kid—you want to accidentally spill a beer on.

As for Capus and Griffin, they gave it their all. Failure cannot go on forever without a moment of relief, if network executives work hard and are willing to grin and bear. Was it worth it to throw NBC News' reputation away for a brief shining moment when the little-network-that-couldn't seemed like maybe it could after all? Was it worth it to be able to say, "That year we had Obama and Olbermann, we had a good run"?

As for Olbermann himself, he's going to have to be satisfied with second place until Bill O'Reilly finally decides to retire. Even then, Fox may pull something out of its hat to deny him that long sought success for another decade.

But Olbermann's swiftboating lies worked. Bush's successes were condemned, daily and loudly. The lies did their job all too well.

Chapter Five

Sixteen Words: The Bogus Storm over Bush's Speech and the Wilson/Plame Affair

"The British government has learned that Saddam Hussein recently sought significant quantities of uranium from Africa."

—PRESIDENT GEORGE W. BUSH, STATE OF THE UNION ADDRESS,
JANUARY 28, 2003

This is the story of how sixteen words spoken by George W. Bush in his January 2003 State of the Union address led to sixteen months of left partisans and media mixing tiny seeds of truth into whole-grain suppositions to arrive at the half-baked conclusion that George W. Bush and senior administration officials had lied to convince the nation that the only solution to the long-standing problem of Iraq was a military invasion and overthrow of the Saddam regime. The very accusation that Bush had lied about pre-war intelligence—particularly Iraq's nuclear ambitions—was the left's big lie in action.

This story was a Russian matryoshka doll of lies. A big one on the outside, with a succession of smaller (but still noxious) lies inside. Thus the "sixteen-words" lie eventually gave way to the lie that the Bush administration had recklessly "outed" one of its own spies in the pursuit of a political vendetta. Her name was Valerie Plame, a twenty-year veteran of the CIA. It was certainly true that Plame was exposed and her clandestine work compromised. But it turned out in the end that the beautiful blonde spy had actually outed herself. Valerie Plame had no one to blame for the sudden end of her CIA career but herself, and her relentlessly self-promoting husband.

This lie about why we went to war was hatched in the earliest days of the pre-invasion period, as the left—facing the double whammy of a popular president and a popular war—meekly challenged long-accepted facts about Iraq's weapons of mass destruction. The big lie was carefully nurtured in its infancy, and into maturity, through the successful invasion and the growing trouble of the post-war period. It was designed to appeal to a small but increasingly vocal component of the American public, which, even at this early date, was turning against both the war in Iraq and George W. Bush.

The story began as rumblings. There were elements in the media and government that didn't believe the Bush case for war. This group—rank national security amateurs working as journalists abetted by career government experts opposed for various reasons to the invasion of Iraq—was troubled by the administration's case against Iraq on the issues of chemical and biological weapons. But it was absolutely incredulous about George W. Bush's assertions, seconded by his vice president, national security advisor, and secretary of state, that Iraq posed a legitimate threat as a potential nuclear power.

Adding fuel to the fire was a report from the IAEA, the United Nations' International Atomic Energy Agency, which in early March 2003—a little more than a month after Bush's controversial assertion in his State of the Union address—declared a key document in Bush's case against Iraq to be a forgery. The document in question was a contract, alleged to have been a sales agreement between Niger and Iraq for Saddam's purchase of five hundred tons of uranium "yellowcake," an essential material for the construction of a nuclear mechanism, either a power generating plant or a bomb. The document appeared to be one of the linchpins in Bush's case, in that it purported to document the sale of material that could be used to make as many as forty-two nuclear weapons.

Bush and Vice President Cheney, as well as National Security Advisor Condoleezza Rice, had invoked images of mushroom clouds in making their case for a military campaign to depose Saddam

Hussein, and the left was embittered over the effectiveness of the argument on public opinion.

Two weeks before the launch of the invasion—and just thirty days after Bush's speech warning of the Iraq uranium purchase— the IAEA was provided a copy of the document, and immediately (within hours!) recognized it as a fake—wrong names, wrong dates, clearly forged signatures.

"The IAEA was able to review correspondence coming from various bodies of the government of Niger and to compare the form, format, contents, and signature of that correspondence with those of the alleged procurement-related documentation," Muhammad al Baradei, head of the IAEA, said in a prepared statement. "Based on thorough analysis, the IAEA has concluded, with the concurrence of outside experts, that these documents, which formed the basis for the reports of [a] recent uranium transaction between Iraq and Niger, are in fact not authentic. We have therefore concluded that these specific allegations are unfounded."

The "specific allegations" had been the basis for the president's assertion in his State of the Union address that Iraq was seeking the material for a nuclear bomb. Suddenly, the media erupted into a loud and red-faced argument about the president's "sixteen words." Who had allowed such faulty information into a State of the Union address? Why hadn't United States intelligence agencies realized the document was a fraud?

Or worse, was Bush trying to flimflam the American public?

Additionally, it came to light that the CIA knew there were problems with the document well before President Bush had uttered the sixteen words. It soon became known that CIA director George Tenet had personally made a call to Deputy National Security Advisor Stephen Hadley to have a similar line removed from a Bush speech to be delivered in Cincinnati only a few months earlier. CIA analysts clearly had deep reservations about the document going back months.

The sixteen words soon became a daily issue in the press, and a nightly issue on the cable television talk shows. What was Bush up to? Had he lied to the American people to launch a war?

In June 2003, Tim Russert had confronted National Security

Advisor Condoleezza Rice on *Meet the Press* about the fact that the uranium purchase document had been exposed as a forgery. She answered with transparent unsteadiness: "The president quoted a British paper. We did not know at the time, no one knew at the time in our circles, maybe someone knew down in the bowels of the agency, but no one in our circles knew that there were doubts and suspicions that this might be a forgery."

Meanwhile another figure was watching this story unfold with growing anger. His name was Joseph C. Wilson IV and he was a former ambassador to Gabon and São Tomé and Principe in the Clinton administration (not exactly a high-level appointment). He had also served as deputy chief of mission in Iraq under the George H. W. Bush administration. Now out of government service, he had gone into the consulting business after marrying another government employee and starting a family. But he never lost his ambassadorial itch.

Wilson's highest professional moments had been as a diplomat in the U.S. Department of State. He was the last American to have had direct face-to-face dealings with Saddam Hussein. Only a year earlier he had gone to the African nation of Niger to investigate allegations of an Iraqi uranium purchase and reported to his CIA contacts that the story was bogus. He now had reason to believe that his report had been transmitted to the vice president of the United States and twisted into a case for war against Iraq. Joe Wilson had a personal stake in the Iraqi uranium story.

Wilson steamed as he watched the sixteen-words story unfold. He started talking to the media, tipping off more than one reporter about what he thought were glaring discrepancies between what he had personally investigated and reported to the U.S. government, and what he saw George W. Bush using as a justification for war—a war that Wilson personally opposed.

Wilson wasn't quiet about it. Within a week of Bush's speech, on February 6, 2003, he published an editorial in the *Los Angeles Times*, titled "A 'Big Cat' With Nothing to Lose," in which he argued that attacking Saddam Hussein would cause him to use WMD on U.S. troops, and perhaps supply WMD to terrorists. "There is now no incentive for Hussein to comply with the inspectors or to refrain from using weapons of mass destruction to defend himself if the United

States comes after him. And he will use them; we should be under no illusion about that."

The anti-Bush media immediately snatched him up in order to amplify his claims. What could be better than a former U.S. ambassador, appointed by the president's own father, coming out against the war? On February 28, 2003, Wilson sat down for an interview with Bill Moyers for PBS, and asked the rhetorical question, Why is the United States turning away from al Qaeda? It was a theme that eventually became the mantra of millions.

"The game has shifted to Iraq for reasons that are confusing to everybody. The millions of people who are on the streets of our country and of Europe, as I said the other day, it strikes me as—it may prove that Abraham Lincoln is right. You cannot fool all the people all the time," Wilson told Moyers. "They have been sold. We have been sold a war on disarmament or terrorism or the nexus between terrorism and weapons of mass destruction or liberation. Any one of the four. And now with the president's speeches, you clearly have the idea that we're going to go in and take this preemptive action to overthrow a regime, occupy its country for the purposes, the explicit purposes of fostering the blossoming of democracy in a part of the world where we really have very little ground, truth, or experience."

The twin ideas of the "selling" of the war on false pretenses and of the "shifting rationales" were being firmly implanted in the public mind, along with the notion that in taking on Saddam Hussein, Bush had "taken his eye off the ball" in Afghanistan. In fact, a coherent case had been made that in order to deal with the terrorist threat, America must "drain the swamps" in the Middle East by confronting rogue regimes that trained, supported, and financed Islamic terrorism, not just hunting down al Qaeda. But this complex case with its multiple rationales was falsely interpreted by a hostile media—abetted by recalcitrant elements in the government itself—as a dishonest and cynical shell game.

In early March, Joe Wilson wrote a bombastic article for *The Nation*, a radical antiwar publication, at the request of Washington bureau chief David Corn, called "Republic or Empire?" In it, Wilson blasted the neo-conservatives—who were viewed as the main architects of Bush's antiterrorism strategy—writing, "American pre-eminence in the Gulf is necessary but not sufficient for the hawks. Nothing short of conquest, occupation, and imposition of handpicked leaders on a vanquished population will suffice. Iraq is the linchpin for this broader assault on the region. The new imperialists will not rest until governments that ape our worldview are implanted throughout the region, a breathtakingly ambitious undertaking, smacking of hubris in the extreme."

Wilson was clearly tailoring his message to suit his audience. Subdued and thoughtful public servant for Bill Moyers, fire-breathing anti-imperialist for *The Nation*.

Up until this point, Wilson had publicly supported the notion that Saddam did in fact possess illegal stockpiles of WMD. After the March 20 invasion it didn't take long for the media to start receiving reports from Iraq indicating that American troops were not finding the promised WMD stockpiles. Within sixty days it became evident that WMD were not going to be discovered in large amounts in Iraq. At that point, with the WMD issue going bust, Bush was vulnerable to attack. Wilson immediately began to back off his consistent support for the idea that Saddam had WMD.

In May, Joe Wilson began to advise the Kerry campaign on foreign policy issues. He was slowly coming out of his nonpartisan shell and publicly embracing the left. The Associated Press reported that Wilson said he'd been a Kerry supporter for some time and had contributed $2,000 to the Kerry campaign earlier in the year. He also promised he would campaign for Kerry, including the all-important New Hampshire primary.

On the second day of May 2003, Wilson and his wife, Valerie Plame, a CIA employee, attended the Senate Democratic Policy Committee meeting in Washington, D.C. (One has to wonder what a woman whose job is supposed to be top secret was doing in this forum.) One of the panelists sitting down the table was Nicholas Kristof, the *New York Times* reporter. The next morning Kristof and his wife, the writer and China expert, Sheryl WuDunn, had breakfast with the Wilsons. Wilson told Kristof about his trip to Niger the previous year, and within days Kristof wrote about Wilson's mission, without naming him, in a May 6 article. Kristof reported that a former American ambassador had been sent to Niger to investigate the story that Iraq had a contract for a uranium sale. "In February 2002, according to someone present at the meetings, that envoy reported to the

CIA and State Department that the information was unequivocally wrong and that the documents had been forged. The envoy reported, for example, that a Niger minister whose signature was on one of the documents had in fact been out of office for more than a decade."

Wilson was getting sloppy. Telling Kristof that he had personally debunked the forged contract was at best an exaggeration, and at worst, a purposeful lie. In either case, the Senate Select Committee on Intelligence investigation, published in 2004, established as fact that Wilson had never seen the documents in question, and was not a part of the exposure of the forgery.

As for the claim that he had determined the Iraq-Niger uranium deal was "unequivocally wrong," the SSCI investigation also reported that Wilson's trip actually *confirmed* for the CIA that Iraq had sought to establish a uranium connection with Niger in 1999, and that Wilson unwittingly delivered information that contradicted what he was now claiming.

The *Washington Post*'s Bob Woodward later reported—somewhat sheepishly considering the circumstances— that in June he had interviewed Richard Armitage, the number-two person at the State Department under Secretary of State Colin Powell, about Wilson's trip to Niger. The Woodward recording of the interview revealed who had been the first person to unmask Wilson's wife, Valerie, as a CIA spy.

WOODWARD: Well it was Joe Wilson who was sent by the agency, isn't it?

ARMITAGE: His wife works for the agency.

WOODWARD: Why doesn't that come out? Why does that have to be a big secret?

ARMITAGE: (over) Everybody knows it.

WOODWARD: Everyone knows?

ARMITAGE: Yeah. And they know 'cause Joe Wilson's been calling everybody. He's pissed off 'cause he was designated as a low-level guy went out to look at it. So he's all pissed off.

WOODWARD: But why would they send him?

ARMITAGE: Because his wife's an analyst at the agency.

WOODWARD: It's still weird.

ARMITAGE: He—he's perfect. She—she, this is what she does. She's a WMD analyst out there.

WOODWARD: Oh, she is.
ARMITAGE: (over) Yeah.
WOODWARD: Oh, I see. I didn't think . . .
ARMITAGE: (over) "I know who'll look at it." Yeah, see?
WOODWARD: Oh. She's the chief WMD . . . ?
ARMITAGE: No. She's not the . . .
WOODWARD: But high enough up that she could say, "Oh, yeah, hubby will go."
ARMITAGE: Yeah. She knows [garbled].
WOODWARD: Was she out there with him, when he was . . . ?
ARMITAGE: (over) No, not to my knowledge. I don't know if she was out there. But his wife's in the agency as a WMD analyst. How about that?

This interview was reported by Woodward much later, after a special prosecutor had spent several years trying to determine who in the Bush administration had illegally revealed the identity of Wilson's wife, and where she worked. Woodward, to his great embarrassment, had sat silent for months as the vice president's chief of staff, Scooter Libby, was dragged through the mud in the press and put on trial for illegally revealing the identity of a covert CIA operative, when in fact Woodward knew all along who had been responsible for the revelation: the much liked but gossipy Armitage.

But that raging controversy was still in the future. Valerie Plame Wilson had not been outed quite yet, though the way Wilson was parading around Washington, D.C., with a spy-wife on his arm, it was shocking she wasn't outed much sooner.

On June 14, Wilson was a keynote speaker at the Education for Peace in Iraq Center, a vocal left-wing group. His wife, Valerie, the CIA official, attended with him.

Wilson was still not directly and publicly identifying himself as the envoy who had gone to Niger a year earlier. But it was clear he wasn't trying very hard to conceal his identity.

"I can assure you that that retired American ambassador sent to Africa, as Nick Kristof called him in his article, is also pissed off, and has every intention of ensuring that this story has legs," Wilson told the group with a broad self-referential wink. "And I think it does have legs. It may not have legs over the next two or three months, but when you see American casualties moving from one to five or to ten per day, and you see Tony Blair's government fall because in the U.K. it is a big story, there will be some ramifications, I think, here in the United States, so I hope that you will do everything you can to keep the pressure on. Because it is absolutely bogus for us to have gone to war the way we did."

Wilson's fuming evidently grew unbearable. He could no longer contain the secret that he had had a personal hand in events leading up to the war. In a watershed moment, Wilson stepped into the spotlight, and in the process, declared war on the Bush administration.

On July 6, 2003, a little over three months after the invasion of Iraq was carried out by General Tommy Franks on orders from George W. Bush, Joe Wilson published an op-ed piece in the *New York Times* headlined, "What I Didn't Find in Niger."

It was not just a public break with the Bush administration—he'd already been very public within the closed circles of Washington, D.C.— but it was a hostile act, meant to undermine a still popular president and a still popular war with an election about eighteen months away.

Wilson came out guns a-blazing. "Did the Bush administration manipulate intelligence about Saddam Hussein's weapons programs to justify an invasion of Iraq?" he asked in the opening paragraph.

His answer was offered promptly, in the second sentence. "Based on my experience with the administration in the months leading up to the war, I have little choice but to conclude that some of the intelligence related to Iraq's nuclear weapons program was twisted to exaggerate the Iraqi threat."

Twisted to exaggerate the threat. This was a serious charge, clearly meant to undermine public support for the war.

To establish his bona fides, Wilson gave a brief history of his diplomatic career—postings to Africa, the last American to personally face down Saddam Hussein on the eve of the 1991 Gulf War—and referred to a couple of newspaper stories that had appeared in the previous weeks telling part of his story without naming him.

"Those news stories about that unnamed former envoy who went to Niger? That's me."

A crucial aspect of Wilson's op-ed piece was the carefully crafted implication that he was sent to Niger to investigate Saddam's nuclear ambitions by the vice president's office.

"In February 2002, I was informed by officials at the Central Intelligence Agency that Vice President Dick Cheney's office had questions about a particular intelligence report," he wrote, carefully avoiding any mention of who precisely had informed him of the report. It turned out later to be an all-important detail that was purposely left in the dark. In fact his wife had sent him, or had arranged to have him sent, not the office of the vice president. That fact was established by the Senate Select Committee on Intelligence investigation. But Wilson has insisted that he was sent at the VP's request, evidently to enhance his status and because the mundane truth of the matter might indicate he was in fact a "low-level guy" sitting around the house with nothing to do until his wife dreamed up a junket to Niger.

"While I never saw the report," he wrote, referring to the forged "contract" for Niger to supply Iraq with five hundred tons of uranium, "I was told that it referred to a memorandum of agreement that documented the sale of uranium yellowcake—a form of lightly processed ore—by Niger to Iraq in the late 1990s. The agency officials asked if I would travel to Niger to check out the story so they could provide a response to the vice president's office."

Vice President Cheney, in reviewing the two CIA reports on the discredited document, had asked his CIA briefer for additional information. Unbeknownst to Cheney, the CIA had gone along with Valerie Plame Wilson's suggestion and asked Wilson to make a trip to Niger for further inquiries. As far as Cheney knew, the agency was following up, but he was not informed exactly how, or who was making the inquiries.

Wilson wrote that he made the trip to Niger, spent eight days talking to officials he knew from his previous ambassadorial experience in the region, and when he returned made a verbal report to two CIA officials who visited him in his home. His conclusion: It was virtually impossible for Iraq to have concluded such a sale. "I spent the next eight days drinking sweet mint tea and meeting with dozens of people: current government officials, former government officials, people associated with the country's uranium business. It did not take long to conclude that it was highly doubtful that any such transaction had ever taken place."

Wilson's reasoning seemed to make sense: first, because Iraq was under UN sanctions at the time, Niger would be loath to break the sanctions. Second, the government-owned mines were carefully controlled by a French mining consortium that had contracts for uranium purchases by legitimate end users—national power agencies, for instance—and it seemed highly unlikely that five hundred tons could be siphoned off for an illicit sale to Iraq.

Wilson claimed to have known about the document purporting the sale and doubted its authenticity. "As for the actual memorandum, I never saw it. But news accounts have pointed out that the documents had glaring errors—they were signed, for example, by officials who were no longer in government—and were probably forged. And then there's the fact that Niger formally denied the charges."

Wilson's long experience told him that there should have been at least four separate reports on his trip circulating in government offices, one of which should have gone to the vice president (though he allowed that report could have been given to Cheney orally by a CIA briefer.) The SSCI investigation later determined that Cheney had never received any report, written or oral.

According to Wilson, he went back to his life, assuming the issue had been put to rest. In later interviews, he allowed that he had taken part in the debate about Iraq, taking the position that rigid containment of Saddam was preferable to a military invasion. He was also quick to question President Bush's motives for going to war. (As an example, when Wilson was interviewed on the Bill Moyers PBS program *Now* on February 28, 2003, just three weeks before the American invasion of Iraq, Moyers asked, "Does it seem to you that the president, George Bush, is prepared to accept a disarmed Hussein? Or does he want a dead Hussein?" Wilson replied, "I think he wants a dead Hussein. I don't think there's any doubt about it.")

In his *New York Times* piece, Wilson addressed what had changed in the Niger story. "In September 2002, however, Niger re-emerged," Wilson wrote. "The British government published a 'white paper' asserting that Saddam Hussein and his unconventional arms posed an immediate danger. As evidence, the report cited Iraq's attempts to purchase uranium from an African country. Then, in January, President Bush, citing the British dossier, repeated the charges about Iraqi efforts to buy uranium from Africa."

Wilson said he asked a friend in the State Department if the president was referring to Niger when he said "uranium from Africa," and the friend reminded him there were three other African nations that mined uranium.

"The vice president's office asked a serious question. I was asked to help formulate the answer. I did so, and I have every confidence that the answer I provided was circulated to the appropriate officials within our government. The question now is how that answer was or was not used by our political leadership."

Wilson's answer to his own question was a shot, not across the bow, but directly amidships of the Bush administration: "If . . . the information was ignored because it did not fit certain preconceptions about Iraq, then a legitimate argument can be made that we went to war under false pretenses."

Twisted intelligence. War under false pretenses. Wilson was bringing out the big guns. Getting such charges into the *New York Times* was a major victory for the antiwar left. A line had been crossed in the debate. Now to the chorus of complaints that Bush had lied about WMD would be added the charge that he (or his warlike vice president) ignored or twisted intelligence that didn't suit their case.

Wilson demanded that Congress investigate. "America's foreign policy depends on the sanctity of its information. For this reason, questioning the selective use of intelligence to justify the war in Iraq is neither idle sniping nor 'revisionist history,' as Mr. Bush has suggested. The act of war is the last option of a democracy, taken when there is a grave threat to our national security. More than 200 American soldiers have lost their lives in Iraq already. We have a duty to ensure that their sacrifice came for the right reasons."

Wilson's revelations were a sensation. The same day his *New York Times* piece appeared, he made an appearance on NBC's *Meet the Press*, repeating much of what he had earlier leaked to Nicholas Kristof, and then expanded upon it under his own name. *MTP* host Tim Russert was off, and Wilson was interviewed by substitute host Andrea Mitchell, NBC's chief diplomatic correspondent.

Ms. Mitchell asked, "What do you think was going on here? *Was this the politicization of intelligence in order to justify a war?*" (italics added)

Wilson answered, "(E)ither the administration has some information that it has not shared with the public or, yes, they were using the selective use of facts and intelligence to bolster a decision . . . that had already been made, a decision that had been made to go to war."

This was another major point in the left-wing arsenal. The idea that Bush had planned to take out Saddam even before 9/11 was taken as prima facie evidence that the whole war had been cooked up to satisfy Bush's personal vendetta against Saddam for trying to have his father killed.

Before the segment ended, Mitchell obligingly asked Wilson for his assessment of the decision made by President Bush to invade Iraq and topple Saddam Hussein. Wilson said that the sanctions were working—"We've got him surrounded"—and that the invasion and war "was the highest risk, lowest reward option we could have possibly imagined, the invasion, conquest, and now occupation scenario."

It was a heady moment for Joe Wilson. He was personally challenging the president and vice president like David confronting Goliath. The left and the liberal media had rallied around him when he was anonymous, and now that he was out in the open he was practically given a parade. He basked in the warm glow of media attention. Wilson was a truth teller. Wilson dared to challenge power. Wilson was a hero.

But there were two problems with Wilson's versions of events. First, the vice president did not send Joseph C. Wilson IV to Niger to investigate an intriguing report, as Wilson had cleverly implied in his *New York Times* piece. As later confirmed by the Senate Select Committee on Intelligence, it was Wilson's wife who brought up his name, and wrote a memo urging her boss to send her husband. The vice president's office had nothing to do with sending Wilson, and was blindsided by his July 6 *New York Times* piece.

The complication was that Wilson's wife, Valerie Plame Wilson, was a CIA official in the clandestine service. Her work life was secret. If anybody, such as the vice president, were to ask who arranged Joe Wilson's trip to Niger, she would necessarily be exposed. Wilson's bellicose stance against the president and the vice president virtually insured that the vice president's office would ask questions—"Who is this guy who says I sent him to Niger?"—and his wife would be outed as an officer of the CIA's clandestine service.

The second problem was that Joe Wilson's original finding was wrong. As the Senate Select Committee on Intelligence also reported, the CIA took his information, but did not agree that he had exposed the Niger uranium story as untrue. In fact, in his interviews with the president of Niger, Wilson was told—and reported to his CIA handlers—that Iraq had sent a delegation to Niger in 1999 to hold talks on "expanding trade" between the two countries. Niger had no trade to speak of other than uranium, and the CIA recognized the discussion of "expanded trade" for what it was: a bid to break the sanctions and illegally sell yellowcake to Saddam. The president of Niger told Wilson he had steered the conversation in another direction. What Wilson didn't recognize, but the CIA immediately grasped, was that Wilson had in fact confirmed Iraq's recent attempts to secure supplies of yellowcake from Niger. This is precisely what President Bush had said in his notorious sixteen words. Not that Iraq had actually obtained uranium, which Wilson's report claimed to debunk, but that Iraq had illegally *sought* uranium from Africa, thus confirming the Bush administration's main contention that containment had by no means induced Saddam to abandon his nuclear ambitions. This is what Bush said, and it was true. Yet the left was determined to turn this simple fact on its head and transform it into a heinous lie.

Mr. and Mrs. Wilson, for their part, failed on two counts. Valerie Plame Wilson brought herself to the very edge of exposure by nominating her husband for the mission, and Joe Wilson made certain his wife's exposure would occur by picking a fight with the very U.S. government officials whose questions are always answered.

The left refused to see that Vice President Cheney had a right to know who sent the envoy who was now publicly attacking him. The left refused to see that the American people deserved to know whether someone was trying to undermine the policies of the United States government. Wilson was cast as a whistleblower by the left, and Cheney was cast as a powerful man trying to exact revenge on Wilson for making embarrassing information public.

The truth was just the reverse. The Wilsons had injected themselves into the political process, and as a necessary result of their own actions Valerie Plame Wilson would be exposed as a member of the CIA's clandestine service.

Nonetheless, despite the facts, of all the lies about George W. Bush and the war in Iraq, the most lovingly told (and retold ad nauseam) was the torrid tale of the beautiful American spy who was betrayed—outed, burned, exposed—by her own government because her courageous husband spoke the truth about what he called the administration's phony reasons to go to war.

The beautiful spy was indeed a striking woman. Valerie Plame Wilson was a slim blond with a winning smile and clear blue eyes. She was a mother of young twins. She lived a quiet life, preserving her cover by telling friends, neighbors, and even family that she was employed by an international energy company when in fact she was a CIA spy. She worked overseas for a time under Non-Official Cover (NOC). Her contacts were especially sensitive to exposure, because they were not aware of her true employer.

While Valerie's husband gloried in media appearances in which he repeated the story of his trip to Niger and reiterated his claims that Bush twisted intelligence to make his case for war, several reporters were asking why Vice President Cheney would send someone to Niger who would betray him in the *New York Times* a year later. Cheney himself, and his chief of staff, I. Lewis "Scooter" Libby, were making the same inquiries. Who is Joe Wilson, and who sent him to Niger?

Meanwhile the White House went into full damage control mode. On July 7, White House spokesman Ari Fleischer formally withdrew the president's sixteen words, saying the statement was not "correct." Four days later CIA director George Tenet conceded that the claims about Iraq buying uranium from Niger were a mistake and that the sixteen words "should never have been included in the text written for the president." But it turned out to be a triple embarrassment a year later when the British government's Butler Report confirmed that the president's sixteen words were "well founded."

There were instances, and this was one, in which the Bush administration contributed to the effectiveness of the left's lies. Wilson's own reporting inadvertently confirmed the accuracy of the sixteen words, and Bush should never have authorized either his spokesman or the CIA to take them back.

On July 8, we now know, Richard Armitage told syndicated columnist Robert Novak the same thing he'd already told Bob Woodward, that Wilson's wife worked at the CIA, giving her name as Valerie Plame. Later the same day, Novak contacted White House advisor Karl Rove seeking a confirmation. Rove answered Novak's question enigmatically: "Oh, you heard that too?" (He had told *Time* magazine's Matt Cooper that Wilson's wife worked at the CIA, but didn't reveal her name or covert status. Rove then cut the call with Cooper short, saying, "I've already said too much.")

Even before Novak published Valerie Plame's name, the trouble was already starting for the vice president's office.

On July 8, the same day Novak was informed of the identity of Wilson's wife, Chris Matthews was on MSNBC taking aim at the vice president's chief of staff, Lewis Libby.

Matthews, who specializes in drawing sloppy connections and then loudly and obtusely repeating them, explicitly stated the lie that would not die: the vice president sent someone to find crucial information in the case for war, then ignored him when the information that came back didn't conform to expectations.

"Why would the vice president's office, Scooter Libby, or whoever is running that office—why would they send a CIA effort down in Niger to verify something," Matthews asked Congressman Curt Weldon, "find out there wasn't a uranium sale, and then not follow up by putting that information—or correcting that information—in the president's State of the Union? If they went to the trouble of sending Joe Wilson all the way to Africa to find out whether that country had ever sold uranium to Saddam Hussein, why wouldn't they follow up on that?"

Matthews, who is not nearly as dumb as he looks, understands his role in the liberal news distortion racket, which is to move the story forward not by making direct accusations but by raising insinuating questions. He also clearly understood the potential of the Wilson/Plame story to drag the vice president out of his lair and hang a scandal around his neck, and maybe more. The prospect of siccing a special prosecutor on Dick Cheney obviously excited him. Accordingly, he set the narrative early: the vice president sent Joe Wilson to Niger (he hadn't), then ignored Wilson's report because he didn't like the information (he didn't).

"The former ambassador, Joe Wilson, said that this was cleared by the vice president's office. They are the ones who sent him to Africa to find out whether it was true or not, whether it was action—there was traffic in nuclear materials between the country of Niger and the country of Saddam Hussein's Iraq. He came back and said there was nothing going on like that six months before the speech. Doesn't the vice president's office hold the greatest culpability here for not acting on that truth?" The number of illogical leaps and unverified assertions in this paragraph is staggering.

Matthews, as is his habit, hammered this story relentlessly night after night. His shows consisted of little else for weeks on end: and he repeated his wrongheaded formulation at least five times in each program.

It was a distorted view of what had actually happened, a misimpression based on a toxic mix of ignorance and animus—not in and of itself a lie. But this erroneous narrative became a lie when the left and its media allies refused to abandon or even revise an incorrect storyline that served their purpose of attacking and undermining Cheney and Bush. And the left never was willing to give that narrative up. Like a willful child demanding to hear its favorite bedtime story again and again, they always wanted Cheney to have been the one who "sent" Wilson to Niger, then ignored his information, and savagely retaliated against his principled antiwar stance by exposing his wife and ruining her career.

But Matthews was right—the story had legs. In mentioning the name of the vice president's chief of staff, Lewis "Scooter" Libby, he set in motion a series of events that would eventually conclude with the conviction of Libby for perjury.

Two days after Matthews began connecting Libby to the Wilson/Plame affair, on July 10, an angry and agitated Libby called Tim Russert at NBC to protest Matthews throwing his name around. Russert begged off, saying he had no management control over Matthews. But the call stuck in Russert's mind, and two years later when called to testify in Libby's perjury and obstruction of justice trial, that call sealed Libby's fate. Libby claimed he had learned Plame's identity from "reporters" and named Russert as the one who had mentioned her to him. In fact, he had learned her identity through official sources, and was either confused or lying when he said it was Russert. The jury believed he lied about it hoping to avoid embarrassment to the White House. That lie constituted the crime of perjury and obstruction of justice.

Meanwhile, Matthews kept it up. On July 9, he put Libby and the vice president's office in the crosshairs again. "He [Wilson] made it very clear he was sent down there at the behest of the vice president's office last year, months, almost a year before the president's State of the Union address, he came back with the information that there was, in fact, no deal. Isn't the vice president's office responsible right now to come out and say why they didn't act on that information?" Again, no one had ever claimed there was a deal, only an attempt to purchase uranium illegally. But these omissions and distortions did their job: the seeds of doubt were planted in the public mind.

Five days later, on July 14, Robert Novak's nationally syndicated column came out, divulging the name of Ambassador Wilson's wife, Valerie Plame, and reporting that she worked at the CIA on WMD counter-proliferation. Novak's column also revealed that it was Plame who had set up her husband's trip, not the office of the vice president.

A day or so later, Wilson later recalled, he got a quick call from Chris Matthews at MSNBC. "I just talked to Karl Rove and he says your wife is 'fair game,'" Matthews said hurriedly, before hanging up.

It was a bombshell revelation, but for the wrong reasons. Instead of focusing on the fact that the vice president's office was not in fact responsible for sending Wilson to Niger, the media whipped itself into a fury over the notion that a CIA operative had been outed by someone, possibly as an act of petty revenge against her husband by Dick Cheney or his surrogate, Scooter Libby. It seemed not to occur to anyone in the media that Valeria Plame had put herself in a position to be outed, first by promoting her husband for a trip to answer a question from the vice president's office, and then by allowing him to go public with his complaints about it, first as an unnamed source and then in his own right. Aren't these people trained to avoid unwanted media attention?

A few days later, David Corn of *The Nation* published an article that expressed outrage over the exposure of a CIA "deep-cover operative," and Joe Wilson—soon to be ubiquitous—provided a tasty quote. "Naming her this way would have compromised every operation, every relationship, every network with which she had been associated in her entire career. This is the stuff of Kim Philby and Aldrich Ames," Wilson said, invoking the names of two of the most famous traitors in the espionage business. Corn asked the leading question: Wasn't the exposure of a "covert" agent of the CIA a breach of national security, and wasn't that a crime? He cited the Intelligence Identities Protection Act of 1982, which made it a crime for anyone with access to classified information to disclose intentionally information identifying a covert agent. "The punishment for such an offense is a fine up to $50,000 and/or up to ten years in prison," Corn wrote.

Novak had reported in his column, and confirmed to Corn, that his sources were administration officials. All eyes turned to Libby and Karl Rove. The person who actually gave up Plame's identity to both Woodward and Novak quietly passed under the radar.

In his interview with Corn, Wilson scoffed at the notion—later confirmed—that his wife had put him up for the Niger trip, joking that with two young children at home it would not have been in her interest to send him to Africa. "His wife's role—if she had one—has nothing but anecdotal value," wrote Corn.

"Stories like this," Wilson told Corn, "are not intended to intimidate me, since I've already told my story. But it's pretty clear it is intended to intimidate others who might come forward. You need only look at the stories of intelligence analysts who say they have been pressured. They may have kids in college, they may be vulnerable to these types of smears." Wilson's suggestion that the administration—particularly Cheney and Libby—was pressuring CIA analysts to come to conclusions that the analysts didn't honestly support was specifically denied by the Senate Selected Committee on Intelligence investigation, which concluded that while some analysts were questioned by the vice president—in person during one of his several visits to CIA headquarters—they did not interpret that questioning to be pressure.

"Will there be an inquiry?" Corn asked.

Evidently, the CIA thought one was warranted. The CIA also thought it was the White House, not their own "covert" operative, who was responsible, apparently taking Novak's cue that "administration officials" had identified Plame. And the CIA had its ways of getting back. Acting on the suspicion that the White House had outed one of its covert operatives, the agency referred the incident to the Department of Justice a few days later for a criminal investigation. A few weeks after that the investigation became official, and eventually Attorney General John Ashcroft recused himself, leaving the case in the hands of Special Counsel Patrick Fitzgerald, with the full powers of the AG.

The public controversy about Iraq's WMD, or the lack of it, was now in full swing. In early August, Barton Gellman and Walter Pincus of the *Washington Post* wrote about Wilson's "information" and concluded that something was seriously amiss in the way it was handled. "The new information indicates a pattern in which President Bush, Vice President Cheney, and their subordinates—in public and behind the scenes—made allegations depicting Iraq's nuclear weapons program as more active, more certain, and more imminent in its threat than the data they had would support."

Referring to Wilson, they wrote, "On occasion administration advocates withheld evidence that did not conform to their views. The White House seldom corrected misstatements or acknowledged loss of confidence in information upon which it had previously relied." Gellman and Pincus also reported, "The National Intelligence Estimate (NIE) of October 2002 cited new construction at facilities once associated with Iraq's nuclear program, but analysts had no reliable information at the time about what was happening under the roofs. By February, a month before the war, U.S. government specialists on the ground in Iraq had seen for themselves that there were no forbidden activities at the sites. . . ."

Some people tried to push back. Paul Leventhal, the founding president of the Nuclear Control Institute, wrote to the *Washington Post* about the Gellman/Pincus article. "Unfortunately, the absence of evidence is not evidence of the absence of a nuclear weapons capability in Iraq," Leventhal reminded the authors, to no evident effect.

The Bush Lied, People Died narrative was being chiseled into the public consciousness by a media increasingly opposed to the war in Iraq.

In September, Keith Olbermann of MSNBC was doing his best to make certain the preferred narrative on Joe Wilson and Valerie Plame stayed front and center. "Somebody revealed that person's work for the CIA to a reporter—'blew the cover,' as the spy novels call it. That agent would be the wife of the former U.S. ambassador to Iraq, Joe Wilson." Oops. Wilson was not the former ambassador to Iraq, though he didn't mind if people thought he was. "He was the man who blew the lid off the sixteen-word story, writing in the *New York Times* that he'd been sent by the administration to Africa to substantiate the claim that Iraq was seeking plutonium in Niger and he could not do so."

Wilson famously demanded that Karl Rove be "frog marched across the White House lawn in handcuffs" because Rove had told Chris Matthews that Wilson's wife was "fair game." At a December dinner where her husband received the Ron Ridenhour Award for Truth Telling, Valerie Plame made her first public appearance among journalists. Timothy Noah of *Slate*, who attended the event, wrote, "Wilson was most emotional when addressing his wife's exposure." "Fighting back tears," Wilson said, "I'm sorry for (your exposure). If I could give you back your anonymity . . . I would do it in a minute."

Noah wrote, "She sat quietly, wiping away a tear, as her husband added, 'Frankly, frog marching is too good for those who decided that their political agenda was more important than either American national security or your life.'"

Noah evidently wasn't buying it. He recited a list of articles from the *Washington Post, Vanity Fair,* and others in which Plame had attended parties or events with her husband, and sat by "quietly" as he expounded on the crimes of the administration in exposing his wife. Indeed, Wilson turned out to be a major publicity hound, and very skillful, too, despite his protestations that he only wanted to protect her privacy. Thus his wife was surprised on coming home one day to find photographers setting up in her kitchen for a big glossy spread in *Vanity Fair.* Wilson had long claimed that his wife would never be photographed—it was part of the mystique he carefully cultivated around her—but he convinced her to pose for a cover photo sitting with him in his Jaguar convertible in front of the White House. She wore large dark glasses and a scarf covering her blond hair.

"My only regret about the *Vanity Fair* photo is that after all my wife and I have been through on this," he told the *Washington Post,* "that she had to be clothed as generic blonde in order to deal with the genuine concern that some wacko on the street might easily identify her. It was just in the interest of personal security."

Who exposed Valerie Plame? Despite the obvious conclusion that she set this inevitable result in motion when she injected herself into national politics by sending her husband on the Niger mission, the special counsel eventually convicted no one of the crime of revealing her identity. The special counsel knew from the grand jury testimony of Bob Woodward and Robert Novak that the actual source of the leak was Richard Armitage and that no crime was involved.

Eventually, Scooter Libby was convicted of perjury and obstruction of justice for not telling the grand jury the truth.

But just to seal the matter, the prosecutor who put 1993 World Trade Center bomber Ramzi Yousef in prison for life, Andrew McCarthy, pointed out that the CIA had already blown Valerie Plame's cover long before Bob Novak published her name.

During the Libby trial, Special Counsel Patrick Fitzgerald demanded testimony of several reporters, including Matthew Cooper of *Time* and Judith Miller of the *New York Times*. Refusing to testify, Miller spent eighty-five days in jail for contempt of court before Libby himself convinced her she should give testimony. Cooper was spared the same fate when his boss, Norman Pearlstine, voluntarily turned over Cooper's notes of his conversations with Karl Rove. But during the arguments about compelling the testimony of journalists, a group of publishers and broadcasters filed briefs with the court that revealed that Plame's identity had been compromised by the CIA in a slipup that allowed the government of Cuba to read secret papers that identified her as a CIA operative.

"Thus, the same media now stampeding on Rove," McCarthy wrote, describing in shorthand the media campaign to indict and convict Rove for outing Plame to both Cooper and Novak, "has told a federal court that, to the contrary, they believe the CIA itself blew Plame's cover before Rove or anyone else in the Bush administration ever spoke to Novak about her." McCarthy concluded, "Although the *Times* and its cohort have a bull's-eye on Rove's back, they are breathtakingly silent about an apparent CIA embarrassment—one that seems to be just the type of juicy story they routinely covet."

On the first day of September 2006, the *Washington Post* editorial page tried to end—finally—the sorry Plame/Wilson tale. The occasion was the embarrassing discovery that Bob Woodward had known for years that the person who was telling reporters about Valerie Plame's identity was Richard Armitage of the State Department. (See the earlier transcript of Woodward's conversation with Armitage.)

The *Post*'s editorial board lamented the fact that years had been spent chasing down a "sensational" charge that the Bush White House had set out to leak Ms. Plame's identity to punish Joe Wilson, a charge the *Post* admitted was clearly "untrue."

"All of that might have been avoided had Mr. Armitage's identity been known three years ago." Of course, it *was* known—to *Washington Post* reporter Bob Woodward. Mr. Woodward's lapse in judgment in this matter caused his editor, Leonard Downie, great embarrassment, and Mr. Woodward was forced to apologize in print.

"Nevertheless, it now appears," the editorial continued, "that the person most responsible for the end of Ms. Plame's CIA career is Mr. Wilson. Mr. Wilson chose to go public with an explosive charge, claiming—falsely as it turns out—that he had debunked reports of Iraqi uranium-shopping in Niger and that his report had circulated to senior administration officials."

Here the *Post* arrived at the most important point. "He ought to have expected that both those officials and journalists such as Mr. Novak would ask why a retired ambassador would have been sent on such a mission and that the answer would point to his wife. . . . It's unfortunate that so many people took him seriously."

What the *Post* would not address was why so many on the left found Wilson so convenient to take seriously. His story fit with an anti-Bush narrative the left desperately needed to stir from a mere ember into a raging conflagration. It worked. The lie stuck, even if the liar was exposed.

The American public soon forgot the controversy about the spy who was exposed, but the Joe Wilson line that the Bush administration "twisted" intelligence, and that the country was taken to war on false pretenses—those lies live on even today.

Chapter Six

The Numbers Game: Swiftboating the War with Statistics

The left's swiftboating of George W. Bush on Iraq was nothing if not ruthless. There's no strategy as effective as a lie presented as the truth. Confusion helps the liar.

In the case of the much-debated question of how many Iraqi civilians had been killed in the war, it is instructive to look at the anatomy of the lie. Taking apart how the lie worked and how it affected public attitudes is essential to understand how the left worked the media and the public to *swiftboat* the war and George W. Bush.

Of all the charges leveled against Bush, probably none stung as sharply as the antiwar slogan, "Bush Lied, People Died." It was one thing to have held him responsible for four thousand American military deaths and thousands more injuries; at least those numbers, sad as they may have been, were also true. The issue of his responsibility for those deaths lay in the heart of the voter, and by 2006, as the congressional elections approached, more and more voters seemed to be holding Bush to blame for those American casualties. When the number of American dead passed the number of people killed in the World Trade Center and Pentagon attacks of 9/11, many people began to conclude Bush was throwing a lot of lives on the fire of this war.

But there was also the issue of the number of Iraqi dead. In a way, that number was unknowable. In the chaos of Iraq, it was not certain whose numbers were correct, and whose were not. The U.S.

government didn't even try. "We don't do body count," General Tommy Franks famously remarked.

But others did. An antiwar organization in Britain, calling itself the Iraq Body Count, or IBC, began keeping track in 2003 and posted its results online. It followed rigorous rules: figures could not be added to the total that were "estimates," but had to be a record of documented deaths; only violent deaths were recorded; only civilian—noncombatant—deaths were recorded.

As of the end of 2003 it had counted between 10,077 and 12,010 Iraqi civilian deaths. By 2007 those numbers, statistical extrapolations called the "interval," had risen to a low of 22,586 and a high of 24,159 for a total on the high end of about 85,000 Iraqi civilian deaths for all the years of the war to the close of 2007.

The IBC records gave in incident number, the kind of incident—gunfire or car bomb, for instance—and the number of people killed, and if possible their names and other personal information.

For instance, IBC case number K-13184 notes the bodies of a kidnapped woman and her daughter were found near Rubieya al-Saadiya on April 8, 2009. The report notes two deaths, and makes an entry for "type": "Executed."

The records are incomplete in many cases. Names are unknown, and the exact circumstances of the deaths may not be known. But the IBC did display a level of meticulousness that engendered a certain confidence in its reporting. Still, the IBC total through 2007 was regarded by most experts to be a fairly high number. And other organizations tracking civilian deaths were reporting lower numbers.

Yet in October 2006, a startling and shocking new claim was revealed to the world that turned out to be one of the slickest lies the left told about the war.

With election day in the United States about a month away, the prestigious British medical journal *The Lancet* published a study by researchers at the Johns Hopkins Bloomberg School of Public Health that claimed that since America launched its invasion of Iraq, 655,000 Iraqi civilians had been killed. The study also claimed that most of these deaths were caused by gunfire, implying that American soldiers had done most of the killing.

What this meant in political terms was simple enough: it gave concrete support to the idea that George W. Bush had launched a war that had killed—meaning *he* had killed—between half a million and a million Iraqis. Set against a total population of 25 million, that meant Bush had killed 2.5 percent of the population.

These estimates were met with universal horror. A death rate of 655,000—and 601,000 seemingly attributable to American soldiers—was a staggering number. It was twenty times the number President Bush had used only a few months earlier (30,000) and ten times the number used by the Iraq Body Count Web site (50,000).

It was a number large enough to induce immediate shame on the part of the American people, hostility and fury in parts of the rest of the world, and not enough incredulity and skepticism among the journalists who covered the story from the start.

It was one of the more transparent lies about the war in Iraq, but the news came at a crucial moment and the damage was done quickly and permanently, before anyone could look at the study closely and figure out why these numbers were so much higher than previous estimates.

To be sure, it was a very difficult job to keep count of how many Iraqis were being killed in the aftermath of the invasion, and no one was certain whose numbers were right and whose were wrong. As was demonstrated on the news every night, there were so many ways to die in Iraq. A person could be shot. A person could be too close to an air strike. A person could have his head cut off. A person could be executed by his enemies. A person could have holes drilled in his head. A person could be at the market when a car bomb was set off. A person could be in a café when a suicider pulled the cord on his vest.

There were other, more mundane ways to die. Run over by an American military vehicle. Shot for disobeying rules at a checkpoint. A kidnapping gone wrong. Yes, there were American bombs sometimes falling out of the sky, sometimes on terrorist safe houses tucked away among the homes of innocent civilians. Yes, there were firefights in which Iraqis might have been caught in the cross fire. Yes, the American and coalition forces had killed many, many al Qaeda and insurgents and sectarians. But a hot war zone is always a particularly difficult place to keep a body count. The hospitals and morgues complained constantly of a tide of bodies, stacked wherever, endlessly flowing in.

The timing of the report—October 11, 2006—was hardly coincidental. With election day three weeks away and the war not going particularly well, these two prestigious medical institutions—Johns Hopkins and *The Lancet*—plainly intended to influence American voters. This alone should have engendered a healthy skepticism about the report. Instead the press uncritically accepted the estimates and indulged in an orgy of blame.

The CBS *Evening News* led its broadcast that evening with a report from correspondent David Martin, a veteran Pentagon reporter.

"Now we're learning that the war has been a lot more deadly than we knew." Martin opened. "A new and stunning measure of the havoc the American invasion unleashed in Iraq. A study published in the British journal *Lancet* estimates 655,000 Iraqis—2.5 percent of the entire population—have died as a consequence of the war. To understand how large, consider this: The same percentage of the much larger American population would be 7.5 million dead."

CNN's lead (online and on air) was authoritative and dire: "War has wiped out about 655,000 Iraqis, or more than 500 people a day since the U.S.-led invasion, a new study reports."

The headlines hit the American public like a car bomb in a Baghdad market. Public attitudes toward the war shifted sharply in favor of the Democrats who were campaigning for congressional seats against Bush and against the war. The story was so strong—five hundred people a day dead!—any explanation or denial seemed weak and mealymouthed. When President Bush was asked about it in a televised news conference by Suzanne Malveaux of CNN, he said he didn't believe the study was "credible," and that General George Casey, commander in Iraq, agreed.

The *New York Times* played the story of *The Lancet* study as a credible report that deserved serious attention. "The figure breaks down to about 15,000 violent deaths a month," the *Times* reporters wrote, "a number that is quadruple the one for July given by Iraqi government hospitals and the morgue in Baghdad and published last month in a United Nations report in Iraq. That month was the highest for Iraqi civilian deaths since the American invasion." That United Nations report put the number at about 3,500 Iraqi civilian deaths.

The *Washington Post* likewise uncritically regurgitated the study's claim: "A team of American and Iraqi epidemiologists estimates that 655,000 more people have died in Iraq since coalition forces arrived in March 2003 than would have died if the invasion had not occurred."

In an NBC *Nightly News* report, correspondent Jim Miklaszewski said, "An independent study released today by Johns Hopkins University claims that more than 650,000 Iraqis have been killed in the war, more than ten times U.S. military estimates. President Bush dismissed the report as not credible because he says the way in which the numbers were compiled has been discredited."

On ABC's *World News*, anchor Charles Gibson at least described the estimate as "controversial," as he used it to set up a story from Iraq on the impact of the ongoing murders: "There is a controversial new study about civilian deaths in Iraq that was released today. Researchers from Johns Hopkins claim more than 600,000 Iraqis have died in violence since the U.S. invasion. That number is a good deal higher than other estimates, and President Bush maintained today that the new study is 'just not credible.' But he also said that too many innocents are dying, and in our 'Closer Look' tonight, ABC's Terry McCarthy reports the widespread killing is affecting every aspect of life in Iraq."

Predictably, the antiwar American left went berserk with rage. Rosie O'Donnell on ABC's *The View* spoke to millions of American women (women being by far the bulk of the program's audience): "I just want to say something: 655,000 Iraqi civilians are dead. Who are the terrorists?" It was clear who she thought the real terrorists were: American troops.

Co-host Elisabeth Hasselbeck reacted with shock. "Who are the terrorists?" she asked O'Donnell. "Wait, who are you calling terrorists now? Americans?"

O'Donnell wouldn't back down. "I'm saying if you were in Iraq, and the other country, the United States, the richest in the world, invaded your country and killed 655,000 of your citizens, what would you call us?"

Hasselbeck asked O'Donnell, "Are we killing their citizens or are their people also killing their citizens?"

O'Donnell wouldn't answer the question. "We're invading a sovereign nation, occupying a country against the UN . . . ," Rosie paused, changing directions. "Because people no longer—the vast majority of Americans no longer are falling for the trick of the bad terrorists are out there to get us."

The *Village Voice* said about the large number *The Lancet* had reported, "That's more than twice the 290,000 humans that Saddam Hussein is said to have killed during his 25-year reign."

Antiwar activist and professor Juan Cole wrote on his blog, which is a frequent read among the left in the news business, "I follow the violence in Iraq carefully and daily, and I find the results plausible."

The *Malden Observer* (of Malden, Massachusetts) wrote in an unsigned editorial: "When Bush this week dismissed a new estimate of the number of civilian deaths in Iraq, it was totally in character. 'I don't consider it a credible report,' he said, without further explanation. Bush can only envy the credibility of the report's authors, a team of epidemiologists from Johns Hopkins, and *The Lancet*, the 182-year-old journal in which it was published."

The authors of the study, and the journal itself, would ultimately be revealed as part of a left conspiracy to lie with science. But for now they got respect and credibility. And the story achieved its effect, rocketing around the globe at the speed of digital transmission.

In Europe, the story seemed too obviously true to generate much shock or surprise. The UK *Guardian*'s lead paragraph ("The death toll among Iraqis as a result of the U.S.-led invasion has now reached an estimated 655,000") took care to repeat the implication of the study that it was the Americans who inflicted the death toll.

"The findings provoked an immediate political storm," the *Guardian* added in its follow-up the next day.

In Edinburgh, the *Scotsman* said "Such a figure would mean that 2.5 percent of the Iraqi population has died because of the invasion and ensuing strife."

On a Web site called Islamcity, a man named Hannan posting from Germany wrote, "When does 'collateral damage' so dwarf combatant deaths that war becomes genocide? Bush's 'war on terror' is, in fact, a war on Iraqi civilians."

The Bangladesh newspaper the *New Nation* editorialized: "President Bush and his administration should realize that truth can't be suppressed and it shall prevail."

Muslim commentators in America and overseas not only embraced the story enthusiastically, they sprinkled magic dust and made the number grow. The *National Journal* quoted an Al Jazeera debate in which an Egyptian cleric said the Americans had "killed *one and a half million people* . . . [and] killed a million Iraqi children during the [1990s sanctions] siege, left traces of enriched uranium from the weapons that were used [in 1991], and destroyed the environment for the next *35 billion years*, according to American estimates."

The Nation's Eric Alterman, writing on *Huffington Post* a week after the study was released, was angry that its methodology was being questioned. He cited an Associated Press report that quoted "expert" Anthony Cordesman characterizing the study as "politics" in advance of the upcoming election. Alterman also quoted Christopher Hitchens, who had written that the figures were "almost certainly inflated." He asked, "What the hell kind of society kills all these people and cannot be bothered to care? Cannot be bothered to count them and when someone does, risking their lives in the process, lies to discredit them—and no one cares about that either?"

Alterman used the story, as many others did, as a jumping off point to again attack the entire war effort. "The sad fact is that Hussein could have been contained militarily without all of these people dying unnecessarily. Easily. But our leaders couldn't prove themselves sufficiently macho for chickenhawk neo-cons to take the necessary steps, and so we have all this blood on our collective hands, to say nothing of our own soldiers' deaths, an increased terrorist threat, a trillion dollars wasted, and the hatred of the world toward our citizens."

A post on the *USA Today* Web site by a person called "Disgusted by Rightards": "Iraqi deaths far exceed the 3,000 killed in the WTC attacks. Even American deaths will soon top that number! It's also clear that WMD claims were lies, since both Rice and Rumsfeld said before the war that Saddam had no meaningful weapons capability left. So the war's bogus too! Shame on you, America!"

This person—and you can never tell much more when reading notes from people who don't use real names—who is so disgusted by *rightards* posted at 7:40 in the evening on the day the story broke in the morning. The anger must have been stewing all day.

The San Francisco–based, very left-wing Salon.com picked up the theme a week later. Gary Kamiya sobbed out a piece headlined "Shame," in which he argued, "When we chose to invade Iraq, we made ourselves morally responsible for the consequences." Kamiya proposed a national day of apology. "A day simply to say we're sorry. And to say it, figuratively or literally, on our knees."

Columnist Phillip Adams headlined his comment in *The Australian*, "Blind Eye to Political Genocide": "The lies and disinformation that got us into the war continue and the Iraqis pay an intolerable price for the wish-fulfillment fantasies of armchair generals and neocons."

The reaction, suffice it to say, was volcanic, and if nothing else proved that the study results had successfully worked their way into public consciousness. Radio talk show hosts were confronted by angry callers wanting justification for the "655,000 deaths in Iraq."

When President Bush immediately questioned the study's "credibility," his sinking position in the polls allowed some people to take his doubts as their own confirmation. If Bush said it was wrong, it must be right.

The number had what politicians call "resonance." It bounced off the walls of the nation. "Within a week the study had been featured in 25 news shows and 188 articles in U.S. newspapers and magazines," Neil Munro and Carl Cannon wrote in the *National Journal*.

Did America really kill half a million Iraqis? "Even more," said the left, "even more."

But there were problems the left didn't want to notice. The study was riddled with trip wires of suspicion. To begin with, the number itself was grotesquely high, as any of the major media should have known. But they were happy to let the headlines do maximum damage and move on.

Soon the story drifted off the front pages and network newscasts, as the media moved on to cover a North Korean nuclear test, and the red-faced Republican story of the hour, GOP Congressman Mark Foley's sex emails with a boy in the House Page dormitory.

In the meantime, others began looking more closely at the Hopkins study, and predictably, alarms began to go off. Digging into the substance of the study uncovered enormous problems. Reporters discovered people in the scientific community who objected to flaws in what statisticians and scientists who specialize in population surveys call "methodology." These were the methods of working in the war zone, and actual mathematical calculations the researchers used to arrive at a reliable number of Iraqi civilian dead.

The study's authors had employed a two-step process: First data (numbers of deaths) had to be gathered in the field, in face-to-face interviews in Iraq; that would establish the basic data. Then a mathematical extrapolation for the entire Iraqi population would be made to arrive at a credible number of Iraqi civilian deaths. That part, at least, was accepted basic science.

The study involved sending teams to randomly selected Iraqi homes to interview whoever was in the house about who lived there, who was born and who died in the year and a half before the invasion, and the year and half after. In each neighborhood the survey team visited, they would interview people in thirty to forty houses and assemble the data for that "cluster." Survey teams went to a total of forty-seven of those thirty-house clusters at various places around Iraq. The information from those clusters was subsequently expanded by mathematical extrapolation to arrive at a total estimate of Iraqi civilian deaths.

The study's authors required the survey teams to ask for and see a death certificate on the person reported dead. Over 90 percent of the respondents were able to produce a death certificate.

The Iraq Body Count organization—not a pack of Bush supporting neo-cons, to be sure—had also weighed in with criticism of an earlier Hopkins study back in 2004. At that time, Johns Hopkins researcher Les Roberts was rushing a preliminary study into print that showed 100,000 excess deaths when the IBC showed no more than 22,000. As IBC's statisticians noted, "Because the researchers did not ask relatives whether the male deaths were military or civilian, the civilian proportion in the same is unknown (despite *The Lancet* Web site's front-page headline '100,000 excess civilian deaths after Iraq invasion'). The authors clearly state that 'many' of the dead in their sample may have been combatants."

The 2006 study, an update of the 2004 survey, had expanded the number of households surveyed and claimed a "95% confidence interval" to arrive at the approximation of 655,000 deaths. Les Roberts, Ph.D., and Dr. Gilbert Burnham, M.D., were co-authors of both reports. Johns Hopkins Bloomberg School of Public Health had approved the study, and *The Lancet*, the "prestigious" British medical journal, had approved it. It had been peer reviewed—rushed to be sure, but reviewed and approved.

The outrage was furious, and the vitriol righteous. America had been exposed as a nation of wanton murderers marauding through a benighted nation of innocents.

There was only one problem: The study was a phony and the shockingly high number of estimated deaths was most certainly wrong. The whole thing was a fraud.

The Hopkins study was deeply flawed, yet millions of Americans believed it, and may have voted in November 2006 based in part upon their feelings of disgust, embarrassment, and shame.

This started to become apparent in the days following the release of the study as reputable scientists began to look through the backup information and found it lacking.

Some scientists noted that even though the "cluster" model had been used successfully elsewhere, these results were based on an exceedingly low number of clusters. Many objected that it was unreliable to extrapolate a credible number of deaths in a population of 25 million with just forty-seven clusters. Thus the *National Journal* reported, "The accidental deaths included 15,000 Iraqis killed by U.S. vehicles in road incidents—extrapolated from five death reports."

"It is not science. It is propaganda," said Mark van der Lann, professor of biostatistics and statistics at UC Berkeley. "The estimates based upon these data are extremely unreliable and cannot stand a decent scientific evaluation." In van der Lann's view, it was all conclusion and no support, for the purpose of propaganda, i.e., antiwar. Experts also questioned the number based simply on the fact that it was ten times higher than any other estimate from other organizations that specialized in tracking civilian deaths.

John Zogby, the Arab American pollster, defended the study's methodology. But he couldn't have attacked the methodology without undermining the credibility of his own polling. The Hopkins study had canvassed just over 1,800 people to draw results for a population of 25,000,000. Zogby routinely issued polls for 300,000,000 Americans based on 500 phone calls. How could he possibly criticize?

But others noticed glaring problems. First, it was evident that the primary designer and co-author of the study, a controversial epidemiologist named Les Roberts, was an open and vocal opponent of the war. His partner in the study, Dr. Gilbert Burnham of Johns Hopkins, was equally open in his war opposition.

Roberts actually did nothing to deflect suspicions of bias. He openly admitted that he had rushed out his first study of Iraqi civilian deaths before Election Day in 2004, and had likewise insisted that the study that showed the 655,000 deaths be published before Election Day 2006. He was accommodated in that request by *The Lancet*.

Roberts shrugged off criticism of his motives, saying simply, "I'm a public health doctor. War is a public health hazard."

At the moment the news of the study broke, the doctor was somewhat difficult to reach, as he was running for a congressional seat in New York's Democratic primary. He eventually dropped out of the race. But Roberts was not shy about defending himself. In a personal letter to Dr. John Allen Paulos of Temple University, he responded to criticism of his politically motivated "rush to publish" by Paulos. As Roberts explained:

> We finished the survey on 20 Sept. If this had not come out until mid-Nov. or later, in the politicized lens of Baghdad (where the chief of police does not allow his name to be made public and where all the newly trained Iraqi soldiers I saw had bandannas to hide their faces to avoid their families being murdered . . .) this would have been seen as the researchers covering up for the Bush White House until after the election and I am convinced my Iraqi co-investigators would have been killed. Given that Kerry and Bush had the same attitude about invading and similar plans for how to proceed, I never thought it would influence the election and the investigators never discussed it with each other or briefed any political player.

"So, we rushed to get it out," Roberts admitted again. "I do not understand why the 'study's scientific neutrality' is influenced or the likelihood that the sample was valid, the analysis fair." Here Roberts referred to the criticism that his scientific "neutrality" had been compromised. "What does neutrality mean? Do people who publish about malaria deaths need to be neutral about malaria?"

He signed his letter, "Yours in confusion and disgust." Paulos had been a friend and colleague.

Roberts had earlier boasted about his adventure getting into Iraq to set up the survey teams. He'd hidden on the floor of an SUV with $20,000 stuffed in his clothes and money belt for the dangerous trip into Baghdad. Once there, he had to immediately give up going out with the Iraqi survey teams because of the danger.

In an interview with an Australian news service, he described his time out in the open in Baghdad before holing up in a hotel room for the rest of his stay.

"It was terrifying. You know, some of the interviewers wouldn't ride in the same car as me because I was an American, and we had an agreement that I would never speak on the street," Roberts said. "I did go out to the first couple of neighborhoods where we trained interviewers and then for the first 8 of the randomly picked 33 neighborhoods . . . After that, the Iraqis did the brave chores of going out to Fallujah and elsewhere and interviewing the families."

This frank admission of the limitations imposed by the war lead some critics to question whether the study could have been conducted properly under such dangerous conditions. But Roberts was undeterred and completely confident about his results. During his congressional campaign, Roberts was asked about his harrowing month in Iraq in September 2004. "Of every Iraqi I spoke to . . . I would ask, 'Why do you think the coalition came?' No one, not one person said anything related to Saddam. They thought we had come for two reasons: We came for oil and we came to create a setting of anarchy so that every nefarious element in the region would come and fight us there, rather than fighting us in North America or fighting us in Israel. I think . . . we do not have either the moral high ground or the minimal support to be a force of stabilization."

As for the war itself, he said, "This can't end well. I think . . . we would end up with a better Iraq, a safer Iraq, and less Iraqis dead by getting out quickly."

Roberts' glaring bias fit nicely with at least one of his study's principal funders. Another document search revealed that almost half the money came from anti-Bush billionaire George Soros.

Soros had spent $30 million of his personal fortune to beat George W. Bush in 2004. He poured more cash into the 2006 congressional races, and publicly plotted with Paul Begala and Rahm Emanuel a $40 million campaign to defeat Senator John McCain. Soros also funded far-left organizations like the Center for American Progress, Moveon.org, and Media Matters for America in order to bring down Bush.

Now it turned out that Roberts was supplied with nearly half the money for his research project by Soros through his Open Society

Institute. Soros contributed $46,000 of the $100,000 budget. As Soros said in 2009, "Defeating Bush policies is my life's work." He'd said much the same in a 2003 interview with the *Washington Post*.

So Soros bought and paid for an incendiary study of civilian deaths in Iraq in order to push the election over the line for Democrats in 2006. True, it was one of many such investments Soros made, but it may have been both the cheapest and the one with the biggest payoff. (Responding later to this charge, the institution funding the Hopkins study claimed that Soros was "likely not even aware of his small donation" and the money was largely used for activities after the completion of the study.)

The left-wing media had trumpeted the headline from day one, but now were tiptoeing away from the scene, so as not to be required to report on the ugly mess the study had become. Tainted studies of this kind were routinely dismissed by left-wing opponents of Big Tobacco. But in this case no one had thought to look under the hood.

It wouldn't have been hard to locate the source of the problem. The editor of *The Lancet* was a man name Richard Horton. It was he who had accepted the study and caused a ruckus by publishing it. Horton was also loudly antiwar and defiantly unrepentant about the study. At a 2006 "Time To Go" rally against the war in Iraq, he took the stage and set to shouting himself hoarse, reading a prepared statement on a folded-up piece of paper.

"Tony Blair told us these numbers were false, impossible, and untrue. Shame! Shame on [his] lies" Horton bellowed to the crowd. "We now know that the civilian deaths in Iraq and Afghanistan have been massively underreported and underrecognized. A mountain of violence and torture going back to the arrogance and delusion of a government that prefers to support the killing of children instead of building hospitals and schools. As this axis of Anglo-American imperialism extends its influence through war and conflict, gathering power and wealth as it goes, so millions of people are left to die in poverty and disease."

Intriguingly, Horton all but admitted that the violent deaths he had reported from "gunshots" were mostly from guns carried by Iraqi sectarians and insurgents: "The souls of justice lie with the mothers and fathers gunned down and blown up in sectarian violence we initiated and continue to sustain." These numbers inflated the study, but Horton's zeal to discredit the war made him blind to this obvious subterfuge.

Horton concluded with a challenge: "Mr. Bush and Mr. Blair, there is a limit to your deception. We are the new resistance!" he shouted, raising his voice in steps. "Let that tempest start to roar! Let the roar continue to grow! It is time to say . . . Stop these wars!"

In other words, Horton opposed both the "bad" war in Iraq and the "good" war in Afghanistan that had toppled the Taliban. This marked him as a member of the far left.

Not surprisingly, *Lancet*'s reputation had suffered under Horton's leadership. He plainly saw his role at the venerable publication as pursuing political ends through scientific means. As a result, he'd been involved in several controversies since becoming the journal's editor in 1992.*

There was also a question about the Iraqi scientist who had gathered the data. How exactly had he and his small survey teams accomplished their work in a war zone? Dr. Riyadh Lafta of Al-Mustansiriya University College of Medicine in Baghdad was listed as a co-author of the study. He insisted that he had been doing this sort of work in Iraq for years, trying to establish child mortality rates, and that his researchers conducted the work properly.

That previous work for the Saddam regime was precisely the point critics raised. According to Neil Munro, who wrote an investigative report for the *National Journal*, Lafta "used to do propaganda journals for Saddam back in the 1990s when Saddam was trying to break the [UN] sanctions. He was sending his flacks and minions out to the United Nations and American universities saying 'Hundreds of thousands of children are starving to death etc.' He would get his Iraqi researchers to do studies that backed up this claim." Lafta was the scientist who performed those research projects for Saddam in an effort to embarrass the United States and the United Nations into lifting the sanctions.

---

* Under Horton's leadership direction, *The Lancet* published a study in 1998 linking the measles, mumps, and rubella vaccine to autism. After an investigation by London's *Sunday Times*, several of the authors of the study withdrew their names and the study was repudiated. In 2005, Horton came under attack for publishing a study that claimed rats suffered organ damage from consumption of genetically modified (GM) foods. Horton has been outspoken in published columns on controversial health-care issues.

Lafta didn't give many interviews, but he made an exception in 2007 when a passport snafu blocked his travel to Canada and Seattle, where he was scheduled to speak to fellow scientists. He was certain it was because of the American government's embarassment over his 2006 study.

"This country is a killing machine," said Dr. Lafta, referring to Iraq in a phone interview from Baghdad with the *Globe and Mail* newspaper in Canada. He explained the fear that he and his teams endured when they were gathering information. "Maybe your adrenaline is going. You have an objective, and the difficult conditions make a special kind of person. It makes you more courageous."

To some experts, these comments seemed to suggest that shortcuts might have been taken to produce the desired numbers. But despite the storm of criticism, Lafta has steadfastly refused to release his raw data.

All of this added up to an abundance of reasonable doubt. But did these crucial details about the credibility of the claim that 655,000 Iraqis had been killed—601,000 by coalition forces—translate into public awareness here in the United States of the study's fatal flaws? Not in the least. Certainly not in the flaming headlines just before Election Day 2006.

Why? It was a busy season for bashing Bush. The election was coming, and the scent of blood was in the air. Bush was being teed up to lose Congress. The media that had declared the United States had been killing 500 Iraqis a day moved on to the North Korean nuclear test, and Florida congressman Mark Foley's gay sex scandal.

The American public didn't hear the news that the bloated 655,000 death toll was a blatant, but damaging, lie. They didn't see how that devastating number had been manufactured by political operatives masquerading as scientists.

A lie had won the day, and the media were walking away from the scene of the crime, softly whistling, pretending they hadn't seen a thing. There were other distractions to chase.

Four weeks later the American people voted and gave the Congress back to the Democrats. The day after the big Republican loss, President Bush accepted the resignation of Defense Secretary Donald Rumsfeld.

The swiftboating strategy worked perfectly. Go in stealthy, blow something up, leave quietly. In and out. Mission accomplished.

And the secondary explosions went up in booms and blooms of fire. The left wanted the study to be true and spent the next couple years continually trying to prop up the thoroughly suspect results.

In 2007, as General David Petraeus was preparing to report to Congress on the preliminary results of the surge, an organization in Britain called Opinion Research Business published its own updated survey of Iraqi civilian deaths. The polling company, which claimed to have been tracking Iraqi public opinion since 2005, said its results showed "more than 1,000,000 Iraqi citizens have been murdered since the invasion took place in 2003."

A million? The Americans had killed a million Iraqis! Some in the media tried to pump up the outrage, get the folks wound up again, but there were not nearly as many takers this time around. Perhaps the use of the word "murdered" in this latest "scientific" study was a tip off that this time the political hit-piece studies weren't even trying to conceal their bias.

Nonetheless, some in the news media felt obligated to report the results. In September 2007, Tina Susman of the *Los Angeles Times*, writing from Baghdad, led her story thusly: "A car bomb blew up in the capital's Shiite Muslim neighborhood of Sadr City on Thursday, killing at least four people, as a new survey suggested that the civilian death toll from the war could be more than 1 million."

It was clever of her to tie a single car bomb to a phony estimate of a million deaths, but it was also deeply misleading. "The figure from ORB, a British polling agency that has conducted several surveys in Iraq, followed statements this week from the U.S. military defending itself against accusations it was trying to play down Iraqi deaths to make its strategy appear successful," Ms. Susman wrote, evidently trying to prove that the military was wrong.

There certainly were scads of people online willing to start an argument over the two studies. A supporter of the 2006 study named Tom Welsh insisted in an online posting, "No one has ever published a convincing criticism, let alone a refutation, of the survey published in *The Lancet*. And please note that, although *The Lancet* is a British publication, the work was done by experts from Johns Hopkins University. They employed exactly the same methods as were used to estimate the number of dead in Rwanda and Darfur." Mr. Welsh was wrong about the notion that the study had not been challenged, but correct about the last point—Roberts had used the same methodology to estimate deaths in those genocidal campaigns. But he failed to recognize the implication that the faulty methods also called into question the millions of deaths Roberts reported—and the world accepted!—in both Rwanda and Darfur.

Journalist Michael Fumento reported in the *Weekly Standard* on the ever-escalating and wildly exaggerated claims about Iraqi civilian deaths. He was astonished that the most recent was being taken seriously. But of course it was being used to retroactively support the flawed 2006 study. "The key importance of the [ORB] poll," Fumento quoted one leftist British "media watch" organization, "is that it provides strong support for the findings of the 2006 *Lancet* study, which reported 655,000 deaths."

Swiftboat technique #1012: Phony up an even bigger number to make an equally phony but smaller number appear more credible. And repeat as often as possible.

Online the rage was *en fuego*. A man named Bill Flarsheim—and it was rare that people used their real names in these online diatribes—wrote in the comment section of the *New York Times*'s Opininator blog in January 2006 that he had no problem assigning these large numbers of deaths to sectarian violence, but still blamed the United States. "The reason the U.S. is culpable in the excess deaths from insurgents is that in addition to starting a war to remove a dictator, we (led by Rumsfeld) tried to remove a dictator and show how few troops could be used to do it. The intent was to show how powerful we were. By trying to do it 'on the cheap' instead of recognizing that casualties in war can be minimized by using the most overwhelming force possible (i.e., the Powell Doctrine and the first Gulf War), we created the worst possible situation for both our troops and the Iraqi people."

"War on the Cheap" was a potent criticism of the Iraq War, along with its twin argument that the war cost many billions of dollars more than anticipated and effectively broke the national treasury. Critics tended to want to level both contradictory criticisms. And the idea that by rejecting an option of "overwhelming force" the United States created "the worst possible situation" rests on the notion that a huge force of American troops would have kept the violence down. Would more troops equal less sectarian violence, or was the urge to settle old scores so strong more troops would have equaled more troop deaths and casualties?

War planners not unreasonably decided it was the latter. But Colin Powell's maxim of maximum force haunted the discussion.

Events intervened, American casualties declined, and *The Lancet* study issue drifted to the back of the public mind. The 2008 presidential election and the various ensuing coronations for the new leader of the Western world distracted everyone.

But eventually, the game was up—at least as far as the truth of the matter.

In early 2009, one of Roberts' co-authors was censured for the faulty study. The American Association for Public Opinion Research announced in February 2009 the results of an eight-month investigation of Dr. Gilbert Burnham, who supervised the work of Les Roberts, and Dr. Riyadh Lafta for John Hopkins Bloomberg School of Public Health. Dr. Burnham was the supervisor of Roberts' 2006 work published in *The Lancet*. (Though he later withdrew his name as a "co-author" of the 2006 study, he remained listed as a co-author of the initial 2004 study.) The AAPOR charged that Dr. Burnham had provided "only partial information [on the study] and *explicitly refused* to provide complete information about the basic elements of his research." The American Statistical Association later wrote a letter in support of the AAPOR action.

In short: Roberts' research was repudiated by the very associations that monitor the published science of statistical sampling. He would not reveal, as is the custom in such matters, the field notes for his work so that other scientists could double check his results. His conclusion and assertion that 655,000 Iraqi civilians were killed by coalition troops should now have been judged to be flat-out wrong. Only the authors and their acolytes still believed any of their numbers.

The last shoe dropped in February 2009, and the lie was finally and entirely exposed.

The Associated Press announced it had obtained secret records from the Iraqi Health Ministry, which had been carefully kept since the start of the war. The AP compiled those figures with its own records kept by its Baghdad bureau. The AP concluded that the actual death toll since the American invasion was 110,600 civilians.

It could have been that Roberts and company were just wrong. It could have been that Dr. Lafta just didn't cover enough clusters. It could be that the danger of the war zone meant it was just not possible to gather accurate data.

Except that the Iraq Body Count numbers matched the Iraqi Health Ministry numbers, which matched the AP numbers, all of which were in the same zone as a new study from the World Health Organization that put the number of Iraqi deaths at about 150,000. But when the biases of the people who put forward the higher numbers were taken into account, it does not seem possible that all of these agenda-driven scientists would just happen to be in synchronous but innocent error. Anything less than a willful conspiracy among the parties did not seem possible.

Which meant the left had lied when it reported a number five times higher in the Hopkins/*Lancet* study, and ten times higher in the ORB study.

Moreover, as radio host and author Michael Medved wrote in his syndicated column, the AP study had one major flaw. "The analysis failed to note that the overwhelming majority of the 110,600 dead met their demise at the hands of terrorist violence or sectarian strife; only a tiny minority (perhaps 10 percent or less) of all casualties occurred at the hands of Americans or other coalition forces." Medved came to that conclusion because the report acknowledged that 59,957 of the deaths had occurred in 2006 and 2007, "when sectarian attacks soared and death squads roamed the streets . . . [a] period marked by catastrophic bombings and execution-style killings."

"The story might have added that the Americans perpetrated none of these mass killings," Medved wrote, "and instead fought heroically to bring them to an end."

So let's add up the elements of the story: antiwar researcher Les Roberts teams up with antiwar colleagues Gilbert Burnham of Johns Hopkins and Riyadh Lafta, a former Saddamite child mortality researcher, in a conspiracy—of conscience, perhaps?—to sell a biased study to *The Lancet*, which happens to be run by the rabidly antiwar Richard Horton. These four individuals cobble up a study and twist its results to "prove" that the Americans have killed 600,000 Iraqi civilians—mostly by gunshot. And they sold it to the public with the willing connivance of a compliant liberal media establishment. Got away with it, too.

The Associated Press story of its own meticulous study that showed the true number of Iraqi civilian deaths made the news for a few days, but not the big news. Not big enough to erase from the minds of Americans that they had killed over half a million Iraqis. No matter how much shouting flies around talk radio—"It's been disproved, dammit!"—the American people remember the headlines and don't hear what isn't on television.

Who could blame them for beginning to think, "No wonder they're mad at us." Who could blame them for changing their minds on the war?

It was a lie that got very good mileage. It helped get a new left-wing Congress elected, it set up a national guilt fest that got a left-wing president elected, and it is a lie that lives to this day in bar arguments and talk show shouting matches.

In short, the study turned out to be a phony political stunt for a rabidly antiwar faction of the public health community, and a classic instance of successful swiftboating: 655,000 Iraqi civilians did not die. But too many Americans think they did.

Chapter Seven

Katrina and the Bush-Hating Left

Hurricane Katrina was George W. Bush's fault.
Hurricane Katrina was caused by George W. Bush. At least, as far as the left in America was concerned. The hurricane was not an act of God; it was an act of George W. Bush. Bush and Bush alone willed it to happen. Bush set the climate wheels in motion, and it was Bush who stirred the massive storm into a raging hurricane that eclipsed all before it. Bush did it because George W. Bush didn't like black people. Bush killed 1,400 people, a disappointing and low number because the left had managed to pump the number of dead into the thousands, and each and every one was blamed on George W. Bush. When the real numbers turned out to be much lower, well, 1,400 was still a lot of deaths, but thousands would have been so much worse, and therefore so much better.

As for the living, in the left's narrative of the massive hurricane named Katrina, Bush pushed more than 30,000 New Orleans residents into their attics to escape the rising floodwaters. He forced them to chop holes in the roof for air, and to be seen pitifully waving sheets and T-shirts in order to be rescued by the inadequate number of helicopters sent to help. With the pitiless inundation, Bush forced many more thousands to wade out of their below-sea level neighborhoods to high ground through chest-deep water that was a frightening brew of industrial toxins, sewage, and snakes. Those were the lucky ones.

When the waters rose to fifteen feet those who couldn't or wouldn't swim through the filth were on the roof or trapped in the attic.

The pictures of the plight of the storm victims were particularly revealing, as far as the left was concerned. It was the storm that targeted black people, and it was all the fault of George W. Bush.

The massive storm came ashore August 29, 2005. A day later the storm surge pushed water over the top of the delicate and barely adequate levee system that kept most of New Orleans dry. The levee system was pushed hard by the surging waters and by the time the heaviest pressure had crested the system suffered over fifty breaks to levees. The city of New Orleans and some surrounding parishes were inundated with water over ten feet deep in many places. State and municipal emergency services were overwhelmed. At one point emergency radio systems were knocked out, officials' personal cell phone batteries were drawn down to dead and there was no way to recharge. The city was without communication in the most critical hours and days when thousands were still trapped by the rising waters. People were without water and food, crowded into inadequately prepared emergency shelters, and medical assistance was unable to get to them. Chaos reigned.

The hip-hop artist Kanye West famously said on NBC's "Concert for Hurricane Relief" two days after the hurricane hit, "George Bush doesn't care about black people." What he might actually know about George W. Bush was anybody's guess, but the theme took hold.

"Oblivious. In denial. Dangerous," said Representative Nancy Pelosi, Democrat of California and the House minority leader, of President Bush.

The city of New Orleans and its mayor, Ray Nagin, failed to evacuate poor black people, despite its own emergency plan that predicted thousands would need to be bused out. The state of Louisiana and its governor, Kathleen Babineaux Blanco, failed to supply basic necessities—food, water, medicine—despite its own emergency plan that foresaw the dire situation when a storm such as Katrina hit. But instead Bush was blamed for the state's and city's inadequate preparation for the storm. He was blamed for the people who ignored evacuation orders, for the woeful shortfalls in preparing the evacuation centers at the New Orleans Superdome and the New Orleans Convention Center, and for the levees that could not hold back the rising waters of Lake Pontchartrain.

Senator John Kerry of Massachusetts, the Democratic presidential nominee in 2004, said, "What you see here is a harvest of four years of complete avoidance of real problem solving and real governance in favor of spin and ideology." The state of Louisiana had obviously dithered. The City of New Orleans and its garrulous mayor had not been able to execute its own simple evacuation plan. No matter. The person at fault was George W. Bush.

"Our government failed at one of the most basic functions it has— providing for the physical safety of our citizens," declared Senator Evan Bayh, an Indiana Democrat who was considering a run for president in 2008.

"It's more than thousands of people who get killed; it's about the destruction of the American community," said Howard Dean, the one-time insurgent Democratic candidate for president.

Senator Edward M. Kennedy, Democrat of Massachusetts, said: "The powerful winds of this storm have torn away that mask that has hidden from our debates the many Americans who are left out and left behind."

The left's politicians could be expected to take shots at George W. Bush. After all, the hurricane came just nine months after they had been handed a stinging defeat by Bush, in an election they were certain they could win. The confidence of the Democrats challenging President Bush for the White House bubbled up from their conviction that the war in Iraq was a neon-lit demonstration of Bush's bad faith and incompetence, and they were stunned the American people had stuck with a president they believed to be simply not up to the job.

Normally, politicians could be expected to calibrate their statements, on the odd chance events would later prove them wrong, or if not in error, jumping the gun on placing blame for what was obviously a natural disaster. But not in the case of Katrina. When it came to blame heaped on George W. Bush, the left's politicians went all in.

Assisting the anti-Bush political movement, the left-wing media joined in with gusto. This was the media that had worked so hard for Bush's defeat, and was still reeling from the stunning realization that the American people had not listened to them, that their influence had not been a decisive factor in the 2004 presidential election.

Contributor Nancy Gibbs said on the CBS *Sunday Morning* program, "If the majority of the hardest hit victims of Hurricane Katrina in New Orleans were white people, they would not have gone for days without food and water, forcing many to steal for mere survival. Their bodies would not have been left to float in putrid water. . . . We've repeatedly given tax cuts to the wealthiest and left our most vulnerable American citizens to basically fend for themselves. . . . The president has put himself at risk by visiting the troops in Iraq, but didn't venture anywhere near the Superdome or the convention center, where thousands of victims, mostly black and poor, needed to see that he gave a damn."

The dreaded and dreadful Keith Olbermann used NBC airtime to launch another of his many tedious jihads against President Bush. "For many of this country's citizens, the mantra has been, as we were taught in social studies it should always be, whether or not I voted for this president, he is still my president. I suspect anybody who had to give him that benefit of the doubt stopped doing so last week. I suspect, also, a lot of his supporters, looking ahead to '08 are wondering how they can distance themselves from the two words which will define his government, our government: New Orleans." The puffed-up pontificator concluded by calling Bush "a twenty-first-century Marie Antoinette."

The theme that the disaster would not have befallen white people in the same way it hit black people became ubiquitous. CNN's Wolf Blitzer, normally a studious adherent to the notion that a news anchor should try to restrain his or her biases, asked Congressman Elijah Cummings Jr., "Do you believe, if it was, in fact, a slow response, as many now believe it was, was it in part the result of racism? There are some critics who are saying, and I don't know if you're among those, but people have said to me, had this happened in a predominantly white community, the federal government would have responded much more quickly. Do you believe that?"

Bush found himself being blamed for a hurricane because he cut taxes. On the television program *Inside Washington* four days after the storm hit, NPR's Nina Totenberg declared, "And let us say one other thing. For years, we have cut our taxes, cut our taxes and let the infrastructure throughout the country go, and this is just the first of a number of other crumbling things that are going to happen to us." Fellow guest Charles Krauthammer blurted out, "You must be kidding here." The show's moderator, Gordon Peterson, interjected, "She's not kidding." And Totenberg confirmed, "I'm not kidding."

The fluffy Hollywood star-watcher program *Access Hollywood* got in on the orgy of Bush bashing courtesy of actor Colin Farrell, who said, "If it was a bunch of white people on roofs in the Hamptons, I don't have any fucking doubt there would have been every single helicopter, every plane, every single means that the government has to help these people."

Actor-comedian turned faux anchorman for the youth of America, Jon Stewart, managed to work the word "vagina" into his criticism: "Hurricane Katrina is George Bush's Monica Lewinsky. One difference, and I'll say this, the only difference is this: That tens of thousands of people weren't stranded in Monica Lewinsky's vagina. That is the only difference."

The *Boston Globe* op-ed columnist Ross Gelbspan made the hurricane a global-warming issue, and the culprit was, of course, Bush: "In 2000, big oil and big coal scored their biggest electoral victory yet when President George W. Bush was elected president—and subsequently took suggestions from the industry for his climate and energy policies. As the pace of climate change accelerates, many researchers fear we have already entered a period of irreversible runaway climate change." Not only was global warming George W. Bush's fault, Katrina was a warning to the world that unfairly made thousands of black people suffer rather than the real culprit. Innocents were made to pay for George W. Bush's crimes.

CBS morning anchor Harry Smith turned the hurricane into a reason to criticize George Bush's well-known Christian faith. Talking about "church people" taking in refugees from the storm, Smith asked pastor Rick Warren, "Do I need to be concerned that I'm going to go live with a church family, are they going to proselytize me, are they going to say, 'You better come to church with me or else, I'm, you know, you're not going to get your breakfast this morning'?"

Howell Raines, who had recently been fired from his job running the *New York Times* when one too many of his pet reporters were caught lying in print, demonstrated where the liars might have received their training in mangling the truth. "The dilatory performance of George Bush during the past week has been outrageous.

Almost as unbelievable as Katrina itself is the fact that the leader of the free world has been outshone by the elected leaders of a region renowned for governmental ineptitude." Outshone by the politicians of Louisiana? The mayor of New Orleans ran off to Dallas in the middle of the crisis to set up housekeeping for his family in a reliably dry location. But Raines was positively giddy with glee pitching bombs at Bush. "The churchgoing populism of George Bush has given the United States an administration that worries about the House of Saud and the welfare of oil companies while the poor drown in their attics and their sons and daughters die in foreign deserts." No one questioned the highly tenuous connection between the poor "left to drown" in New Orleans and the poor "sent to die" in Iraq. The *Los Angeles Times* published this calumny on its op-ed pages without a trace of embarrassment.

In all, the hurricane was a one-size-fits-all opportunity to attack George W. Bush: He was a malevolent racist; a greedy oilman responsible for melting icebergs; a religious zealot who would withhold Wheaties in the morning unless the hungry would accept the baptism of the reborn, and a heartless warmonger who sent kids to be shredded by roadside bombs in Iraq while drowning their parents back at home.

Radical black firebrand Michael Eric Dyson in his book *Come Hell or High Water* used Hurricane Katrina to allege that the response to the hurricane was America's most visible evidence of a war on the poor, blaming Bush for both the poverty of New Orleans and the fact that it was the poor who were hit hardest. "Because government took its time getting into New Orleans," Dyson wrote. "Hundreds of folk, especially the elderly, died waiting for help." (Among Bush critics, Dyson had the luxury of publishing a book, which gave him time to avoid the common misstatement that "thousands" had died.)

Dyson seemed to blame Bush not only for the storm, the failure of the levees, the plight of poor blacks who suffered and some of whom died, but also for the fact that the poor of New Orleans didn't have cars. "Children and the elderly made up 38 percent of the population of New Orleans, but they accounted for 48 percent of the households without access to cars," he wrote. "These facts make it painfully clear just why these folk could not evacuate before Katrina struck . . . They simply couldn't muster the resources to escape destruction, and for many, even death."

In Dyson's view, the America of George W. Bush had committed a group offense: "The deeper we dig into the story of Katrina, the more we must accept culpability for the fact that black citizens of the Big Easy—a tag given New Orleans by black musicians who easily found work in a city that looms large in the collective American imagination as the home of jazz, jambalaya, and Mardi Gras—were treated by the rest of us as garbage."

Dyson was not the first or last to overstate the case about the response to Hurricane Katrina. Considering the damage to the city of New Orleans and surrounding parishes like Saint Bernard and Plaquemines, and the dislocation of tens of thousands of people, escaping through extremely harrowing conditions, it would take a champion of overstatement to beat reality. Nonetheless, all sorts of people did precisely that: A disaster of monumental proportions was not allowed to stand on its own. Katrina, bad as it was, was relentlessly and unnecessarily hyped. It was an emergency so dire that the true facts would have shocked the nation and the world, but in the political atmosphere of the moment a simple gold strike wasn't good enough. The Bush-bashers wanted Eldorado. They wanted a Bush-caused disaster of mythic proportions.

There is no question Hurricane Katrina was horrific, and that the inadequate government response made the disaster many times worse. There is also no question that the failed response included agencies controlled by the president of the United States, George W. Bush. He admitted as much himself in the immediate aftermath of the final evacuation of the victims of the flood, saying he took responsibility for the shortcomings of the Federal Emergency Management Agency (FEMA) despite his ill-timed public praise of his executive appointee at the height of the crisis.

But the narrative about Katrina and George W. Bush was set in concrete in the first few days, when facts somehow became subservient to wild rumors and blatant lies.

In the confusion of the first few days, endlessly repeated rumors took on the appearance and force of truth. News people and commentators writing about the disaster routinely spoke of "thousands" dying. By the time calm prevailed, it turned out just over 1,400 died. Fourteen hundred largely preventable deaths is an enormous number, but to overstate it by a factor of ten, if not more, was a terrible disservice not only to the people who suffered and died, but to those who ended up being blamed.

There was virtually no question that many, if not all, the deaths were attributable to exposure to oppressive heat, stress from the chaotic escape from the floods, lack of food and fresh water, widespread lack of medicines and medical care—all of which should have been preventable. But in the days immediately following the break of the first levee that began to inundate New Orleans, certain "facts" became accepted by virtually everyone, and almost every one of those so-called facts were later shown to be untrue.

Scores of murders were reported in the New Orleans Superdome, a chaotic, dangerous, extremely uncomfortable, and inadequately supplied impromptu emergency shelter. Twenty thousand people were packed into the Superdome, which had lost power and had turned into a sauna of sweat, the stench of human waste and rotting garbage, with virtually no security presence to protect the weak and innocent from well-armed street thugs.

A reporter from the *New Orleans Times-Picayune* quoted an Arkansas national guardsman who said he'd seen thirty to forty bodies in a walk-in freezer in the Ernest N. Morial Convention Center, including elderly people who had been bludgeoned to death, children who died of dehydration, and the shocking claim he'd seen one child whose throat had been cut. The story quickly spread through the newsrooms of America and beyond. Anchors began throwing the death reports and mortality figures around, including the detail of the seven-year-old whose throat had been slit.

But it wasn't just a credulous local reporter. New Orleans police chief Eddie Compass said, "We have individuals who are getting raped, we have individuals who are getting beaten." He told Oprah Winfrey (incredibly) of babies being raped, and on the same program New Orleans mayor Ray Nagin said, "They have people standing out there, have been in that frickin' Superdome for five days watching dead bodies, watching hooligans killing people, raping people."

The news media, including the Associated Press, began to distribute these unverified stories as if they were fact: the baby with the slit throat, women being dragged off and gang-raped, murders, corpses piling up in hallways and basements.

When it was all over, the New Orleans Superdome and the city's convention center were swept for the corpses everyone believed were there. They could not find the reported forty bodies—not in the basement, not in a walk-in freezer, not anywhere. Out of the 20,000 packed into the Superdome without water, air-conditioning, food, or medical assistance, ten had died. At the chaotic convention center, where 19,000 were packed in for days, four had died.

In all, only two were believed to have been murdered, and one appeared to have been brought to the building after being killed somewhere else. One death was ruled a suicide. Most of the deaths were among the elderly and the very young from stress, heat, and dehydration.

Hospitals and nursing homes were also vulnerable, located in the bowl of New Orleans and neighboring parishes, below the level of a mountain of water held back by fragile levees. Memorial Medical Center was flooded. Thirty-four patients died when power went out, rescuers didn't arrive, and besieged health-care workers frantically moved patients and beds to higher floors in a scene of life or death chaos. Two nurses and a doctor were later accused of murdering patients—euthanizing them because medical personnel could not move them and could no longer effectively care for them. (Later, the public rallied behind the nurses and doctor and the charges were dropped.)

Thirty-five patients at St. Rita Nursing Home in Saint Bernard Parish died when the facility flooded. The owners of the nursing home, an elderly couple themselves, were later put on trial for not evacuating patients as required by the state government. The owners were accused of dereliction of their duty to the patients, but they claimed they thought it was safer for the patients—many in delicate health—to stay in the facility, which was situated on high ground and had not flooded in the last big hurricane, Betsy, in 1965. Their calculation was a fatal error and when the levees broke and Lake Pontchartrain emptied into New Orleans and Saint Bernard Parish, St. Rita's was inundated, trapping the helpless patients.

There was no question that thousands suffered extreme misery at the New Orleans Superdome and convention center. At both locations, crowded with thousands of evacuees, including elderly, children, tourists, and street thugs, there was little or no security, no food or water; the power went out leaving everyone in the dark; and the stench of human waste was overwhelming. Armed men roamed the darkness, stealing food and other valuables at gunpoint, and arguing amongst each other. Police sent to restore order stumbled through the dark trying to find the troublemakers. They located trigger-happy evacuees by spotting muzzle flashes in the darkness. A national guard member was shot in the leg when an evacuee tried to take his gun. The situation was awful, but even a bad situation can be made worse by exaggeration and rumor.

Eighty percent of New Orleans had been successfully evacuated by car, but about 40,000 had been unable to leave because they either didn't have their own automobiles or evacuation buses didn't arrive until after they had spent days in horrific conditions without food, water, or medicine.

The narrative that George W. Bush had abandoned New Orleans to its fate, and worse, had left thousands of African Americans to die in the flood and heat and disease was so precious to the left—and the victims themselves—that it was well-nigh impossible to scrub away. For the media and the left, the story of Bush's incompetence fit too well with the general theme that Bush had led the country into the wrong war at the wrong time, and had compounded the errors by his personal incompetence. Katrina was used to prove this point.

When Congress held hearings on what went wrong in New Orleans three months later, the exaggerations and myths persisted. Victims of the flood told their harrowing tales to members of a congressional committee, and said the reason they were left to fend for themselves was race. George Bush was a racist.

"No one is going to tell me it wasn't a race issue," said New Orleans evacuee Patricia Thompson. She was still living in distant College Station, Texas, far from her home city on the banks of the Mississippi. "Yes, it was an issue of race. Because of one thing: When the city had pretty much been evacuated, the people that were left there mostly was black."

The witnesses not only testified that they were abandoned to drown because they were black, but that national guardsmen pointed machine guns at their small children, and that the federal government brought the flood on New Orleans' black residents on purpose. "I was on my front porch," Diane Cole French said at the hearings. "I have witnesses that they bombed the walls of the levee."

When Congressman Chris Shays expressed disbelief, Ms. French did not back down. "You believe what you want," she replied, petulantly.

Bush accepted the brunt of the blame for what went wrong in New Orleans. The Federal Emergency Management Agency, which had been folded into the Department of Homeland Security, was conspicuous by its absence in New Orleans. Buses to evacuate people were slow to arrive, trucks with water and ice were held up short of the city while FEMA officials demanded "tasker" numbers, which truck drivers and suppliers had never heard of. Firemen volunteering for search and rescue efforts were kept sitting in a hotel in Atlanta for two days listening to earnest FEMA lecturers instruct them on public relations and sexual harassment. Boat drivers who showed up in New Orleans wanting to help rescue people trapped in their homes were turned away because of FEMA-ordered roadblocks.

New Orleans mayor Ray Nagin was interviewed by a local radio reporter five days after the storm hit. He was angry about televised briefings from Washington, D.C., bureaucrats. "I don't want to see anybody do anymore goddamn press conferences. Put a moratorium on press conferences. Don't do another press conference until the resources are in this city. And then come down to this city and stand with us when there are military trucks and troops that we can't even count," Nagin said, his voice rising. "Now get off your asses and do something, and let's fix the biggest goddamn crisis in the history of this country."

Nagin's helplessness and his passion for his city and his people turned the spotlight on George Bush and FEMA. The president didn't help himself when he spoke at a news conference with FEMA director Michael Brown, and said, "Brownie, you're doing a heckuva job."

The president also didn't help himself when he was photographed looking out the window of Air Force One like a curious tourist as it made a low pass over New Orleans while en route to the White House after his customary August vacation at his ranch in Crawford, Texas.

The president was also hammered by the left for cutting from the budget of the Army Corps of Engineers $71 million for upgrade work on the levee system protecting New Orleans. The fact that the projects would not have been finished in time to protect the city from Katrina, and were also not slated for sections of the levee system that actually failed, did not seem to matter. Sidney Blumenthal, the former Clinton White House enforcer known as "Sid Vicious," wrote in the U.K. *Guardian* newspaper, "Federal funding for the flood control project essentially dried up as it was drained into the Iraq war." His piece, headlined "Nobody Can Say They Didn't See It Coming," attacked Bush by laying out the recent history of corps of engineers budget cuts.

Once the narrative was set, it was almost impossible to erase. *Time* magazine—no friend of Bush—sent its reporters to figure out who was to blame and for what. It published a piece thirteen days after the storm hit and named four places (people) where "the system failed." Bush wasn't on the list.

Number one was the mayor of New Orleans. "Did C. Ray Nagin do everything he could to save his city? Despite all appearances to the contrary, New Orleans had a plan. A week after the storm, Nagin summarized it for the *Wall Street Journal*: 'Get people to higher ground and have the feds and the state airlift supplies to them—that was the plan, man.' But in fact, the plan was more substantial. And it makes clear that the mayor was in charge when disaster struck." Nagin's job was to prepare the city for a hurricane and use his Office of Emergency Preparedness to evacuate the sick and elderly. He was also supposed to ask the state to request national guard troops. After dire warnings from the National Hurricane Center, Nagin did call for an evacuation at a news conference, but he did not make the evacuation order mandatory, according to the *New Orleans Times-Picayune*, because his staff was still "researching" whether he had the authority to issue a mandatory order. *Time* magazine reported, "In fact, the city's plan clearly allows the mayor to do just that." But according to the *Times-Picayune*, Nagin hesitated because the city might be held liable for unnecessarily closing hotels and other businesses.

Even so, there are always people who won't go, or for one reason or another cannot evacuate their homes. *Time* confirmed that the city's own emergency plan "estimates that 100,000 residents would have no means of transport." Nagin told people that the New Orleans Superdome would be the shelter of last resort, but evacuees were instructed to bring their own food and water—enough for three or four days—and to "eat a full meal before arriving."

The Superdome had been used as a shelter in 1998's Hurricane Georges, and the 14,000 people who showed up trashed the place, stealing equipment and furnishings, and causing nearly $50,000 in damage. Consequently, the official attitude was, "Don't make the place too comfortable," since it was safer to leave the city anyway. Thus, the city had not stockpiled food and water—or generator fuel—for the emergency.

Dr. Max Mayfield of the National Hurricane Center made a personal call to Nagin to make sure the mayor had a proper warning. "It was only the second time I've called a politician in my life," said Mayfield, "but I wanted to be able to go to sleep knowing I had done everything I could do."

With less than twenty-four hours before the storm's expected landfall, Nagin finally called for a mandatory evacuation. Some city buses were used to ferry people to the Superdome, but *Time* could find no evidence they were used to get people out of the city. In fact, a fleet of city school buses was left unattended in a parking lot that was eventually flooded, rendering the buses inoperable and useless.

Time asserted, "We still don't know what happened to New Orleans' $7 million grant in 2003 for a communications system that would connect all the region's first responders." Shortly after Katrina came ashore, the emergency radios used by police, firefighters, and the mayor himself drained their batteries and were out of service. The *Wall Street Journal* reported their satellite phones would not recharge, and landline and cell phones lost service in the hurricane-force winds and flooding.

For two days the mayor and his emergency team were marooned in the Hyatt Regency, in *Time*'s phrase, "fending off gangs of looters." *Time*'s investigators concluded, "We don't know why the mayor and his emergency team did not use the city's Mobile Command Center—meant for just such a disaster—or join the other local officials at the emergency center in Baton Rouge."

The second entity on *Time*'s blame list was the governor of Louisiana, Kathleen Babineaux Blanco. Early in the emergency situation, she finally reached President Bush after a series of frantic phone calls. She later said she had left messages, but didn't insist on being put through. When they finally connected, she said, "Send everything you got." Bush told her, "Help is on the way." Bush was right: help was on the way, but Blanco would find out later that it was not the help she needed most—transportation for those stranded at the two hellish emergency shelters.

There were aspects of the emergency that the governor handled well—putting the preparedness plan into effect, evacuating 80 percent of the city by opening both directions of the freeways for evacuees to get out. But there was one area where her instincts seemed to have failed her: requesting help from the federal government.

Blanco was not very specific with federal officials about what she wanted rushed to New Orleans, but that would be an unfair criticism. Should she have asked for X thousand blankets and cots, or X tons of ice, or X truckloads of water? Perhaps not, but she should have been able to give federal officials an estimate of how many people were in need. But she also expected FEMA to be able to deliver buses to evacuate the Superdome in a timely manner, and that probably was not possible. FEMA's buses were miles—states—away, and the only way to evacuate the Superdome and the convention center quickly was to use the buses at the disposal of local government, many of which had already been rendered inoperable, and for which there were not drivers anyway. School bus drivers, most often middle-aged women, simply refused to be involved after hearing the fearsome tales of chaos at the emergency shelters.

Governor Blanco also found herself in a turf war with the White House when Bush officials requested she turn over command of the state's national guard troops to federal authorities. Worried the feds would sweep in, clean up the mess, and then blame locals, she refused.

Time magazine said of the governor, "No one would mistake Blanco for Rudy Giuliani. In the first week after the storm hit, she came across as dazed and unsteady, at one moment in despair over 'people probably who are on drugs, who are threatening other people, who are causing our rescue effort to stall'; at another, declaring her troops had 'M-16s, and they're locked and loaded.' "

By the time Blanco steadied herself, federal aid had arrived, and thousands of people were evacuated from the Superdome and convention center.

Time named two others as primary culprits worthy of blame, and both were Bush administration officials. First was Michael Brown, the Bush appointee to head FEMA. Brown had no experience managing an emergency agency. His previous job had been the director of an Arabian horse association, and it seemed he was hired to run FEMA because he was a friend of Bush confidant Joe Albaugh. Brown seemed overly concerned about his television appearances and his press relations (remember Nagin's outburst about the "news briefings"), and overly bureaucratic in fulfilling the needs of embattled Louisiana officials and the mayor. He would send them what they wanted, if they asked for it. The later congressional investigation identified the principal problem as a "Lack of Initiative." Brown regrettably fit the description. Bush can fairly be criticized for making this unqualified appointment.

Also to blame was Department of Homeland Security Secretary Michael Chertoff, who didn't seem to understand the dire conditions that people in New Orleans were dealing with. Slow of foot, it took Chertoff days to get the wheels of federal largesse moving toward Louisiana, and he didn't seem to understand the extent to which all eyes were on him and his team.

Bush gave a news conference a few days after the situation had stabilized and took responsibility for the slow federal effort. Eight days after being designated leader of the federal relief effort, Brown was replaced by a coast guard vice admiral, and three days after that he resigned as head of FEMA. To add insult to injury, embarrassed federal officials were subjected to public offers of international assistance from Cuba and Venezuela, among others.

But the question remains, why did Bush absorb so much of the blame for New Orleans while local officials so obviously fell down on the job and were overwhelmed from the first moment? No one has ever intended the federal government or FEMA to be a first responder. New Orleans, like any other city in America, is expected to be able to handle the first forty-eight to seventy-two hours of a disaster before federal help can arrive, especially one for which there was more than adequate warning. That standard was not met in New Orleans; yet the media's attention turned to George W. Bush. Why wasn't he there to intervene when the water slopped over the top of the first failing levee?

Paul Krugman, the *New York Times* columnist who won a Nobel Prize on the strength of his consistent hammering of President Bush, wrote, "I don't think this is a simple tale of incompetence. The reason the military wasn't rushed in to help along the Gulf Coast is, I believe, the same reason nothing was done to stop looting after the fall of Baghdad. Flood control was neglected for the same reason our troops in Iraq didn't get adequate armor." For Krugman the answer was simply that "our current leaders just aren't serious about some of the essential functions of government."

For Krugman and the like, it always comes back to Bush. Bush can give them good reasons—diminishing the importance of FEMA by making it part of the mammoth Department of Homeland Security, and loading it with political appointees like Brown—or he can provide evidence of good stewardship. But it doesn't really matter. For the left, any opportunity to attack Bush is a terrible thing to waste.

Even when there is ample evidence others should shoulder the blame, if George W. Bush is even remotely in the picture, the blame shifts to him.

It was all part of the campaign to undermine the president in order to undermine his other initiatives. In New Orleans, thousands of people were fighting for their lives. Outside New Orleans, thousands more were fighting to convince the rest of the country that George W. Bush was a miserable failure, and that all his choices were wrong.

As far as the left was concerned, Katrina was just another way to fight the war in Iraq. If Bush were a competent chief executive, the left argued, he would not have gone to war; if he were a competent chief executive he would have prosecuted the war better and quicker; and since Katrina proved he was not a competent chief executive, the left was able to square the circle on its war arguments.

If Americans did not believe the war was Bush's fault, they could see with their own eyes that Katrina *was* Bush's fault. With that point proved, the left could—and did—argue that a straight line could be drawn from the incompetence of Katrina, back through the execution of the war, and even the decision to go to war itself.

Americans disgusted with what they saw from New Orleans on their television screens could do the math themselves. If Bush couldn't handle a hurricane in his own backyard, how could he be trusted to manage a war in a far-off country?

With a national election a year away, it was yet another "case closed" argument for the left.

Chapter Eight

The Echo Chamber: Dailykos and the Left-Wing Noise Machine

At the dawn of the age of Internet politics, bloggers were nothing more than a gleam in a left-wing bomb thrower's eye. The heady days of mobilizing thousands of bloggers to ridicule, mock, denigrate, undermine—swiftboat—George W. Bush and the war in Iraq lay years ahead. Early on the entire point of the Internet was raising money. The discovery of the Internet's effectiveness on political messaging came later. For instance, John McCain surprised everyone, including himself, when he raised an eye-popping $1.5 million on the Internet during his run for the Republican nomination in 2000 against Texas Governor George W. Bush.

McCain's Internet windfall was a hint of things to come. Eight years later McCain would be swamped in his run for the White House by an insurgent democrat, Senator Barack Obama, whose Internet fund-raising machine amassed nearly half a billion dollars.

In between McCain's near-miss in 2000 and his crushing defeat in 2008, another candidate came along to show the political world how to use the Internet. It was Vermont governor Dr. Howard Dean, whose run for the presidency in late 2003 and 2004 was driven almost entirely by the Internet—including fund-raising and political messaging through an explosion of both professional and citizen bloggers. It was Howard Dean who showed everybody, including a young Barack Obama, how to do it.

Dean's campaign came upon the Internet almost by accident. His campaign manager, Joe Trippi, was a Silicon Valley alumnus (he went to college at San Jose State and later served on a tech startup board) who played around with stock trading on the net, played around on Google late at night, and was keenly aware of the potential of driving a campaign around the power of laptop people. But the power of the Dean phenomenon on the Internet surprised both Trippi and the candidate himself.

"We fell into this by accident," Dean admitted to *Wired* magazine ten weeks before the 2004 Iowa caucuses. "I wish I could tell you we were smart enough to figure this out. But the community taught us. They seized the initiative through Meetup. They built our organization for us before we had an organization."

It was a Web site called Meetup.com that proved to be the key to the Dean Internet insurgency. Meetup was a site designed to allow people who held a common interest to get together online and make arrangements to meet in person. Small groups of people intensely interested in a subject were able to quickly organize a meeting of the like-minded thru Meetup.com.

In early 2003 Dean himself was convinced by his campaign to go to a Meetup gathering of supporters in New York. Not expecting much, he was shocked to find 300 enthusiastic Deaniacs. At that point the largest group using Meetup.com to organize gatherings were *witches*.

"I was obsessed with beating witches," Zephyr Teachout, the director of the Dean campaign's Internet Outreach, told *Wired* magazine about the campaign's obsession with Meetup.com. "Witches had 15,000 members, and we had 3,000. I wanted first place."

It didn't take long for Dean to find himself in first place by a wide margin. It all started with one New York member of Meetup issuing a "Dean Meetup Challenge" in March 2003. By mid 2003 Dean had 31,000 Meetup members, and in November of 2003 the Howard Dean group on Meetup.com had 140,000 members. "The largest component spreading the word—both in money and organization—are the Meetup folks," Joe Trippi told CBS News' Douglas Kiker. "Meetup has been incredible. Just incredible."

In the third quarter of 2003 Howard Dean raised $15 million online, in large part through the power of Meetup members spreading the word online and encouraging their friends and contacts to take a look at Dean.

But the blogging side of the equation was still in its infancy, as the media noted at the time. The USC Online Journalism Review looked at the Dean Internet operation in August 2003, and noted that Dean's "blog has become a cross between a focus group and cheering section, with supporters sending ideas via the vast array of comments."

Markos Moulitsas Zuñiga, founder of the Dailykos, worked for the Dean campaign during this period, advising the campaign on Internet strategies, including the use of Meetup. "The important thing in blogging is not to have people show up, it's getting them to return," he told USC's OJR. "Because the more they return, the more intimate they become with the campaign. And the more intimate they become, the more likely they are to volunteer and/or donate money. And once they invest their time or money, they have a vested interest in the campaign's success and will do *everything* in their power to see their investment pay off."

Dean's official campaign blog was dated March 15, 2003 (The Ides of March!). The second paragraph conveyed the campaign's idea of what a blog should be. "The most important thing you can do right now is let everyone know about this blog. Email your friends, other Dean supporters, and anyone else you think might be interested, and let them know to check this site," the blog pleaded. "Please post a link on any blogs or Web sites that are appropriate, and make the link prominent on anything you maintain yourself. Get the word out!"

In these early days of political blogging, "Get the word out" was the most important message. That soon changed. The reality that a blog could be used to tear down—swiftboat—the opposition by retailing rumors, myths, and lies soon became the entire point of the blogging world. Matt Stoller, a pioneering left-wing blogger and Internet organizer, put it this way in a fund-raising appeal: "Help us continue to undermine the right."

The Dean campaign used its Internet capabilities and strategies brilliantly, but ultimately Dean had to stand down in favor of the party's nominee, Senator John Kerry of Massachusetts.

The Dean bloggers were immediately furious with Kerry for the

crime of timidity. Kerry refused to say Bush lied the country into a
war—a common theme of the left-wing blogosphere—and his hesitant attacks on Bush quickly led to a vicious reaction in the left-wing
blog world populated by former Dean supporters. Taking a cue from
their angry and aggressive candidate, the Dean blog world soon exploded with the echoing chant "Bush Lied, People Died." The days
of the nicey-nice blogging world were over, and swiftboating Bush on
the Internet began in earnest.

IT WAS IN those heady days of the primary season, when the Dean
machine was scoring its greatest triumphs, that the left began to formulate its strategy of online political destruction. On the first day of
2004, ex-conservative journalist David Brock published a book called
The Republican Noise Machine, in which he set out a theory of how conservatives had amassed significant—seemingly unstoppable—political
power. Brock described the national network of conservative think
tanks, publications, talk radio, and television as an infrastructure for
disseminating and popularizing conservative ideas. Laying out the
architecture of conservative intellectual dominance, he compared liberal efforts to proselytize their own ideas and found that they came
up short.

In order to make this argument, of course Brock had to ignore
many years of liberal ownership of the news media and liberal dominance of universities and think tanks. He also neglected to mention
that at the time the book was published, the tide had already turned.
The left's own "noise machine" was picking up steam and creating
its own echo chamber, in which its charges against Bush and conservatives would soon gain the status of accepted truth, not to be
challenged.

But overall, Brock's point was correct: Liberals, or the left, pos-
sessed levers of media power that were old, boring, and stodgy. In the
modern media game they had been outmaneuvered by conservatives
and needed to play catch-up.

Perhaps the finest hour of the right-wing blogs—demonstrating
their surprising new power to challenge mainstream media—was the
incident known as "Rathergate." Just before the presidential election
of 2004, CBS anchorman Dan Rather aired a report on CBS's *60*

Minutes in which he purported to have authentic documents from the personal files of the commander of young George W. Bush's Texas air national guard unit. In those documents, the air guard commander was highly critical of the young Bush.

The story that Bush was a slacker in his youth had been floating around for some time. During the 2000 election, rumors were floated that Bush had pulled strings to avoid going to Vietnam and had been AWOL from his air national guard unit. Now, as election day 2004 approached, CBS set out to prove these rumors true by demonstrating that Bush had indeed gotten into the air guard through family connections, had barely if ever shown up for duty, and used those same connections to cover up his tarnished record.

Bloggers on the right were immediately suspicious of the documents and began checking details that CBS apparently never considered, including the typeface of the old-model IBM typewriter that had purportedly been used, and other details. The supposed author of the documents, Lt. Col. Jerry Killian, had died some years earlier, so he was not available for comment. Questions about the authenticity of the so-called Killian Papers soon migrated from the blogs to the major media because the issue was the president of the United States, and his accuser was respected CBS anchorman Dan Rather.

The very day Rather's Bush exposé appeared on *60 Minutes*, a posting on a forum at FreeRepublic.com began vetting the documents. Matthew Sheffield of Ratherbiased.com later explained that within minutes various bloggers were researching the Internet and taking a close look at the documents. "Forty-seven posts later," Sheffield told an audience gathered in Washington, D.C., "a person who called himself 'Buckhead' offered the proposition that he thought the documents were forgeries."

The *Los Angeles Times* tracked down Buckhead and revealed he was Harry MacDougald, an Atlanta lawyer who was a member of the conservative groups the Federalist Society and the Southeastern Legal Foundation. He had also helped draft the petition urging the Arkansas Supreme Court to disbar President Clinton after the Monica Lewinsky scandal.

What MacDougald had discovered was that the Killian documents were in a proportionally spaced font that was not available on ordinary typewriters such as the one Killian would have used in the 1970s.

"The use of proportionally spaced fonts did not come into common use for office memos until the introduction of laser printers, word-processing software, and personal computers," MacDougald wrote on the freerepublic Web site. "They were not widespread until the mid- to late-nineties. Before then, you needed typesetting equipment, and that wasn't used for personal memos to file. Even the Wang systems that were dominant in the mid eighties used monospaced fonts."

Because of MacDougald's connection to conservative groups, the left raised suspicions that the entire thing had been a set up by Republican operatives to distract from the substance of the CBS report on Bush's shirking his military obligation, and undermine and embarrass CBS, a pillar of the liberal media. But the swiftboating strategy failed. The evidence of fraud was just too plausible.

Initially, Rather defended the documents, saying, "We are told they are from Lt. Col. Killian's files," and claiming CBS had consulted experts in authenticating the documents. It later turned out CBS had done no such thing. (Later, even after their falseness had been exposed, he would continue to defend the memos as "fake but accurate.")

Meanwhile, *USA Today* undertook an analysis of the documents—they were faxes; the originals were said to have been destroyed—and raised questions about their validity. CBS belatedly started its own authentication process, and concluded, like others in the media, that there were major problems with their credibility.

Two weeks after airing the story that relied on these documents, Rather and CBS publicly repudiated the documents. Rather said, "If I knew then what I know now—I would not have gone ahead with the story as it was aired, and I certainly would not have used the documents in question."

Producer Mary Mapes was fired, and in the end Rather himself was forced to step down from the CBS *Evening News*; he broadcast his last program on the twenty-fourth anniversary of his ascension to the anchor chair. Eventually he left CBS altogether, launched a lawsuit, and signed on to do reporting for an obscure cable channel owned by billionaire Mark Cuban.

One can only conclude that ingrained animus to George W. Bush caused Rather and his CBS colleagues to push the envelope on their own reporting standards. Why would they take such a chance?

Because they had bought into the many stories about Bush's misspent youth—some true, some mythical. And because before the advent of the world of bloggers they might not have been caught in their sloppy and erroneous reporting.

But it wouldn't be long before the strength of conservative blogs would be confronted by a highly organized challenge from the left.

In 2002, after Democrats lost the congressional elections, a passionate young leftist named Markos Moulitsas Zuñiga was so crestfallen that he decided to create a new base for liberal politics on the Internet. He'd already done a stint in the army, earned undergraduate degrees, completed law school, and taken a flyer at making millions in Silicon Valley. Now he founded a Web site called the Dailykos, named after himself, which set out to defeat conservatives and help the left win power.

"The simplest fact about American politics," the frustrated young man told the *Washington Monthly* in 2006, "is that Republicans have a noise machine and we don't." As he spoke, that young man's Internet start-up was four years old and was already judged to be the most important left-wing political blog on the Internet. The *Washington Monthly* reported that he decided his Internet business "would become the Democratic noise machine, pressing the case against the Bush administration and the Iraq war in the strongest terms possible."

Dailykos never fell short of its goal. His fanatically loyal followers went after Bush and Cheney with the zeal of crusaders, determined that nothing—not even the truth—would stop them from running Bush and his neo-cons out of office.

Dailykos (or dkos) fought against Republicans, conservatives, neo-cons, President Bush, Vice President Cheney, the response to 9/11, the reasons for the Iraq War, the war itself, and anything else connected to Bush, with a steady stream of news, comments, and updates. Republicans were bad, and Democrats were foolish if they did not listen to the "netroots." Democrats were not spared if they were judged wanting in the qualities of toughness, aggression, and resistance to George W. Bush.

"I'm all about winning," Moulitsas said to the *Washington Monthly*. He refused to describe himself as a journalist, but proudly called himself an activist. Much of his personal blogging was on particular races he thought a Democrat could win, and he encouraged his many readers to donate to their campaigns. He raised half a million dollars for a slate of Democrats in 2004, and none of them won. By 2006, he raised three times that amount, and this time about half of his candidates won, including senators John Tester of Montana and James Webb of Virginia.

A blog poster named Jeffrey Feldman set down the rule on the Dailykos, far and away the most active, influential, and powerful of the poltical blogs on the left: "Remember the power of repetition: If you remember one thing from the last four years of blogging about election debate rhetoric and what it takes to win, remember this: *What we repeat is what the country remembers.*"

Feldman had put in a short paragraph what David Brock spent an entire book accusing Republicans of having done. In fact, however, it was a strategy that the left had been employing even before Brock published his book.

The secret for the left in creating its own noise machine, its own echo chamber, was to set up an apparatus that could level charges against Bush, or the neo-cons, or the war in Iraq, and then repeat, repeat, repeat.

The left had television in the form of MSNBC, the big network newscasts, and virtually all entertainment products including television and movies and pop music stars like Bruce Springsteen and the Dixie Chicks. They had newspapers and news weeklies. But Moulitsas gave them all a failing grade. They didn't investigate 9/11, they didn't question Bush's spin in the run up to war, they acted as a cheering section during the invasion, and as a cover-up team in the chaos that followed. When the press and mainstream media finally found that there were no WMDs in Iraq, Dailykos mocked the media and attacked the Democrat politicians who voted for the war.

But the right-wing had talk radio, and the left didn't even know it wanted something as powerful and aggressive until Dailykos came along and gradually began to fill that role. Dkos' million of pageviews became the eyes of network news executives, and their moral anchor. Among the pageviewers were newspaper editors and reporters, and the editorial staffs of the newsweeklies. And as a special bonus, the Dailykos fans—Kossacks as they were called—were an army that seemed to stretch to the horizon, sitting at attention at their laptops. Opinion flowed from the Dailykos in a molten torrent, and it began to affect the way stories about the war, the president, and a dozen other related subjects were reported in other, more influential media.

Weblogs, or blogs, come in a few very different sizes and shapes. Pure political Web sites like Thinkprogress.org and Moveon.org appear to traffic in news and information. But their purpose is clear and unambiguous: They are partisan sites designed to popularize the left's message ("General Betray-us" was a Moveon.org project). Web sites like the *Huffington Post* are slightly different. The *Huffington Post* is decidedly left, but it tries to present itself as a legitimate news site. President Obama called on reporter Sam Stein from the *Huffington Post* during his first White House news conference. Yet despite its acceptance as a legitimate news organization, the Web site of Arianna Huffington is as loudly left as she is, and makes no effort to hide the fact. The columnists range from the tweedy left of the college campus to the bomb throwers of Hollywood's self-reverential intellectual class. Readers are allowed to comment, but it doesn't offer a reader the opportunity to open his or her own spot on the Web site to keep his own "diary," as Kos names it, where the writer can amass a base of fans.

Huffington Post decides who is allowed to write a column. Dailykos gives readers a chance to elbow their way in and have their own say in something close to a featured position. Moulitsas calls it the "democratization" of the process of criticism of the right.

Dailykos, *HuffPost*, Democratic Underground, and other sites soon joined together to forge a powerful and effective noise machine of their own. Added to the mix was Air America, a lefty radio network; the increasingly partisan MSNBC cable network; and of course a host of best-selling books and left-wing magazines. This left-wing echo chamber reverberated daily with attacks on its bête noire, the hated George W. Bush.

One of the truly significant swiftboating lies about the war in Iraq was that President Bush and officials of his administration "misled" America into war, that the intelligence was "manipulated" to convince the American people that Saddam Hussein was a threat, and that consequently, in the familiar left-wing catchphrase, "Bush Lied, People Died." In the formulation of Dailykos poster Jeffrey Feldman, this notion became a fixed and accepted idea by pure repetition.

This popular catchphrase acquired a life of its own early on, but in early 2005 it received a major boost from an explosive story originating in Britain. The story concerned the release of some incriminating documents—quickly labeled the Downing Street Memos—and they had an enormous effect on the major American media. Among liberal reporters, editors, pundits, and radio talkers, the memos were a smoking gun that proved that George W. Bush had lied and manipulated intelligence to get Americans to support his immoral imperialist war.

Late at night on April 30, 2005, a Kos diarist named Smintheus noticed bombshell news breaking in the *Sunday Times* of London, where it was already May 1. The news was the leak of the minutes of a meeting of British Prime Minister Tony Blair and his chief national security advisors in late July 2003 in which they discussed the American preparations for invading Iraq that were already well underway.

The scandal was that the American plans were revealed to have been much farther along than American officials admitted at the time. President Bush's public statements conveyed a readiness to go to war if Saddam Hussein did not comply with reasonable demands of the international community. The memos revealed secret plans to go to war no matter what Saddam Hussein did or said.

Many in the media had already worked the story of former Treasury secretary Paul O'Neill's book, *The Price of Loyalty*. O'Neill claimed the Bush team was talking about invading Iraq in the very earliest days in the White House, well before 9/11. Former Clinton counterterrorism official Richard Clarke's book *Against All Enemies* alleged the same.

Nonetheless the first of what became Downing Street Memos was an eyepopper. The document recorded the views of Britain's national security team in preparation for an upcoming trip to the United States by Tony Blair for a meeting with President Bush. The minutes were taken and signed by Matthew Rycroft, a foreign policy aide. In attendance was the British secretary of defense, Geoff Hoon, head of British Intelligence (MI6) Richard Dearlove, Foreign Secretary Jack Straw, the attorney general Lord Goldsmith, head of the Joint Intelligence Committee, John Scarlett, and others.

Dearlove, who was just back from Washington, D.C., reported that in America's corridors of power, "There was a perceptible shift in attitude. Military action was now seen as inevitable. Bush wanted to remove Saddam, through military action, justified by the conjunction of terrorism and WMD. But the intelligence and facts were being fixed around the policy." Headlines: War inevitable. Intelligence fixed. The scandal deepened when it appeared that Dearlove, who had met with George Tenet, head of the CIA, was merely repeating what he'd been told by the American spy chief.

The Dailykos posting characterized the *Times* of London story as bombshell material, mainly for the revelation "that after consulting with Bush and his administration, the British leaders met to strategize about an invasion of Iraq that Bush had already decided upon (months before the congressional resolution)!"

There was more. Foreign secretary Jack Straw was quoted as describing the U.S. case against Saddam as "thin." The attorney general expressed doubts as to whether a war based on the idea of regime change would be legal. The defense secretary assessed Iraq's WMD capability as less than that of Libya, Iran, and North Korea. It all raised the questions, why Saddam, and why now?

Equally shocking to the British public, it was made clear that Blair had already decided Britain would join the Americans months before: "When the prime minister discussed Iraq with President Bush at Crawford in April," the briefing paper stated, referring to a Bush and Blair meeting three months earlier, "he said that the U.K. would support military action to bring about regime change."

That was a genuine bombshell in Britain, where Blair was already being characterized as Bush's "poodle" for his apparent willingness to follow wherever Bush led.

At the Dailykos, the blogger Smintheus was beside himself. "This is colossal in my opinion." Smintheus addressed all left-wing bloggers who had been fighting Bush and the war for four years, and had already lost a round of congressional elections in 2002 and a presidential election in 2004. "What is needed is a plan of action to make this story the center of political debate in the U.S. I encourage you to shift discussion to that topic."

The left-wing blogosphere duly exploded with denunciations of Bush and outraged calls for his impeachment. Yet Smintheus had to be disappointed with the reaction from mainstream media. It took a week for the *Washington Post* to get around to the story, and even then the news was not that Bush seemed to have made up his mind to go to war, but that intelligence was being "fixed around the policy," in Rycroft's intriguing phrasing.

The *Washington Post* characterized the importance of the document as showing "U.S. policymakers were trying to use the limited intelligence they had to make the Iraqi leader appear to be a bigger threat than was supported by known facts."

Representative John Conyers of Michigan, one of the Democrats who later became fixated on the impeachment of George W. Bush, noticed the Smintheus posting on the Dailykos and immediately sent a letter to President Bush asking for an explanation of the charges in the *Times* of London story. Still, the U.S. media didn't seem to be interested in the story, even with the "news hook" that Conyers, an important member of Congress, was demanding answers.

The left-wing Web site Fairness and Accuracy in Reporting (FAIR) complained bitterly about the lack of coverage. "At the first Bush press conference . . . since the memo was leaked," Julie Hollar and Peter Hart wrote on FAIR's Web site about a Bush news conference a month after the news of the memo broke, "not one of the nearly 20 reporters called on asked Bush to respond to its damning contents." Hollar and Hart tracked coverage and found that it was two weeks until the story made the front page of any American newspaper.

Left-wing bloggers were outraged. Within a week many had jumped on the story in what they called a "blogstorm" of online focus, forming what they called "The Big Brass Alliance," a Web site dedicated to moving the Downing Street story into the mainstream. The site was outfitted with a logo of two big brass balls. This "alliance" asked bloggers to direct all correspondence to a central clearing house blog called afterdowningstreet.org and feature that Web site on their main page. The goals of the Big Brass Alliance were to spread awareness of the Downing Street Memo, pressure the major media to cover the story, gather 250,000 signatures on a petition demanding the president answer questions raised in the memo, and urge people to sign a petition for a congressional "resolution of inquiry" into President Bush's handling of prewar intelligence. By June a blog tracking service owned by the Nielsen Research Company gauged "impeachment" postings had shot up from almost zero to over 2 percent of all blog postings.

When this news broke in 2005 the bumper sticker slogan "Bush Lied, People Died" was already showing its age. But the Downing Street Memo gave it new life.

Within a few weeks, more memos emerged from the deepest secret places of the Blair government, further inflaming the left and providing fodder for the blogs.

A March 25, 2002, memo from foreign secretary Jack Straw was viewed as extremely important if for no other reason than Straw had characterized the case against Saddam as "thin." A March 22, 2002, memo from Peter Ricketts, who was political director for the British Foreign and Commonwealth Office, reported, "[the] U.S. [is] scrambling to establish a link between Iraq and Al Qaeda" and it is "so far frankly unconvincing."

David Manning, the foreign policy advisor, reported on several days of talks with Condoleezza Rice at the White House. "Bush has yet to find the answers to the big questions: How to persuade international opinion that military action against Iraq is necessary and justified; what value to put on the exiled Iraqi opposition; how to coordinate a U.S./allied military campaign with internal opposition (assuming there is any); what happens on the morning after?" To the left, Manning's note indicated that the Bush team was unprepared and ready to proceed without knowing the answers to key questions.

A letter dated March 18, 2002, from Britain's ambassador to the United States reported on a meeting with Deputy Secretary of Defense Paul Wolfowitz, one of the strongest voices in the Bush administration for regime change in Iraq. It contained one solid gold left-wing nugget: "Wolfowitz said that it was absurd to deny the link between terrorism and Saddam." The left eventually came to regard a connection between terrorism and Saddam as one of the more absurd assertions of the Bush administration, and to them this was another sign of a disconnection from reality.

A memo to the members of Blair's cabinet sent July 21, 2002, contained this bombshell: "The U.S. Government's military planning for action against Iraq is proceeding apace." There had not been a congressional resolution permitting war, and the president had not announced his intentions, but the war buildup had been well underway. The left thought Bush had been caught red-handed.

The left-wing blogosphere actively pushed the story. Smintheus wrote, "This story blows wide open Bush's pretense of being a straight shooter. Most fundamentally, it exposes his contempt for democratic process."

The minutes of the July 23 meeting concluded: "[American] Military action was now seen as inevitable. Bush wanted to remove Saddam, through military action, justified by the conjunction of terrorism and WMD. But the intelligence and facts were being fixed around the policy. The NSC had no patience with the UN route, and no enthusiasm for publishing material on the Iraqi regime's record. There was little discussion in Washington of the aftermath after military action."

Smintheus wrote on the Dailykos, "This of course makes even more understandable the consistent opposition and mistrust the Bush administration encountered in the buildup to war, especially in Europe; many leaders in Europe were in a position to know that the war already had the green light, and therefore the posturing before the U.N. by the Bush administration must have been deeply galling for them."

Eventually, the story ran out of steam. There was only so much outrage that could be whipped up by the left, and ultimately both the media and the American public went back to its normal pursuits. Even the Dailykos moved on to other issues. But the proof offered by the Downing Street Memos was now firmly fixed in the minds of media personnel who would be setting the agenda in the 2006 and 2008 elections, in which the war in Iraq figured to be a major factor.

An army of Webmasters and contributors kept up the left's repetitive mantra during the 2006 congressional election campaign, and the Obama campaign that followed in 2008.

The swiftboating storm had its intended effect. The notions that the Bush team had committed a basic error going after Saddam Hussein was fixed in the public mind and seemed impervious to reason or history.

MANY INTERNET OPERATIONS measure success by the number of "pageviews," which is the number of pages viewed by individuals moving through the Web site. When DailyKos first began counting its readers in July 2002, it had just over 5,000 pageviews. During the Obama-McCain campaign's final months, DailyKos pageviews hit 30 million a month. Kos himself likes to calculate the high point by the week, an "audience" that competes with the numbers posted by big cable shows, and even some network news programming. His critics (and there are many) and proprietors of rival Web sites have tried to minimize that achievement, but in terms of Internet traffic, no other political Web site even comes close.

Part of the reason DailyKos was so successful is that it filled a need not met by other sites: It allowed users to post their own opinions and commentary that then elicited comments from readers, and thus developed an independent base of fans who returned again and again looking for new entries from their favorite writers. Comments themselves sometimes took the form of long essays, and the subject was always some aspect of the Bush administration.

It was a winning formula of community involvement that appealed to thousands of frustrated leftists who had watched their party fail repeatedly and felt they had no way in to the inner circles of power, where decisions were made and bad decisions could be corrected, or at the very least criticized. DailyKos exploded because it served the needs of the many leftists whose pent-up anger had nowhere else to go.

The other aspect of DailyKos that set it apart from any other Web operation was the founder himself. At thirty-seven, Markos Moulitsas Zuñiga was able to boast that he had played a pivotal role in the election of Barack Obama and the earlier takeover of Congress by the Democrats. His style is combative, encouraging aggressive language and attitudes among his many diarists and commenters. The Daily Kos engaged in total political warfare, employing ridicule and repetition together, and an in-your-face style of debate that often feels like an argument in a bar just before bottles and chairs start flying.

In the world of DailyKos, Bush could do no right, the war could not go well, and the issues were useful to discuss only insofar as they further undermined Republicans and conservatives.

On March 20, 2006, Moulitsas was interviewed by a young reporter for a student blog funded by the Center for American Progress. The writer introduced him as a "mythic figure" who "sat atop the Pantheon" of political activists on the Web, "casting his blogposts as Zeus once cast thunderbolts." He was asked, Are there any right-wing bloggers you enjoy?

"Oh my god I don't . . . I hate 'em all. . . . the right-wing blogosphere is like the sewage of the conservative movement. They're all absolutely terrible."

The readers and writers of DailyKos revere their leader. And since the sincerest form of flattery is imitation, they also use him as a model for the proper left-wing activist.

Moulitsas' attitude may have been formed in part by his training as a member of the U.S. Army, or his short stint with the CIA just before starting the Dailykos, or his time as a law student (he received a JD, but never practiced). He is a highly combative bomb thrower whose strategy is to encourage thousands of others to bloom.

When the four American contractors were ambushed in Fallujah, and their bodies were dragged through the streets, burned, and hung by ropes from a bridge, Moulitsas was characteristically disdainful. "I don't feel anything for them. Screw 'em." He later apologized and explained that he was angry that the deaths of five soldiers that same day hadn't warranted the coverage of the contractors' deaths, but he called them "mercenaries" and declared he had no sympathy for them.

Moulitsas happily rejects the role of journalist. It's not what he does, he says. He is an activist for causes of the left and works to get Democrats elected. At a session at Simon Rosenberg's New Democratic Network meeting in Washington, D.C., in early 2008, Moulitsas issued a warning—not to Republicans but to Democrats.

"Establishment Democrats have three choices. One, they can join us, and a lot of people have," he said. "Two, they can get out of the way, or [three] we're gonna roll 'em." Moulitsas put the Dailykos square in the zone of partisan political action. "Because quite frankly we're tired of losing and we're not going to do that anymore."

It was not an empty threat. During the 2008 primaries, Moulitsas quickly sided with Barack Obama, and started a campaign against Hillary Clinton. Yet there were many Hillary supporters among his Dkos community, and as the calls for Hillary to leave the race became more heated, many women felt she was the victim of unfair treatment. A group of female bloggers went on "strike" against Dailykos. Moulitsas dismissed them with a wave of his hand. "First of all it's a boycott, not a strike, and they're welcome to go find what they want. It's a big Internet."

"We're gonna roll 'em," probably came to the minds of a few of these women who had been shut out of the Moulitsas community. They could only look back in anger, perhaps reminded of how George W. Bush and his (successful) war had been "rolled" by the same Moulitsas operation.

By this time the Dailykos Web site had become an encyclopedia of supposed Bush offenses. There were miles of outraged copy about the run-up to the war, about Joe Wilson's charges against Bush and Karl Rove's role in exposing Valerie Plame, about the Mission Accomplished speech on the deck of the USS *Abraham Lincoln*, about the very bad years of the occupation, shrieking accusations about the bogus charges that half a million Iraqis had been killed, and much, much more.

Dailykos kept a special section of daily reports—dozens of them—through the entire Katrina disaster. Democrats Kathleen Blanco and Ray Nagin were not blamed for the aftermath of Katrina; Bush was. Moulitsas enforces a rule against conspiracy theories on his site, but the collected diatribes against Bush over Katrina came very close to stating that Bush made the disaster happen, and didn't care enough about the black people who lived there to save them. Hysterical reports were featured on Dailykos of murders and rapes in the Superdome in New Orleans, as were carried on other mainstream news outlets. When these stories turned out not to be true, not much was said about the mistake.

It was the same approach with the surge. It was condemned, along with General David Petraeus, and countless commenters wailed about the crime of sending more American boys to their deaths. When the surge turned out successfully, it was silence at Dailykos—if not outright denial.

The beauty of the situation was that it didn't matter if events didn't pan out as he predicted. The surge could go well, a Democratic government could get on its feet in Iraq, a sectarian civil war could be avoided, the courts could decide there had been no violation of the law with eavesdropping on phone calls, the enhanced interrogations could be something less than torture, and it didn't matter. Kos, the *Huffington Post*, My DD, Talking Points Memo, Moveon.org, Thinkprogress.org, had proved to their own satisfaction that it was all bad, and all wrong, and they weren't going to take it anymore.

During the campaign, Dailykos not only went after John McCain in as brutal terms as possible, it also targeted Alaska governor Sarah Palin. Thousands of posts filled diary sections of Dkos, and thousands more comments followed, mocking and attacking Governor Palin. Dailykos was one of the prime purveyors of the story that Palin's daughter Bristol had not given birth to her baby, but that her mother Sarah had. She was likewise criticized for going ahead with the birth of a baby she knew in advance was afflicted with Down Syndrome. She was attacked for her clothes, her looks, her bungled interviews, and she was mocked incessantly, along with the Republicans who nominated her. In October 2008, novelist Mark Sumner, who writes under the pseudonym Devilstower, wrote about Sarah Palin, "They've created the smirking dolt who wears silk jackets and *kicky* little hats. *Just look pretty and memorize the talking points, dear.*"

In 2009, flush with victory, and hungry for more, Moulitsas taunted Republicans.

"Dear Conservatives," he wrote about the tax protests known as Tea Parties. "If having hilarious tea-bagging parties keeps you guys from shooting people up, then I heartily endorse them. Hugs and kisses, kos."

Moulitsas showed up at the ABC News Bureau in Washington to pitch his new political action committee and warn that if incumbent Democrats didn't, in the words of an ABC reporter, "toe the line," they were going to lose.

We don't want a repeat of 1994 and we don't want our own version of 2006," said Markos Moulitsas, publisher of the liberal DailyKos blog, invoking two recent elections in which the congressional party in power was voted out of office through the work of his new Accountability Now political action committee. It would be supported by DailyKos, by MoveOn.org, the Service Employees International Union (SEIU), ColorofChange.org, Democracy for America, 21st Century Democrats, and BlogPAC, a powerful array of leftist Internet activists.

"Asked to defend the wisdom of backing challenges to incumbent Democrats, given that Connecticut senator Joe Lieberman managed to get re-elected even after Ned Lamont denied him the Democratic

Party's Senate nomination in 2006," the ABC report said, "Moulit-sas said Lieberman was saved by a 'quirk in Connecticut law' that allowed him to appear on the general election ballot as the candidate of his own party."

Moulitsas said he wouldn't stand for that anymore. "2012 is the last of Joe Lieberman," said Moulitsas. "My fear is he will retire. I want to take him out in an election."

The bully boy of the left had taken down a president and replaced him by repeating half-truths, untruths, and out and out lies about the administration and the war. Swiftboating had worked on a Republican incumbent in the White House, it would work again on a Democrat incumbent of the Congress who had not measured up.

Kos had given fair warning.

Chapter Nine

The Torture Myth: How the Left Spun Bush's Restrained and Successful Interrogation Techniques into the Spanish Inquisition

"We knew that (al Qaeda operative Abu) Zubaydah had more information that could save innocent lives. But he stopped talking . . . it became clear that he had received training on how to resist interrogation. And so, the CIA used an alternative set of procedures . . . Zubaydah was questioned using these procedures, and soon he began to provide information on key al Qaeda operatives, including information that helped us find and capture more of those responsible for the attacks of September 11, 2001."

—President George W. Bush, September 6, 2006

"Waterboarding violates our ideals and our values. I do believe that it is torture . . . And that's why I put an end to these practices. I am absolutely convinced it was the right thing to do, not because there might not have been information that was yielded by these various detainees who were subjected to this treatment, but because we could have gotten this information in other ways, in ways that were consistent with our values, in ways that were consistent with who we are."

—President Barack Obama, April 29, 2009, White House news conference

The gap between these two presidential statements was much more than a matter of a few years. The chasm between the positions of these two presidents represented the argument that was slowly building in America since 2004 about the U.S. government's official use of tactics that have been decried on the left and around the world as torture.

George W. Bush gambled with his nation's reputation when he ordered tactics used on al Qaeda captives that seemed to skirt the edges of, and sometimes cross into, the forbidden zone called torture. And Barack Obama's absolutism in assuring the American people that lifesaving information could be gained by other means represents another kind of gamble. For now, the American people have chosen Obama's way. Bush's methods seemed to have passed into history, an approach to terrorism based on the inducement of fear and pain, and on the vivid memories of what al Qaeda did to us in September 2001.

Now the people who swept Obama into office want a price paid for the controversial Bush approach. They have insisted it was illegal and immoral, and that it is past time to enforce the law and prosecute the guilty parties.

The left had political scores to settle, and for many simply banishing Bush and his followers from power wasn't enough. It was a situation that seemed to call for, well . . . a little torture.

Was Bush's policy official United States government sanction of torture? Or was it something else, something not quite torture, and therefore not really illegal?

The left decided long ago to control that argument with a basic deception that would function just like its other swiftboating lies: Bush's interrogation policies were, at their core, torture. Case closed. Nothing left to do but put sheets and toothbrushes in the cells, and lock them down.

In his 2008 book *Law and the Long War*, Benjamin Wittes wrote about the morality fever that swamps any conversation about coercive interrogations. "Few issues provoke the kind of high-minded moral rhetoric that interrogation does, and with good reason. Torture is one of the hallmarks of totalitarianism, antithetical to liberty and consequently corrosive of democratic values," Wittes wrote. "Yet dig deep enough—and often it does not take much digging—and the most categorical opposition to coercive interrogation gives way to consequentialism." That is, what are the consequences of *not* engaging in coercive interrogation?

Illustrating just that point, in the very news conference in which

President Barack Obama was quoted explaining why he had ended the practice of waterboarding, he was quick to add, "I will do whatever is required to keep the American people safe." This statement was tucked between two others that emphasized Obama's strongly held position that the best way to keep Americans safe was "not taking shortcuts that undermine who we are." But it also underscored another paragraph from Wittes' examination of the twin subjects of interrogation and torture.

"There are not many truly principled opponents of all coercion in all interrogations at all times," Wittes began. "And whatever rhetorical pose politicians adopt, categorical opposition to coercive interrogation is not a tenable position for anyone with actual responsibility for protecting a country." One can only hope that Obama has read Wittes' book, if only for the following thought: "The real question is not whether coercion is ever appropriate but how much coercion, how rarely, and with what, if any, degree of legal sanction."

Bush had tried it his way. Now it was Obama's turn.

But in a way it will be harder for Obama, precisely because he rode to office—at least in part—condemning root and branch the practices Bush had instituted. Obama had not only to determine whether and when he would violate his own rules, but somehow had to control the firestorm of lies about torture onto which he himself had thrown great heaps of fuel.

At its heart, the left's story on Bush-era "torture"—a story Obama was happy to be the beneficiary of during the campaign—was a lie, representing itself as the truth. The lie was that Bush tortured. The truth was he did not.

The left's *swiftboating* lie began with the Abu Ghraib scandal, when the outrageous and illegal practices discovered there were held up as Bush administration policy. The left's moralistic campaign started with that deception, and while it was polished and honed over the next five years of public debate on the practice of enhanced interrogation, that lie remained the centerpiece of the public indictment of George W. Bush for torture.

Torture is illegal, and under U.S. law that prohibition applies to its agents anywhere in the world. There is no gray area in discussion of the facts of what the U.S. military personnel did to detainees at Abu Ghraib: it was a crude and unsophisticated brand of torture. So said the president, the public, and the military courts. Six U.S. military personnel were convicted of crimes, and one, Charles Graner, is still serving a lengthy prison sentence.

Speaking out in a television interview almost as soon as the world learned of the abuses at Abu Ghraib in news bulletins that appeared instantly around the world, on April 28, 2004, Senator Ted Kennedy said that America had "reopened Saddam's torture chambers under U.S. management."

It was a line designed to make the headlines, and it did. But the actual truth was lost in the rhetorical zinger. The acts of depravity that were visited on the detainees by criminals in military uniforms were not the carefully vetted and meticulously spelled out practices that had been deemed legal and acceptable by the Bush Justice Department. Those techniques of coercive or harsh interrogation came to be lumped in with what the public already knew about Abu Ghraib. Over a period of years the left erased these distinctions and declared virtually anything done to a captured al Qaeda operative to be illegal, immoral, inhuman, and incomprehensibly cruel.

Swiftboating the nation on torture was all about selling the lie that there was no difference between legal, restrained, closely supervised, but tough interrogations and the horrors of Abu Ghraib.

As Wittes pointed out in a chapter called "An Honest Interrogation Law," one of the biggest obstacles to public understanding of what the United States was doing to elicit intelligence from captured al Qaeda operatives was that it was kept secret, or something like secret.

True, the United States had announced it had captured 9/11 conspirator Khalid Sheikh Mohammad, and that it had captured fellow conspirator Abu Zubaydah a year earlier. But it was immediately obvious something secret was being done to them, as they promptly disappeared into . . . well, *somewhere*. That gave rise to the reasonable suspicion that the United States had created one or more secret locations where it was questioning these very important captives.

The earliest reports of these "secret" prisons appeared in the *Washington Post*, the day after Christmas 2002. The *Post* described a secret facility in one corner of Bagram Air Force Base in Afghanistan that consisted of a group of metal shipping containers. In March 2004, the British newspaper the *Guardian* reported that three British citizens were being held in a secret facility at Camp Echo in Guanta-namo Bay, Cuba. The *Washington Post* broke the story of the so-called CIA "black sites" in 2005, and President Bush finally confirmed the secret prison story in a speech to the nation in September 2006: The point being that the secret wasn't secret all that long, but that some-times what turned out to be valid reports were ignored or not noticed by the news media and the public.

With so many people already putting two and two together about what might be happening with these prominent al Qaeda captives, it was somewhat surprising that the great American torture saga kicked off—to the gasps of a shocked planet in the last week of April 2004—not over the discovery of a series of "black sites" where the CIA could question people like KSM without restraint, but when *60 Minutes* broke the story of Abu Ghraib, a perfectly ordinary and not at all secret prison near Baghdad.

The story aired on a Sunday night, and the next day, the *New Yorker* magazine hit the nation's newsstands like a bomb. That issue con-tained an investigative report by journalist Seymour Hersh, which included revelations from an official army probe that had already resulted in the arrest of several military personnel. The army inves-tigation, called the Taguba Report, was devastating. The details, described at length in the official investigation and in Hersh's article, sent shudders through Washington, D.C., Baghdad, and far beyond.

Reactions from around the world rolled in hot and heavy for all of May 2004. In Egypt, NBC News correspondent Fred Francis declared: "In Cairo, anti-U.S. sentiment is so strong many here see no difference between the actions of Saddam Hussein and George Bush . . ."

That hurt. The war had not been going especially well. Ameri-can death totals were steadily rising in the latter months of 2003 (which was likely the reason Abu Ghraib's night guards seemed to have gotten the message to "soften up" detainees for dayside CIA interrogations attempting to disrupt the insurgency). This scandal made every bit of bad news about the war so much worse. But it was like manna from heaven for the American left, which had been seek-ing a safe means of denouncing Bush's war.

In the great national breast-rending over torture, Abu Ghraib was the vehicle used by the left to tell important truths about what happened at Abu Ghraib but simultaneously lie about American interrogation methods by branding them all as torture. Eventually, torture came to be defined as almost anything that any American did to any Iraqi or al Qaeda detainee that made the detainee uncomfortable. Detention itself amounted to torture, as far as some on the left were concerned.

The left lied about what torture was and was not. It also lied about whether the techniques the left deceitfully called torture actually worked to produce intelligence that saved American lives.

It was the dishonest conflation of these two entirely separate sets of facts that let the left swiftboat the truth and leave the American people with the impression—false through and through—that the United States government ordered people held in its custody to be ghoulishly tortured.

Anchoring NBC *Nightly News* in early May 2004, Brian Williams said, "The damage is clear: After no weapons of mass destruction showed up in Iraq, the U.S. justified the war by saying that at least the human rights violations would stop—the torture, the abuse, and the murders. Tonight, although the scale of this is much different, it is increasingly difficult for the U.S. to make that moral case around the world."

The crimes of those convicted at Abu Ghraib must include the belated charge that their actions allowed the antiwar left to gain power by hammering a perfectly legitimate set of interrogation techniques into a public perception of torture. The Abu Ghraib defendants allowed America to be portrayed as a regime of latter day Torquemadas, feeding their sadistic appetites with hot pokers, drowning tanks, and the rack.

The Abu Ghraib story created a sensation around the world. Largely overlooked in the hysteria was the fact that it was a three-month-old story that had previously been ignored: the U.S. Army Central Command (Centcom) had announced to the media three months earlier on January 16 that soldiers assigned to Abu Ghraib were being investigated for mistreatment of prisoners. Another media release a little later offered updates, but no one followed up on the story.

Lt. General Ricardo Sanchez, then the senior commander in Iraq, had assigned Major General Antonio Taguba to investigate, and his report was completed in late February of that year. The Hersh *New Yorker* story, based on Taguba's report, came two months later. It detailed stunning instances of detainee abuse at Abu Ghraib at the hands of an inexperienced unit of military police reservists. Seven service people ended up charged with crimes that included "breaking chemical lights and pouring the phosphoric liquid on detainees; pouring cold water on naked detainees; beating detainees with a broom handle and a chair; threatening male detainees with rape; allowing a military police guard to stitch the wound of a detainee who was injured after being slammed against the wall in his cell; sodomizing a detainee with a chemical light and perhaps a broom stick, and using military working dogs to frighten and intimidate detainees with threats of attack, and in one instance actually biting a detainee."

And that wasn't the worst of it, believe it or not. Owing to the fact every American soldier seemed to have gone to war with a digital camera in his or her pocket, there were pictures. Many, many horrifying and incriminating pictures.

A series of photographs was said to show grinning soldiers posing with an Iraqi corpse, a man who had died during rough questioning and whose battered body was being kept on ice in an unused shower. There were pictures of soldiers posing next to a pile of naked, hooded detainees, stacked in a human pyramid. "Yet another photograph shows a kneeling, naked, unhooded male prisoner, head momentarily turned away from the camera, posed to make it appear he is performing oral sex on another male prisoner, who is naked and hooded," Hersh wrote.

And of course, the photographs also included the famous image of a detainee—Iraqi or foreign al Qaeda is not clear—standing on a box, wearing a black sheet and hood, his arms extended crucifixion style, with wires dangling from his outstretched fingertips as if he is about to be electrocuted.

"Such dehumanization is unacceptable in any culture, but it is especially so in the Arab world," wrote Hersh.

Coming as it did at the end of April, the *60 Minutes* and *New Yorker* revelations turned May into Abu Ghraib month in the United States. The media was starting to have its doubts about the war, but the charge of "torture" sealed the fate of the Bush administration.

On ABC's *World News Tonight*, Peter Jennings said: "The International Red Cross says the Bush administration knew about allegations of torture and humiliation in Iraqi prisons more than a year ago."

NBC's Tom Brokaw had the same story: "A confidential report suggests the U.S. knew abuse was standing operating procedure in Iraqi prisons and did nothing to stop it." Brokaw promised: "The Iraqi prisoner-abuse scandal is a long way from over."

Brokaw was right. The torture story was just ramping up and was years from being over.

The confidential report to which Jennings and Brokaw referred was a study by the International Committee of the Red Cross— the ICRC—that was submitted confidentially in February 2004 to the commanders of coalition forces, advising them of human rights abuses in the prisons housing Iraqi and al Qaeda detainees. It outlined much the same material as Hersh, though differing slightly from the Taguba Report, Hersh's main source.

In its report, the ICRC said that based on interviews with detainees, whom the organization insisted on referring to as "persons deprived of their liberty," those incarcerated by the United States and coalition forces were "under supervision of the Military Intelligence [and] were at high risk of being subjected to a variety of harsh treatments ranging from insults, threats and humiliations to both physical and psychological coercion, which in some cases was tantamount to torture, in order to force cooperation with their interrogators."

It took almost no time for the report to leak to major news organizations, and it served as confirmation that the United States—in its fury—had stooped to torture.

The lie had thus begun: Reports of abuses, the army's own investigation of abuses, and suggestions of abuse from a respected international body led the media and the public to jump to the false conclusion that torture was an official U.S. policy.

CBS's Dan Rather reported that there was more coming, in the form of pictures. "The president today saw for himself unreleased images of Iraqi prisoners being abused by some American soldiers, images soon to be seen by Congress." Correspondent John Roberts added that the public would soon see the pictures the president had seen. "We caution you," Rather said in his rumbling baritone of doom, "you may not want your young children to hear the graphic descriptions in John's report."

Roberts reported that the unreleased video and pictures were "of prisoners naked, being forced to masturbate before the camera and pornographic video of sex between two guards."

Defense Secretary Donald Rumsfeld said in congressional hearings that, yes, more pictures were coming. Keith Olbermann of MSNBC said of the secretary's admission: "Given tonight's new charges, perhaps Saddam's rape rooms were not closed after all."

Over on NBC's flagship broadcast, *Nightly News with Tom Brokaw*, Andrea Mitchell held a copy of the ICRC report in her hands, and her narration followed words displayed on the screen: "Physical and psychological coercion . . . appeared to be part of the standard operating procedures to . . . obtain confession and extract information at Abu Ghraib. This despite George Bush's promise last year that Iraqi prisoners would be treated properly as he expected Americans to be treated." Coercion and the name George W. Bush were linked for the specific purpose of establishing a connection between the misbehavior at Abu Ghraib and the president of the United States.

From overseas, more bad news. NBC News correspondent Fred Francis reported from Egypt: "In the Arab street and much of the world, outrage has produced a consensus: Rumsfeld must go." Francis interviewed a "moderate" Egyptian journalist who said Arabs rejected the Rumsfeld apology—which had been issued almost instantly when the news broke—as it "seemed more arrogant than contrite."

Francis quoted another Egyptian: "that is not Jeffersonian democracy. It's more like a lesson from Hitler's book, *Mein Kampf.*"

NBC's Bob Faw did a "provocative" think-piece comparing photos of the My Lai Massacre, and the famous photo of a naked Vietnamese girl running away from a napalm bombing. "No, the prison photos are not as gruesome as torture inflicted by Saddam or the My Lai Massacre by Americans soldiers"—then why dredge up these old inflammatory images?—"but in the Arab world and at home they are drawing blood, piercing hearts and changing minds." Sure—but in the public mind, Abu Ghraib had been equated with My Lai, and Donald Rumsfeld was the new Lt. Calley.

Within days, NBC's Campbell Brown was reporting an exclusive: the legendary Delta Force kept a secret "battlefield interrogation facility" at Baghdad Airport, referred to as the BIF. "According to two top U.S. government sources, it's the scene of the most egregious violations of the Geneva Conventions in all of Iraq's prisons. A place where the normal rules of interrogation don't apply." Torture, it seemed, was an American disease and it was spreading rapidly.

The growing scandal also put one of Bush's chief lieutenants in the dock. The left and its media allies smelled blood. If Donald Rumsfeld could be linked to these abominable practices, they would soon have his head on a stick.

May 2004 was all Abu Ghraib all the time. The May 17 cover of *Time* was headlined "Iraq: How Did It Come to This?" and *Newsweek*'s cover read, "Is He to Blame?" over a photograph of Secretary of Defense Donald Rumsfeld.

The photos were bad, no doubt about it. But it was now the task of the press to integrate them into a sustainable story line, one that would make them a symbol of opposition to Bush and the war in Iraq. A godsend to the left, the photos allowed them virtually overnight to transform their stubborn recalcitrance on Iraq into a patriotic defense of America's moral standing and traditions. *Time*'s Nancy Gibbs noted that human rights had become the reason for the war after WMD were not found. "Psychologically, if not in fact, these pictures shred the last good reason to feel righteous about having gone to war."

Prophetically, during that first month of what became a highly damaging years-long narrative, Gibbs set the stage for all the self flagellating and wailing from the left that would follow: "We must recalculate the cost of the post–9/11 instinct to change the rules we play by, detain whomever we need to, forget due process and forgo the Geneva Convention. If this is indeed a fight to the death, what is it we are fighting for, if not the values we seem so ready to sacrifice on the grounds that this is a different kind of war? There will be other causes and threats, and we will need not only the power to confront them but the moral authority as well."

Thus was born the "American values" issue that President Obama cited to end coercive interrogations.

NBC's Brian Williams, waiting patiently in the wings for Brokaw to retire later in the year, reported, "The damage is clear: After no weapons of mass destruction showed up in Iraq, the U.S. justified the war by saying that at least the human rights violations would stop—the torture, the abuse, and the murders. Tonight, although the scale of this is much different, it is increasingly difficult for the U.S. to make that moral case around the world."

Fareed Zakaria of *Newsweek* was already looking forward to November, and the chance that this scandal would put George W. Bush out of office. "Whether he wins or loses in November," Zakaria wrote. "George W. Bush's legacy is now clear: The creation of a poisonous atmosphere of anti-Americanism around the globe. I'm sure he takes full responsibility."

As Fred Francis had reported, the outrage in the Arab world was immediate, and it soon turned brutal and ugly. Within two weeks, the world was shocked again when a video was released by al Qaeda in Iraq that showed Abu Musab al Zarqawi beheading captured American contractor Nick Berg—slicing off his head with a long knife, on camera, to the sound of Berg's anguished screams. The masked figure—Zarqawi—claimed it was an act of revenge for the "brothers" in Abu Ghraib—as if Zarqawi needed a good reason to cut off the head of an American.

Shamefully, network anchors quibbled about whether the man cutting off Berg's head was really Zarqawi (he later boasted of the gruesome deed) and if Zarqawi were really an al Qaeda operative. This was evidently deemed necessary to counter the pro-war backlash that resulted from the airing of the video, whose apparently unforeseen result was not to discredit Bush but to confirm the existence of an implacably evil foe in Iraq. Three months later the Senate Select Committee on Intelligence confirmed that Zarqawi had indeed been a fighter with bin Laden in Afghanistan and had escaped to Iraq at least a year before the U.S. invasion of Iraq, where he had founded a branch of the terrorist organization.

The conflation of real news (Abu Ghraib) and rank speculation from news people—especially anchors—took a serious turn for the worse in early June 2004, about six weeks after the Abu Ghraib abuses were made public.

On June 8, Dana Priest and R. Jeffrey Smith of the *Washington Post* revealed that at least two years before the Abu Ghraib abuses, the Bush administration had decided that "torturing al Qaeda terrorists in captivity abroad 'may be justified,' and that international laws against torture 'may be unconstitutional if applied to interrogations' conducted in President Bush's war on terrorism."

The reporters had obtained a 2002 memo that had been used in a 2003 report by Pentagon lawyers assessing interrogation rules at the Defense Department's detention center at Guantanamo Bay, Cuba. The key memo was identified as a fifty-page document written by assistant attorney general Jay S. Bybee, which the reporters said asserted that "inflicting moderate or fleeting pain does not necessarily constitute torture."

Bybee's memo said that torture "must be equivalent in intensity to the pain accompanying serious physical injury, such as organ failure, impairment of bodily function, or even death." Such hairsplitting distinctions where torture was concerned gave the appearance that the Bush White House was in a kind of moral free fall.

The *Washington Post* quoted the Bybee memo selectively and not extensively. It compared his analysis of the law with the Army Field Manual, which at that time prohibited pain induced by chemicals or bondage, or forcing an individual to stand, sit, or kneel in abnormal positions for prolonged periods of time, which were some of the very techniques Bybee's memo discussed as acceptable for al Qaeda detainees in certain circumstances. (The Army Field Manual has since been updated to allow military interrogators much more latitude.)

The memo also set out the conditions under which U.S. personnel could be exempted from the provisions of the Geneva Convention, which protects captured enemy soldiers, and the Nuremburg rule, which imposes on any military man or woman the obligation to refuse to carry out an order from a superior—even a commander in chief—that he or she knows is wrong.

Tom Malinowski of Human Rights Watch was quoted saying, "It is by leaps and bounds the worst thing I've seen since this whole Abu Ghraib scandal broke." (Malinowski was later denied a position in the Obama Department of State as a human rights advocate because he had been a registered lobbyist for HRW, and the president had forbade lobbyists from serving his new administration.)

Churchill's famous dictum that a lie can get halfway around the world before the truth pulls on its boots was precisely borne out here.

During MSNBC's live coverage of the Republican convention in June, *Newsweek* editor Jon Meacham was interviewed by Chris

Matthews: "The work of the evening, obviously, is to connect George W. Bush to the great war leaders of the modern era. You're going to hear about Churchill projecting power against public opinion . . ."

Chris Matthews: "But Iraq was a popular cause when he first started it. It wasn't like Churchill speaking against the Nazis."

Meacham: "That's not the way the Republican Party sees it. They think that all of us and the *New York Times* are against them."

Matthews: "Well, they're right about the *New York Times* and they may be right about all of us." (One of Matthews' few laudable traits is that he often says exactly what he thinks even if it is a self-indictment.)

The three elements that combined for a classic swiftboating lie had come together in quick succession: the discovery of actual torture by U.S. military personnel, followed by the revelation of a report from the ICRC alleging abuse of detainees, and the final confirmation, a Justice Department document that could be portrayed as an official government guidebook on torture.

Who to blame? The left had a ready answer. It was George W. Bush—or at minimum Donald Rumsfeld—who ordered the torture and knocked the United States off its long-held moral high ground.

Actor/comedian Richard Belzer, appearing on HBO's *Real Time with Bill Maher*, October 2004: "[John Kerry is] running against the worst president in the history of the United States! [audience applause] And that's not hyperbole. That's not hyperbole. The environment, the demonization of gays, the repression of black voters, the favoritism of Halliburton, this unending war. . . . We can't consume everybody's life with this fear when we've been attacked twice in twenty years."

Al Qaeda was certainly satisfied with the results of its years of planning—two attacks on New York in twenty years, one quite spectacular—so why was an actor/comedian minimizing the record? The answer was simple and timeless: The left hated Bush and anything he touched.

First came Guantanamo Bay prison, shortly after the invasion of Afghanistan in 2001, then the revelations about Abu Ghraib, and next news of memos that showed President Bush was angling for exceptions to the anti-torture laws and treaties that the United States had adhered to for decades.

The left exploded in an orgy of outrage and indignation.

An exchange on ABC's *The View*, between guest Sean Hannity, a conservative radio and television talk show star, and Rosie O'Donnell went like this:

Hannity: "Rosie, you guys, all you guys on the left, you demonize this president. You once called George Bush a war criminal."

O'Donnell: "He is. He should be tried at the Hague!"

The View has a daily audience of four million people, mostly women.

Another five million were watching NBC's *Today* show as Matt Lauer said to White House aide Dan Bartlett: "Dan, in the past, the president and the administration have been tough on the Chinese over the subject of human rights. Now the administration itself is under the spotlight over the subject of torture of prisoners in U.S. custody. Does this make it any trickier for the president to go and address this issue with the Chinese?"

It was as if America's opinion leaders felt a personal imperative to declare to the American people—and the world—where they personally stood on torture, as if it were a pass/fail test that each felt they simply must pass. In this great moralistic outpouring, all memories of what the 9/11 plotters had done to Americans were wiped away, any attempt to explain why the treatment of these prisoners was *not* torture was ignored. Good people had to be against torture. Anybody who would not stand and declare themselves to be against torture was not good.

Thereafter, as if by magic, the detainees—incarcerated and isolated though they might be—seemed to control national and international opinion about how they were to be questioned by American authorities: If the detainee thought there was something untoward about the way he was treated, it was ipso facto torture.

Events intervened, and torture moved from the forefront of attention to somewhere in the back of the public mind. In the summer of 2004, Republicans and Democrats held their national conventions and nominated their candidates, George W. Bush and Senator John Kerry. Abu Ghraib still lingered in the background because of the news from Iraq, where al Qaeda violence was literally exploding dozens of times each day. But the candidates did not talk much about Gitmo, Abu Ghraib, and the torture memo. MSNBC's Chris

Matthews complained on his program one night that John Kerry seemed to be gun-shy about confronting Bush "with the torture issue."

The election came and went, and President Bush was returned to office by a handy margin.

The next big break in the torture story came in early 2005 when Jane Mayer of the *New Yorker* reported that the United States had a secret program of "extraordinary rendition," which was used to whisk suspected terrorists to countries like Egypt, Morocco, Syria, and Jordan for special interrogations well beyond the reach of U.S. law. She mentioned that the suspects might be subjected to "waterboarding," the technique of simulated drowning. She quoted former CIA officer Cofer Black, who issued the famous quote, "After nine-eleven the gloves came off." A legal expert explained how "right-wing" administration lawyers were writing memos that essentially took the detainees and "cast them outside the law."

A few months later, on November 2, 2005—almost a year to the day after the Bush reelection—Dana Priest of the *Washington Post* broke the story that the CIA was holding terror suspects in its own secret prison. The so-called "black site" was a Soviet-era compound in Eastern Europe—and wait, there's more!—it was part of a "covert prison *system* set up by the CIA nearly four years ago that at various times has included sites in eight countries, including Thailand, Afghanistan, and several democracies in Eastern Europe."

To the left, it was the unveiling of an American gulag.

CBS *Evening News* anchor Bob Schieffer on MSNBC's *Imus in the Morning,* June 9, 2005: "This [the Guantanamo Bay prison] is just a boil. It's a cancer. This thing is not doing anybody any good. . . . They had a showing up here in New York before Memorial Day, this film about John McCain when he was [tortured] in the North Vietnamese prison camp. And to see what those people did to him, it just, it made me rethink this whole thing about how we treat these prisoners in Guantanamo. . . . We need to think about what separates us from the people who are trying to take our freedom away from us. . . . I don't want my kids to think this is how Americans are."

If Schieffer didn't want his kids to think America was as bad as the North Vietnamese Communists, he shouldn't have drawn this highly misleading analogy. In fact there was no comparison between the treatment of detainees at Gitmo and John McCain's five-year nightmare at the Hanoi Hilton. The left was swiftboating not by inflation but by conflation.

MSNBC's Keith Olbermann introduced former Nixon aide John Dean, author of a hyperbolic book called *Worse than Watergate*, as follows on his *Countdown* program on April 5, 2004: "John Dean, who was at the center of the greatest political scandal in this nation's history, has produced a book with perspective, and that perspective is simply terrifying. The bottom line: George Bush has done more damage to this nation than his old boss, Richard Nixon, ever dreamt of." Turning to Dean himself, he said: "The feeling that I had been left [with] after reading *Worse than Watergate* was that this could have been the historical, essentially, prequel to George Orwell's novel *1984*, that if you wanted to see what the very first step out of maybe fifty steps toward this totalitarian state that Orwell wrote about in his novel, [President Bush's policies] would be the kind of thing that you would see. . . ."

Under the heading of "torture" several distinct issues became one: Abu Ghraib, Guantanamo Prison, enhanced interrogations, extraordinary renditions (including "waterboarding" beyond the reach of U.S. law), and now a gulag of secret prisons where many suspected torture was being inflicted. If not, then why the secrecy? Within a short period of time public figures—many of them actual news people—felt duty bound to inform the public they were personally opposed to all of it. We are against torture, they cried, like a chorus of frogs.

National Public Radio Supreme Court correspondent Nina Totenberg weighed in for the nation's elite intellectuals. Interviewed about the *Washington Post* story on the television program *Inside Washington*, she blurted out: "I just want to say: Who are we? We are people who have always been for inspections of prisons, for some degree of human rights and now we're defending neither. . . . We have now violated everything that we stand for. It is the first time in my life I have been ashamed of my country."

Now it all came back. Five days after the 9/11 attacks, Vice President Dick Cheney had appeared on *Meet the Press* with the late Tim Russert and explained that the government needed "to work through, sort of, the dark side." Cheney continued, "A lot of what needs to be done here will have to be done quietly, without any discussion, using sources and methods that are available to our intelligence agencies, if we're going to be successful. That's the world these folks operate in. And so it's going to be vital for us to use any means at our disposal, basically, to achieve our objective."

Journalist Rosa Brooks—a former George Soros aide turned Georgetown Law professor turned *Los Angeles Times* columnist—now recalled Cheney's comment. "Within months of Cheney's 'dark side' comments, Guantanamo filled up with hooded, shackled prisoners kept in open-air cages. The Justice Department developed legal defenses of torture, we opened secret prisons in former Soviet bloc countries, and the president authorized secret 'enhanced' interrogation methods for 'high-value' detainees," Brooks wrote, damning the entire enterprise.

Another revelation shocked the public late in 2005: the *New York Times* revealed that the National Security Agency had been secretly cleared to eavesdrop on phone calls by suspected terrorists coming in and going out of the United States. The NSA's massive listening stations around the world had tuned in to America, to learn what was being said on millions of electronic transmissions. *New York Times* reporters James Risen and Eric Lichtblau had been tipped off by a career bureaucrat in the Justice Department named Thomas Tamm, who had heard scuttlebutt about a surveillance program that might be illegal. Tamm agonized over the story, and finally picked up a pay phone in a D.C. Metro station and called the *New York Times*. Risen and Lichtblau eventually published the story—and each subsequently published a book—that set off a firestorm of protest from civil libertarians and politicians. It was the first time the NSA had conducted surveillance of domestic telephones and computers. "This really is a sea change," they quoted a former senior official who specialized in national security law. "It's almost a mainstay of the country that the NSA only does foreign searches."

"Defenders of the program," Risen and Lichtblau wrote, "say it has been a critical tool in helping disrupt terrorist plots and prevent attacks inside the United States." But that didn't matter to the left. For them all that counted was that for the first time, the U.S. government was "spying" on its own citizens.

The White House asked the *Times* not to publish the story, "arguing that it could jeopardize continuing investigations and alert would-be terrorists that they might be under scrutiny." The newspaper did delay publication a year—meaning the reporters had known about it since December 2004—and eventually omitted some material that could have been helpful to terrorists.

In September 2006, President Bush gave a prepared speech at the White House in which he explained that, yes, there had been secret prisons, yes, there had been extraordinary renditions, and yes, some al Qaeda detainees had been subjected to harsh interrogations, including three who had been waterboarded. But he said that he did not consider the techniques used on these detainees to be torture, and justified the methods used as successful, insofar as they provided information that led directly to the disruption of al Qaeda plots that could have killed many—perhaps thousands—of Americans. In particular, he cited the al Qaeda plot, using an Indonesian terrorist cell, to fly another airliner into the Library Tower in Los Angeles.

The left immediately set to work trying to prove the plot Bush cited as a nonexistent threat, and continued its condemnation of him for sanctioning what they insisted on describing as torture.

In late 2007, the *New York Times* reported what many had suspected for some time: the United States had secretly approved "severe" interrogation techniques on al Qaeda suspects that included "waterboarding," an offense for which the American government had prosecuted Japanese soldiers after World War II.

Or so it was commonly said. In reality, waterboarding as practiced by the Japanese was a much more brutal practice, by no means comparable to the techniques adopted by American interrogators and commonly used to train American soldiers; nor was it the sole offense for which these prisoners were tried. Rather, they were tried and executed for their various beheading, disembowelment, starvation, and savage beating of prisoners, not to extract information but (apparently) for sport. But such distinctions were lost on the historically ignorant and morally obtuse spokesmen of the American left.

NBC's Meredith Vieira began an interview with GOP Senator Chuck Hagel on the *Today* show in the fall of 2007: "Senator, good morning to you. Let me ask you right out off the bat—when the president speaks about Iraq tonight, do you believe that he will have any *credibility*?"

The drip drip drip of leaked and subpoenaed memos was starting to form a picture for the public. The entire secret effort to make war on al Qaeda had begun as early as 2002 when the CIA first captured an al Qaeda operative named Zayn al Abidin Mohamed Hussein, also known as Abu Zubaydah. He had proved difficult to crack, and the CIA had asked for legal advice as to what they could do to make him talk.

Those early memos from the Department of Justice Office of Legal Counsel formed the justification for enhanced interrogation, including waterboarding, for the string of secret prisons, for the detainee encampment at Guantanamo Bay, Cuba—supposedly beyond reach of the U.S. Constitution—and for the practice of swooping into a foreign country, picking up a suspect off the street, and whisking him away to another country where he might be indefinitely detained and tortured, perhaps never to be seen again: the so-called "extraordinary renditions."

At the time of the 2007 *New York Times* "waterboarding" report, the pre-primary season was in full swing, and a phalanx of anti-Bush Democrats were headed for the first primaries in Iowa and New Hampshire. The war in Iraq was a big issue, and torture was mentioned from time to time. Over the course of the campaign, Barack Obama made it a signature issue, treated frequently in stump speeches with the promise "I will not torture." Beyond that, the issue was not big in the public consciousness; but if it wasn't big, it was certainly constant.

On September 28, 2007, Bruce Springsteen appeared before a live audience of about six million people on NBC's *Today* show and introduced his song "Living in the Future" as follows: "Over the past six years we've had to add to the American picture: rendition, illegal wiretapping, voter suppression, no habeas corpus, the neglect of our great city New Orleans and the people, an attack on the Constitution, and the loss of our best young men and women in a tragic war. And this is a song about things that shouldn't happen here, happening here. And so right now we plan to do something about it—we plan to sing about it."

In December 2007, columnist Rosa Brooks asked, "So . . . who really done it?" She wanted someone prosecuted. "Cheney, presumably, and the sinister little gnomes on his staff, and the checked-out Decider, who either knew and didn't care, or didn't care to know. And the CIA leadership and a whole cadre of operatives, who were willing to try a long list of discredited shortcuts they could borrow from our enemies," referring to practices of the Chinese Communists who used torture tactics on Americans captured during the Korean War. "And blame the conservative punditocracy, which eagerly defended enhanced interrogation methods. And let's not forget the GOP leadership in Congress, which gave the administration a whole book of blank checks." Brooks aimed mainly at conservatives, but she reserved some of her ire for a fellow leftist.

"But save some blame for House Speaker Nancy Pelosi, who apparently uttered not a word of dismay when briefed in 2002 on enhanced interrogation methods that included waterboarding, and for quite a few other congressional Democrats as well, who thought that ignoring and overlooking administration criminality was a legitimate form of congressional oversight," she wrote, referring to Jay Rockefeller in the first instance, and later a whole host of Democrats on the intelligence oversight committees, who were completely informed of what the administration had approved and CIA officers carried out. "And we can blame ourselves too, collectively. After all, we're the nation that made *24* a hit show."

Brooks would settle for no less than a full investigation, followed by a multi-defendant trial, followed by a hanging that would require several stout ropes.

A month earlier, Brooks had been more forgiving of the wider American public, and much less forgiving of the Republicans, her favorite target. Brooks was writing about the confirmation hearings for Michael Mukasey as attorney general, following the exit of Alberto Gonzales. Mukasey had created something of a firestorm when he refused to call waterboarding torture, and New York's Charles Schumer and California's Diane Feinstein were the only Democrats on the Senate Judiciary Committee to vote for his confirmation. Both soon found themselves under attack from their own side.

Brooks wrote, "They shouldn't have been so surprised by the rapid blowback. Far more than the abortion debate ever did, the debate about torture goes to the very heart of what (if anything) this country stands for." Brooks asked if Americans wanted to be a nation "committed to a vision of human dignity and unalienable rights . . . and the rule of law?" Or, she asked rhetorically, "would we rather bring back the methods of the Spanish Inquisition?"

Comparing the carefully calibrated and closely supervised use of coercive techniques to the horrifying abuses suffered by Americans in Japanese or North Vietnamese POW camps was bad enough—but really, now . . . the Spanish Inquisition?

Many on the left had come to believe that waterboarding was so clearly a matter of torture that it should not have been used on either Abu Zubaydah or Khalid Sheikh Mohammad. In his book, *Law and the Long War*, Benjamin Wittes had written that the classic test of whether an official would order waterboarding—torture—was the ticking bomb scenario, in which a captive knew when a bomb was going to go off and interrogators had to get the information out of him fast. But Wittes said that was not really the right hypothetical. The true test, he wrote, "is Khalid Sheikh Mohammad, and it is not a hypothetical scenario at all, but a very real one." Wittes argued that KSM was the perfect test case: "His potential importance lay not in his knowledge of any single impending attack but in his knowledge of the organizational structure of Al Qaeda and its plans for *many*, presumably future, attacks . . . KSM is far more than a single ticking bomb. He is *all* the bombs."

Yet Rosa Brooks, like others on the left, refused to see that horrific truth about KSM. She rejected waterboarding even him; and in fact, of course, he was one of only three men ever to have been waterboarded by the U.S. government.

Even though she was entirely in error about how to treat al Qaeda detainees—as criminal defendants rather than as enemies engaged in war—Brooks was right to single out KSM as the most important issue in the waterboarding debate, one that would explode only a few months after the new president took office.

BEFORE HIS FIRST one hundred days were completed, Barack Obama took two steps that seemed both contradictory and unexpectedly inflammatory.

On April 19, 2009, his chief of staff, Rahm Emanuel, appeared on *This Week* with George Stephanopoulos and stated that the president was not interested in prosecutions of either CIA officers and officials nor former Bush administration officials, over the issue of waterboarding and torture. "The president wants to look to the future," Emanuel said.

Yet two days later, the White House inexplicably decided to make public four key memos in the long torture saga going back to early 2002. These were the memos that had placed detainees in American custody beyond the Geneva Convention protections, and redefined what was considered cruel and inhumane punishment. At the same time, the Senate Armed Services Committee investigation into the treatment of detainees in U.S. custody was released. The 236-page document covered everything from Abu Ghraib to Guantanamo to the still mostly secret prison at Bagram Air Force Base in Afghanistan.

The one-two punch of these document dumps was like an earthquake. Suddenly Obama found himself losing control of his base—angry Democrats who wanted people prosecuted for what they had written in legal opinions, and for carrying out White House–approved procedures on captives held in U.S. prisons.

"Waterboarding" became a central issue overnight. Again. The left no longer seemed to care what happened to the man had who planned and carried out 9/11. Now they wanted the people who had captured and interrogated him put on trial.

Former vice president Dick Cheney stirred things up by doing a television interview in which he said that actions taken by President Obama would make America less safe, and after the release of the so-called "torture memos" he demanded the CIA release other memos that would show what information had been gained using the waterboarding techniques.

Chris Matthews went on the air to ask Howard Fineman of *Newsweek*, "I wonder, Howard, if the Republican Party really wants to be branded right now as the party of tax cuts and torture? I mean that's what they're selling. I mean tax cuts are always happy to be heard about, even if they're not possible. But the torture part—the image of, of a party that seems to have attached itself to this method, this difficult, hard to justify, sometimes perhaps necessary, method of getting to the truth in, in urgent circumstances. Is it what you want to be known for?"

Interviewing Congresswoman Debbie Wasserman Schultz of

Florida, Matthews mused on the possible outcome: "Well if it turns out that those who drew the lines and said it was okay to use waterboarding and other coercive techniques, violated the law, and those people who did so include the vice president and the president, what do we do? You say we might consider prosecuting them. But how do we do it? Under what law do we go after them? Under international law? Under U.S. law? What do we hit 'em for? If we do it?"

The left was now demanding that the former president and vice president of the United States be prosecuted for policies they developed to keep the country safe for seven years. The enhanced interrogation techniques had worked, and worked dramatically. The former director of the CIA, George Tenet, said that "half of all the information the CIA had on al Qaeda" came from those three 'waterboarded' interrogations. Only thirty-three al Qaeda detainees—out of thousands—were subjected to enhanced interrogation techniques, which stopped short of waterboarding. Another former CIA director, Michael Hayden, said "I know there are people walking around alive today who would have been dead had we not used those methods on KSM and gotten that information."

Yet the left called it torture and demanded an accounting.

As an example of how the left routinely twisted facts to suit its purpose, a story emerged in this period that KSM and Abu Zubaydah had been waterboarded a total of 226 times, Zubaydah alone getting 183 treatments. A hue and cry went up on the left that sadists were running the CIA. Why would anybody think it was necessary to waterboard someone 183 times? How could that possibly be justified? Wouldn't you know much short of that very large number of treatments that he wasn't going to tell you anything more, that he didn't know anything more?

Within a couple days, the truth came out. Both prisoners were waterboarded a total of five times each; the numbers cited referred to the total "pours" of water during the several sessions, each lasting a couple of seconds. But it was too late: the left had convinced the public of yet another lie: that these men were subjected to prolonged, sadistic treatment, practically drowned, and were lucky to be alive.

The interrogations of Khalid Sheikh Mohammad, the planner of 9/11, and his cohort Abu Zubaydah, the 9/11 paymaster, included the use of the technique that has come to be called "waterboarding," in which Mohammad and Zubaydah, and one other 9/11 plotter were held down, and water dribbled over cellophane stretched across their mouth to give them the feeling they were drowning. All three were self-professed key 9/11 plotters. The decision to subject them to this technique was reached in each case only after traditional tactics had failed. For instance, Khalid Sheikh Mohammad was asked repeatedly what other plots al Qaeda had in planning stages; each time he responded with a smile, "Soon you will find out."

It was only after the "traditional methods" that President Obama said would have worked just as well had actually *failed* that Khalid Sheikh Mohammad and the others were subjected to waterboarding.

None of the three were in any actual physical danger of drowning; the technique merely induced the *sensation* of drowning. The process had been tested for many years in the army's SERE program (Survival, Evasion, Resistance, and Escape), which trains U.S. military personnel how to resist torture if they are captured by the enemy. Thousands of American soldiers had been waterboarded by the time the tactic was applied to Khalid Sheikh Mohammad and Abu Zubaydah; those who went through it during training found it very uncomfortable, but none died, or even came close.

The waterboarding sessions were closely monitored and constrained by specific guidelines. Medical personnel were standing by each time to intervene in the event of a serious problem. The whole procedure adhered to exacting rules laid out by U.S. legal counsel, following the advice of doctors, psychologists, and experts from the SERE school.

The information gained from those waterboarding sessions constituted fully half of the high-value information the CIA learned about al Qaeda, including organizational details, and the names of individuals involved in a "Second Wave" plot to crash an airliner into the Library Tower in Los Angeles, whose disruption undoubtedly saved thousands of American lives.

Nonetheless, the swiftboaters of the left seized on waterboarding and other harsh interrogation techniques (including openhanded slapping, and "walling," which involved slamming the person being interrogated into a fake, breakaway wall) as torture, with no further discussion.

To the left there was no reason for discussion. All of these methods were torture, plain and simple. Consequently, the debate was not about the effectiveness of the techniques that were used, but whether the United States is a nation that tortures—as if America had suddenly morphed into something out of the Spanish Inquisition, to use Rosa Brooks' comparison.

These were demonstrably swiftboating lies. When President Bush and others in his administration said the United States does not torture (and the president said it many times), he was telling the truth. But he was mocked and belittled for those statements because according to the left, any tactic used on a detainee that he did not want applied was ipso facto torture.

The president's critics also committed the grievous error of assuming that interrogations should be conducted as if the detainees were criminal suspects, the information gained from said interrogations would be used in a criminal trial for a conviction.

But that was not the purpose. Khalid Sheikh Mohammad and Abu Zubaydah were not criminal defendants. They were commanders in a war, and the United States needed information from them about what else they were planning, how their organization was structured and funded, and who were the people enlisted to attack America.

The torture meme became a central thrust of the left as it campaigned to discredit George W. Bush, and Republicans in general, and win the election for Obama. After President Obama declassified and publicized previously secret documents about how tough interrogation procedures were developed and approved, the torture wildfire flared up again, as if driven by a fierce wind.

The tempest was advertised as a struggle to restore American morality and leadership as a "beacon for the world." John Winthrop's 1630 "City on a Hill" was invoked again. But the controversy was obviously and primarily for the purpose of settling political scores and carrying out congressionally mandated show trials intended to forever blacken the names of the people and the party who had ordered those interrogations.

The debate took many years to build to a head, but by the time the Obama administration released the so-called torture memos, the lions of the left were striving to outdo each other in their indignation—their horror and shame!—that Bush had authorized such tactics. Leading the parade was anti-Bush drum major Joe Klein of *Time* magazine.

On February 7, 2002, George Bush had signed a memorandum stating that the Third Geneva Convention would not be applicable to members of al Qaeda or the Taliban. "That signature led directly to the abuses at Abu Ghraib and Guantanamo Bay," Klein thundered. "It was his single most callous and despicable act. It stands at the heart of the national embarrassment that was his presidency."

The interrogation of the three 9/11 conspirators had suddenly become the worst thing the former president had done—worse by far than the awful decision to invade Iraq, worse than the shameful reliance on phony evidence to "sell" the war to a credulous public, worse than the incompetent prosecution of the war, worse than even the unconscionable wiretapping of American citizens in its misguided and illegal attempts to catch terrorists planning more attacks on the homeland.

Klein, like others before him, rested his anti-torture argument on a gold-plated falsehood. "It should be noted that there was, and is, no evidence that these techniques actually work," Klein wrote, adding, "Patient, persistent questioning using subtle psychological carrots and sticks is the surest way to get actionable information."

This statement was plainly not true, and the interrogations of Khalid Sheikh Mohammad proved it. KSM was extensively interrogated using traditional methods and refused to give anything up. As noted earlier, he merely smiled and repeated one phrase: "Soon you will find out." How were interrogators supposed to interpret that statement but in the most ominous possible light? Were they simply to wait him out? Were they to keep this up for months, even years, until in good time he realized he was never getting out of this? And in the meantime, what damage would be done?

But ignoring this truth was central to the left's outrage over the so-called "torture" techniques, and those who designed and approved them. Any number of commentaries from the left took special pains to deny the utility of these techniques, but a specific denial of the "West Coast Plot" or "Second Wave" of al Qaeda attacks was crucial.

. . . .

THE LEFT'S ARGUMENT was that the administration had already captured a key plotter a year earlier, and by the time of KSM's capture and later waterboarding, already knew that the scheme had been called off. This claim is the very bedrock of the lie that waterboarding KSM accomplished nothing.

The trail of people and information reveals the truth for anyone willing to actually examine the details.

According to former speechwriter Marc Thiessen, who wrote a number of important national security speeches for Bush and has published numerous articles on the subject since leaving the White House, the following chain of events occurred:

- Majid Khan was captured in March 2003. He gave up nothing.
- When KSM was captured a month later, he knew Khan was in custody and assumed he'd confessed to the "West Coast plot," though he refused to provide more information, telling his interrogators: "Soon you will find out."
- After waterboarding, KSM revealed that Khan had been told to give $50,000 to people working for a terrorist named Hambali, the leader of al Qaeda's Southeast Asian affiliate called Jemmah Islamiyah (JI), and that Hambali was KSM's partner in plotting the Library Tower attack.
- The CIA confronted Khan. He confirmed the money had been delivered to an al Qaeda operative named Zubair. He gave up a physical description and a phone number. Zubair was caught in June 2003.
- Zubair was then interrogated and gave up information that led to the capture of Hambali.
- KSM was told of Hambali's capture and revealed to interrogators that Hambali's younger brother Rusman Gunawan (aka "Gun Gun") was the leader of the JI cell that was to carry out the West Coast plot. Gun Gun was captured in Pakistan in 2003.
- Gun Gun led CIA operatives to the seventeen others who were to carry out the plot, and they were captured and detained.

The left worked hard to make this story go away, to declare it a lie. But Thiessen's narratives, and the memos Cheney demanded, prove the truth. There is simply no question that the waterboarding technique that the left condemned had saved American lives.

There was really no coherent argument the left could make to the contrary, but it didn't stop them from making an argument that was completely incoherent.

"George W. Bush and Dick Cheney shouldn't be treated like criminals who deserve punishment. They should be treated like psychotics who need treatment," Rosa Brooks wrote in her *Los Angeles Times* column in 2007. "They've clearly gone mad."

In another column, Brooks wrote, "But all this creates a conundrum. What's a constitutional democracy to do when the president and vice president lose their marbles? Impeachment's not the solution to psychosis, no matter how flagrant. But despite their impressive foresight in other areas, the framers unaccountably neglected to include an involuntary civil commitment procedure in the Constitution."

In the *New York Times*, Frank Rich made a last-ditch effort to prove that waterboarding was not implemented to gain information on future plots, but was rather a futile attempt to force detainees to confess that there was a connection between Saddam Hussein and 9/11, "trying to prove a link that was never there." Like Brooks, he demanded a special inquiry with an eye to trials. "President Obama can talk all he wants about not looking back, but this grotesque past is bigger than even he is. It won't vanish into a memory hole any more than Andersonville, World War II internment camps, or My Lai. The White House, Congress, and politicians of both parties should get out of the way. . . . What we must have are fair trials that at long last uphold and reclaim our nation's commitment to the rule of law."

What the left could never seem to understand was that the rule of law, the high moral ground on which America rests, the beacon to the world that is the United States—all of that means nothing if its leaders won't act to prevent its citizens from being killed.

Chapter Ten

Swiftboating the Surge: How the Democrats Got Married to Losing in Iraq

The left won the 2006 elections because America was losing the war in Iraq. It won the 2008 election because America still thought it was losing the war in Iraq, while in fact it was winning. Keeping that paradox under wraps was key to winning the presidential election and the left seizing complete power in America.

What would the left have done without the Iraq War? How would it ever have won the elections of 2006 and 2008? Why is the left not more grateful it had an Iraq War to denounce and demonize, and to use as a springboard to establish complete and unchallenged power in Washington, D.C., from one end of Pennsylvania Avenue to the other?

These are the questions the left has not answered, and intends to avoid forever, if possible.

Look at what the Iraq War gave the left in America. For starters, it was the almost undreamed of chance to elect a complete nobody to the White House, and the extra bonus that he was African American, solidifying the left's hold on the burgeoning non-white population of the country. It was a chance to push the country farther toward the left's long-held goal of socializing the American economic system. The Iraq War gave the left a good shot at putting the Republican Party out of business, and consigning what few conservatives were still standing to outlaw status.

Without the Iraq War, the left in America would have been just another fringe political movement, with hardly the traction to spin out of the mud of its sloppy politics and greasy financial machinations. It would have been consigned to the far end of the political spectrum, where only nuts and freaks live, which had long been ignored in America.

But the anger over the war, and the way the left in the media manipulated the American public through an almost endless catalog of mischaracterizations, misinterpretations—lies, actually—set the stage for the political opportunity of a lifetime, the big gamble on the proposition that losing a war wins an election. Rushed into the fray, a combination of a vicious left media, left political action groups, and left big money made the big dream come true.

During two years that the United States was not winning the war, the left poured gasoline on the fire, and during the next two years that the United States had turned the corner and was rolling toward success (*winged victory* to the less timid among us), the left media managed to obscure and distract and was able to eventually convince the American public that the war was in fact being lost at the precise moment it was being won.

The moment it should have become clear to everyone was February 27, 2009, when President Barack Obama traveled aboard Air Force One to Camp Lejeune, North Carolina, and outlined his plans for bringing troops home from Iraq.

As Obama entered the room to take the stage, where a group of marines selected for their diverse faces was standing at ease but in the formation of a background for a photo op, the band played "Hail to the Chief," and the offstage announcer boomed, "And now the president of the United States." The troops greeted him with a short golf clap, in sharp contrast to the roar that usually greeted President Bush.

President Obama's speech was a complete capitulation. He outlined a troop withdrawal timeline that was identical to the plan set in place by former President George W. Bush, and backed by Obama's opponent in the previous fall's election, Senator John McCain.

Obama also admitted that Generals David Petraeus and Ray Odierno, and the U.S. troops had won the war. He admitted the goals of the war had been achieved. "And so I want to be very clear. We sent our troops to Iraq to do away with Saddam Hussein's regime—and you got the job done. We kept our troops in Iraq to help establish a sovereign government—and you got the job done. And we will leave the Iraqi people with a hard-earned opportunity to live a better life—that is your achievement, that is the prospect that you have made possible."

Thomas Ricks, the *Washington Post* military correspondent who wrote two books on the war (*Fiasco* and *The Gamble*), said on a national radio program a few days later, "He was probably being polite, not wanting to say you wasted your time and effort on Bush's mistake when [we?] invaded."

Perhaps. But the *Wall Street Journal* called the speech "Obama's Bush Vindication."

Following the speech, President Obama called former President Bush to brief him. The briefing should have started with an apology, but evidently Obama could not bring himself to admit to the man he'd spent years trashing that it had all been nothing but electioneering, undermining the nation for the good of his own personal goals and the goals of his left-wing party.

Candidate Obama's preening on the war was consistently chest-thumping, flamboyant promises to end it. "When I promise that we are going to begin to bring this war to an end in 2009, I want the American people to understand I opposed this war in 2002, 2003, 4, 5, 6 and 2007 so you can have confidence I will be serious about ending this war," he said on the campaign trail in May 2008. It was many of such statements calibrated to play to the 35 percent of the country that was Democrat and against the war, and the 35 percent that had once been supporters of both Bush and the war, but had been convinced to swing left.

Somehow Obama's actual early statements on the war were overlooked by the left in later years. Yes, he opposed the war in 2002, and 2003, but when a Chicago interviewer asked in April 2004, "You said the troops should be withdrawn . . ." he interrupted to correct her. "No, no, I never said that troops should be withdrawn. What I've said is that we've got to make sure we secure and execute the rebuilding and reconstruction process and I don't think we should have an artificial deadline to do that."

Even as late as mid-2006 Obama argued against deadlines in

Iraq that were arbitrary. In a speech to the Senate June 21, 2006, Obama said, "A hard and fast deadline offers our commanders in the field and our diplomats in the region insufficient flexibility" in implementing a winning strategy.

The war bashing from the left was not just Obama, of course. But he was a principle beneficiary of the gloomy mood on the war, and he seldom failed to flog it again to build up his credibility and "judgment" with the left.

The key to turning that overwhelming electorate into an overwhelming win at the polls in 2008 was an all important bit of sleight of hand. It was certainly no trouble convincing people to be against the war during 2005 when the insurgency erupted. In 2006 it was going very badly, but it required much skill and good luck to keep the public convinced the war was going badly in the second half of 2007 and 2008 when the U.S. forces had actually turned the tide and were winning. Obscuring that win until after the election was all important, and while Obama denied reality on the campaign trail, his media enablers went into warp speed to make certain it was not noticed in the public prints and on the airwaves.

Central to this disinformation campaign was the war against the surge. No sign of success of the surge could be allowed to creep into the public consciousness until after the election, despite the fact that glaring, flashing-light signs of success were before the public for at least a year before Election Day.

A lie repeated is the truth defeated. That maxim was put into play every day, if not every hour, as the media swept Obama to victory on a tide of adulation, adoration, and self-delusion. All the while the growing success in Iraq was kept secret by cultlike incantations of defeat, and constant media repetition that Bush could do nothing right.

Of course, at some point the left was going to have to face the facts. The truth about Iraq could be hidden for a while, until after the election, but eventually it was going to have to come out. And so it was that one day short of a month after Barack Obama was inaugurated president of the United States, the left officially embraced the surge. By this late day, of course, the surge and its associated tactics were widely recognized to have worked by professionals in the military and politics in the United States and by most Iraqis. Even al Qaeda complained of its effectiveness.

But for the left in America, the strategy—on display in the public prints and on the airwaves—was to grow the electoral gains of 2006 on war discontent at home. To win the White House in 2008 it was imperative that the lies about the surge and the dismal predictions about the overall situation in Iraq had to keep coming. The two years of the surge were a time of deep denial, and mounting horror on the left as the news from Iraq began to improve. There certainly had been no way any influential and active leftist would have admitted success before the appointed day the American people would reject John McCain, the only one of the two presidential candidates who spoke out loudly in support of the surge.

It also would have seemed just too soon to make a formal acknowledgment until well after the new president had taken office.

But in the chill of mid-February, weeks before Obama made his concession at Camp Lejeune, one of the *grand dames* of the left made it all too clear that the ruse had run its course and been exposed by publicly coming out of her cave of ignorance and willful denial and noted, in print, how magnificently General David Petraeus and his troops had executed the almost impossible task of tamping sectarian violence in Iraq.

That eminence was Joan Walsh, the sharp-tongued editor of Salon, a respected and feared leftist online magazine. After month upon month, year upon year of turning the thumb screws on anyone who supported the war in Iraq, from the president on down, she suddenly flipped. This startling admission came in a column cum review she authored about the latest book from Thomas Ricks, *The Gamble*. Ricks was a long-time military correspondent for the *Washington Post* and had written an earlier book, *Fiasco*, on the confused and chaotic years in Iraq shortly after the invasion.

Walsh lavished praise on *Fiasco* for Ricks' great insights and careful explanation of all that had gone wrong. She said "Ricks was the nation's top expert on the folly of the U.S. mission in Iraq, from inept prewar planning to post-war execution to a botched occupation . . ."

For Walsh, *Fiasco* was perfect bedtime reading. She could drift off to sleep confident George Bush was losing his war simply by reading a few of Ricks' doom-packed pages.

But now Ricks had done something different. *The Gamble* was

about an intelligent and dedicated American general, David Petraeus, and thousands of dedicated and professional young people
who were his troops in Iraq. She titled her piece, "Democrats fought
the surge and the surge—sort of—won. Now what to do in Iraq?"

She described that the drama and "action" of Ricks' new book
involved three men "Ricks respects." They were retired General Jack
Keane, Petraeus, and his deputy, General Ray Odierno.

Brushing lightly over the buildup Ricks gave the three men, fierce
antiwar, anti-Bush, and anti-surge Joan Walsh said, "but it's hard not
to come away admiring what the controversial general accomplished
in just two years."

Walsh admitted she was not a supporter of the surge. And she
certainly was not. In terms designed to boil the skin of her targets,
she had attacked Bush, Cheney, the Pentagon, Petraeus—anybody,
really—who supported an escalation policy she thought had been
closed off, blocked, and barricaded, by the congressional election
that had given both houses of Congress to antiwar Democrats.

In more civil times, you might call Walsh skeptical. But her own
use of language was so distorting and hostile, you would have to
pencil out skeptical and write in "belligerent."

Just to give one example, she wrote about a Bush news conference
in mid-July 2007: "In an administration constantly reaching new
milestones of dishonesty and incompetence, yesterday was a different kind of scary," and, "I also think Bush crossed into a whole new
world of delusion and dishonesty."

Ever sharp of fang and claw, now she was sweetness and light, not
only about the war, but the men leading it, and about the possibility
President Obama might have to consider breaking a few Iraq promises he had made to the left. "It does seem clear from Ricks' reporting that Obama's sober formulation, 'We must be as careful getting
out of Iraq as we were careless getting in,' could be at odds with the
deadline he's set for withdrawal." Translation: Obama should not
keep his promise to march troops out of Iraq, but should hang in to
secure the victory. It all sounded so reasonable, so well thought out,
so prudent, so . . . well, so *Bush*.

Walsh was quick to remind her readers that she was still against the
war, and blamed the war for terrible things such as the budget crisis
in California which was forcing layoffs of state workers, believe it or

not. "I still want troops out of Iraq as soon as possible. But reading this well-reported book may have changed my notion of what that means."

The very same people who called him "General Betray-us" in a *New York Times* full-page ad were starting to come around (Walsh insists she was against the publication of such an insult against Petraeus), and there was a simple reason for such stunning changes in attitude: Much of the opposition to the surge was simple political anger fomented in thousands of hours of television diatribes, and hundreds of thousands of printed screeds, to keep Democrats motivated to become ever more fervent war opponents and elect a Democrat to the White House. Barack Obama eventually became the sole heir to that anger.

Once a full-throated leftist was at the podium in the White House, the left could let down its guard, and "discover" the war had been won while they were looking the other way.

What was so disturbing about Walsh's epiphany on Iraq and General Petraeus was that none of what Ricks described in his book was particularly new. The core story had been reported in newspapers and in previous books that should have been widely read by people intent on arming themselves with the facts on Iraq.

Be that as it may, Ricks' book, *The Gamble*, was released February 10, 2009. The same basic story of how General Petraeus and General Keane and General Odierno tag teamed a solution to Iraq had been laid out five months earlier, with the September 2008 release of Bob Woodward's book, *The War Within*.

In fact, anybody had access to (virtually) the same set of facts and trends in the year's previous reporting by Ricks in the *Washington Post*, and by Michael Gordon in the *New York Times*.

Woodward's book was largely dismissed by the leftoids because a careful reading pointed to an interpretation of events that indicated President George W. Bush had for years sought a strategy and the generals to make an Iraqi turnaround happen. Over and over, Woodward cites instances in which Bush startles his subordinates by asking if a new strategy will help the United States win. *Win* became a word that indicated disengagement from reality.

The War Within related the pressure Bush was coming under from even Republicans to squelch talk of winning. Bush said, "I'm not out of touch. I know how difficult it is. I talk about how difficult it is.

But I've got to make it clear for our troops, for Maliki, for the Iraqi people, that I am committed to winning and to victory."

If the *lefteros* could argue that Bush seemed disengaged, by two months before Election Day a credible record of Bush's determination to succeed was available to everyone who wanted to see. Bush wanted to win.

"I understand that for some people back here," Bush continued in his interview with Bob Woodward, "they don't like to hear it. And they think it's sort of out of touch. But I've got other audiences I have to address."

Bush wanted everybody involved to know he wanted to win.

Why was that an idea so foreign to all serious thinkers about the war? As events unfolded through the end of the Bush years and the start of Obama's, it certainly did appear that perseverance had paid off with success.

In the darkest days at the end of 2006, Bush went to a briefing at the State Department.

American civilians who were members of provincial reconstruction teams were planning to lay out for the president how they planned to help rebuild the country. Woodward reported that Bush told the group, "I want to know how to win."

It was in this meeting that a longtime foreign service officer who was speaking from Anbar province told Bush about the beginning of the Sunni Awakening, the anti-al Qaeda movement in Iraq that became a key element in the success of the surge in the months to come.

Bush was elated at the news, the briefers were dismayed. Nobody was talking about winning except the president, and all the others thought he was fooling himself.

Bush is quoted saying, "We have to do something different," while he continued to get a steady-as-she-goes series of briefings from generals Casey and Abizaid. Bush was about to decide both people and strategy had to go. Something new was needed. And the something new eventually succeeded. Those facts were on the record two months before the 2008 election, which up until the meltdown of the economy was the number one electoral issue.

Yet that would have been an inconvenient takeaway, leftistas thought, coming as it did only two months before Election Day.

Lefties buy books, but mostly books that support their views and validate their opinions. Woodward obliged with some truly strange personal conclusions about the war and about Bush—often dramatically at odds with his own reporting—in a seeming effort to move carloads of books, fatten royalty checks, and continue to get the best television time Washington, D.C., has to offer. Woodward is an author scrupulous about making sure he stays on the right side of the popular politics. A reporter with his finger in the wind, Woodward indicated by his conclusions that he understood there was no percentage in defending George W. Bush, and perhaps even less still in painting a picture in which flinty old John McCain seemed to have a better handle on the situation that the popular young orator Barack Obama.

The left's pet media ran with the book as big news, which it was because the *Washington Post* said so, in a series of Woodward-reported stories on the paper's front page. The book and Woodward's excerpts emphasized the Woodward conclusions, the reporting not so much. The left media tiptoed across the minefield of the revelations in Woodward's book, Election Day the goal. The real story was put away for safekeeping. Ignored. Shunted off.

In reality, the sweeping win of Obama was really the antiwar narrative staggering across the finish line November 7, 2008, events hot on his heels. The left covered up the real story—America wins!—and wouldn't be exposed for ignoring the truth until well after Inauguration Day.

If the years 2005 and 2006 were years of losing the war in Iraq and the president not wanting to know it, the years 2007 and 2008 were years of winning the war in Iraq and the left refusing to believe it.

Owing to high anticipation of an immediate troop drawdown that flowed naturally from the Democrat congressional victories and the recommendations of the Iraq Study Group (ISG), the shock was electric when it became clear at the end of 2006 that Bush was about to choose *more* troops in Iraq not fewer. The new strategy came to be called the surge. It was an idea first suggested by former Senator Chuck Robb in his role as a member of the Iraq Study Group. In fact, Robb's surge of troops was one of the recommendations Bush selected from a list of seventy-nine issued by the ISG, even as he rejected the group's major suggestions.

By the time lefties in D.C. and elsewhere on the group email lists were headed out for New Year's Eve parties, it was pretty clear Bush would choose the option of sending more troops to Iraq, and his announcement would come in early January 2007.

So the left went to war against a surge that hadn't been yet announced.

The din of objection insured January would be Surge Month in D.C. In the first few days of the month, the White House let it be known what the outlines of the surge plans were to be. Twenty thousand additional troops would be moved into Iraq, and billions of dollars more would be allocated to the struggle in Iraq. The media barely noticed that Bush was also changing generals. General George Casey, whose consistent policy was "leave to win," which was clearly not working, was replaced by Lt. General David Petraeus.

Petraeus had led the 101st Airborne in the early days of the war, during the invasion. He was also the author of a book on counterinsurgency tactics, and at the time he was picked for the command in Iraq he was completing the army's new and updated counterinsurgency manual.

First day back at work in the new year, Keith Olbermann launched into one of his vanity-fueled tirades against Bush and the surge, in a "Special Comment." The specialness is that it is long, but otherwise an Olbermann "Special Comment" was a rather *ordinaire* concoction of venom, accusation, free associating fact, comedy level righteous indignation, and spittle-flying certainty. "Your most respected generals see no value in a 'surge'—they could not possibly see it in this madness of 'sacrifice.' Your citizens, the people for whom you work, have told you they do not want this, and moreover, they do not want you to do this. Yet once again, sir . . ." he spit out the "sir" . . ."sir, you have ignored all of us."

Olbermann rose to a crescendo of indignation and delivered a mighty blow of sputtering outrage. "Mr. Bush, you do not own the country!"

You do not own the country!

Olbermann was a sports trading-card collector who took to radio in college and became a sportscaster known for his outrage at play he considered substandard, and management and players he considered stupid. Now by the miracle of transmogrification he had risen to a pulpit from which he could tell off a president.

"In point of fact, even if the civil war in Iraq somehow ended tomorrow, and the risk to Americans there ended with it, we would have already suffered a defeat—not fatal, not world-changing, not, but for the lives lost, of enduring consequence. But this country has already lost in Iraq, sir."

This country has already lost in Iraq, sir. Olbermann's denunciation echoed through the blogosphere. The left swooned.

A few days later, Senate majority leader Harry Reid would use almost the exact words ("This war is lost"), prompting an outcry from Republicans.

On Friday, January 5, the *New York Times*, the *Washington Post*, and the *Wall Street Journal* all carried stories of the plans that Bush would announce the following week in a speech to the nation.

That same Friday afternoon the Democrats in Congress sent a letter to Bush signed by Senate majority leader Harry Reid, and Speaker of the House Nancy Pelosi.

Referring to his speech to the nation scheduled for a few days later, they wrote, "Clearly this address presents you with another opportunity to make a long-overdue course correction. Despite the fact that our troops have been pushed to the breaking point and, in many cases, have already served multiple tours in Iraq, news reports suggest that you believe the solution to the civil war in Iraq is to require additional sacrifices from our troops and are therefore prepared to proceed with a substantial U.S. troop increase.

"Surging forces is a strategy that you have already tried, and that has already failed."

Senators trekked up to the White House to meet with Bush and discuss the strategy with the president. Senator Barack Obama said everybody, Republican and Democrat, wanted the best outcome for Iraq, but he personally opposed sending more U.S. troops to Iraq.

Senator John McCain wondered if the number of troops that would be sent would be enough. "I believe there's only one thing worse than an overstretched military and that's a broken and defeated military," he said, memorably. Senator Joe Lieberman stuck with McCain against his Democrat colleagues, which would become a pattern as the presidential election approached.

CNN reported that the latest polling showed less than a third of Americans still supported the war. Even Republican voters were disgusted, and Republican members of Congress were scared. CBS news reported on January 6 that Republican Susan Collins of Maine was reluctant to support a surge. Republican representative Heather Wilson of New Mexico said she was hesitant to support more U.S. troops, "to do for the Iraqis what the Iraqis will not do for themselves."

The next day, Saturday, the Common Dreams Center, "breaking news and views for the Progressive community," headlined the story as "Bush's Surge Strategy Faces Heavy Opposition."

Jim Lobe of Common Dreams wrote, "[Bush] may find himself in a tougher fight than he expected even a week ago."

Republican senator Norm Coleman, who would later be in a months-long recount fight in a dispute with challenger Democrat Al Franken over a handful of votes, spoke out for reconciliation among Iraqis. He said "[Iraq] doesn't need more Americans in the crosshairs."

Even Lt. Colonel (retired) Oliver North, Lobe said, had reported recent interviews with officers and soldiers in Iraq that "persuaded him that adding more troops to the 140,000 already deployed there would be a mistake."

Lobe asserted that the only political support Bush seemed to have was from the same neo-cons who had advocated the Iraq invasion in the first place. Fred Kagan said he thought it was imperative that no fewer than seven brigades (about 28,000 troops) would be required.

Bush had settled on five brigades, or about 20,000 troops, Lobe said, because it was the most troops "they can get away with."

Lobe's reporting was not the most influential of the day, but it reflected a tone that had permeated almost the entire media. General Casey appeared to be favoring reporters with his opinion that more American soldiers would make the situation worse, and it didn't take a lot of initiative for the left to contact Abizaid, who would have said he agreed with Casey, if he would speak to the press, even off the record. He and Casey were certainly in lockstep whenever they talked to the president by secure link. Woodward's book reported multiple occasions in which Casey made the same pitch for the same strategy of moving troops out, and turning over the responsibility to the Iraqis. Not mysteriously, this line was a common theme among the media.

Not to mention sources at the Pentagon and State Department who all would have said more troops was an ill-advised idea.

Only Bush, Petraeus, General Ray Odierno, and a behind-the-scenes player, retired General Jack Keane, wanted more troops. Woodward's book, a year and a half after the events, reported Bush even had to personally cross the Potomac to talk the Joint Chiefs into his plan.

But an honest reader, one who didn't ignore unpleasant reports, would not have been required to wait eighteen months for the publication of the Woodward book to be aware of these things.

On that next weekend, the Sunday editions weighed in. The *Washington Post* headlined, "Critics Say 'Surge' Is More of the Same." The report cited senior military leaders and commanders worried that the extra troops could "prove inadequate to quell sectarian violence and the Sunni insurgency," and that the move could "backfire."

An unsigned editorial in the *Washington Post* was the very picture of hand wringing, saying even if violence does plummet, "the logic of the surge assumes that while U.S. soldiers ensured security, Iraq's Sunni, Shiite, and Kurdish factions could be pressured into political accord. Yet given their recent behavior, it's hard to believe that the political leadership of any of Iraq's main factions is ready for compromise."

"Recent behavior" was a euphemism for the slaughter Shia death squads carried out on Sunnis in vulnerable neighborhoods. Bodies, sometimes headless, were turning up in the street by the dozens. Some appeared to have been tortured and killed by using electric drills on their heads.

The editorial accused Prime Minister Nouri al-Maliki, probably correctly, as leading a government that "has pursued a sectarian agenda."

The *Post* concluded noting that the Iraq Study Group, the Maliki government, and the outgoing U.S. commanders were all in favor of a strategy that emphasized the U.S. training of Iraqi troops, and Iraqi troops leading the fight against al Qaeda. "If he chooses escalation, Mr. Bush will have to work a lot harder than he has before to explain the mission that justifies the risk and to build support in Congress and with the public."

Two days later, Senate majority leader Harry Reid was reported to be seeking bipartisan opposition to the surge. By the time Bush announced his decision on national television, Reid was able to cobble together a bipartisan resolution condemning the plan to expand U.S. forces in Iraq by 20,000 troops.

January 10, 2007. President Bush addressed the nation and announced he was in fact ordering a surge of five brigades of troops, numbering 21,500, he was asking for another $100 billion for the war, and he was changing generals. Lt. General David Petraeus would be taking the place of General George Casey, who had long fought for a drawdown of troops. Casey moved to the Pentagon, Abizaid retired and Admiral Fox Fallon replaced him at Centcom. Lt. General Ray Odierno would be Petraeus' number two.

The significance of the change of command was ignored by the left media, yet the calculations of why the moves were made should have been easy for an open-minded media person to make. The generals and their views were well known. It was a complete change of direction, not merely an increase in troops. But what was obvious was also ignored.

Barack Obama spoke out in a Capitol Rotunda interview with MSNBC on the same day as the president's speech: "I am not persuaded that twenty thousand additional troops is going to solve the sectarian violence there, in fact I think it will do the reverse. I think it takes pressure off the Iraqis to arrive at the kind of political accommodations that every observer believes is the ultimate solution to the problems we face there. So I am going to actively oppose the president's proposal. I don't doubt his sincerity when he says this is the best approach there, but I think he is wrong, and I think the American people think he is wrong."

Bob Woodward's *The War Within* would later document Bush's growing discontent with Casey's approach, and his insistence that the only way to win was, essentially, to leave Iraq. Casey repeated his belief in a drawdown so many times that Bush had grown visibly annoyed hearing the same thing from Casey. In other words, the *Washington Post*'s own reporter was hoarding news and perspective on the public discussion that would have been informed by his information. The *Washington Post* editor, Len Downie, was supposed to know everything Woodward knew, and assuming Woodward kept up his end of the bargain and Downie was informed, it means Downie was letting his own editorial writers opine without being fully informed.

Woodward knew Bush was placing great faith in Maliki, simply because Maliki was an elected leader, and Bush felt Maliki must succeed.

The public implication of the *Post*'s reporting was that Bush was letting Maliki run amok, enabling Shia sectarian violence. The true story, withheld by the *Post*'s star reporter, was that Bush was personally working Maliki with many phone calls, and a few visits to Baghdad. Ultimately, Bush's faith in Maliki paid off, and one might have guessed it would had Woodward not been sitting on information for his fourth book in the Bush at War series.

The public did not take to the surge. On January 12, two days after Bush's speech, the AP-Ipsos poll showed 70 percent of Americans opposed sending more troops to Iraq. A few days later, a Fox News poll showed that most Americans thought the surge was the last chance in Iraq. Only one third of those polled supported Bush and the plan for Iraq.

The fury on the left was volcanic.

A little more than a week after the announcement, Nancy Pelosi told Diane Sawyer on *Good Morning America* that Bush "has to answer for this war. He has dug a hole so deep he can't even see the light on this. It's a tragedy. It's a stark blunder."

The heavy breathing did not stop the new strategy. The Democrats didn't dare deny funding to troops in the field, and the decision to send the extra troops was not theirs to make. Bush and Petraeus got their five brigades, though Woodward's *War Within* later revealed that Petraeus was not only fighting Democrats, but the Pentagon brass who wanted to dribble the brigades in, and hope that all were not needed.

A few weeks later, in late February, former secretary of state Madeleine Albright spoke at the Carter Center with former president Jimmy Carter at her side. "I think Iraq is going to go down in history as the greatest disaster in American foreign policy," she declared.

Carter chimed in, saying that since Albright was in office "there has been a reduction almost all over the world in trust and esteem by foreigners toward Americans."

While General Petraeus immediately put his new strategy and tactics to work in Iraq and awaited the arrival of fresh troops, the left in America also went to work to make certain public opinion remained opposed to what was happening in Iraq.

In March, *Rolling Stone* magazine convened a panel of eminences to discuss the possible outcomes in Iraq. The group included Zbigniew Brzezinski, Carter's national security advisor; Richard Clarke, former "counterterrorism czar," aka Clinton Guy Who Missed bin Laden; Nir Rosen, author and "expert on Iraq's spiral into civil war"; General Tony McPeak (retired), member Joint Chiefs of Staff during the Gulf War; Bob Graham, former chair, Senate Select Intelligence Committee; Michael Scheuer, former chief of CIA's bin Laden unit; Juan Cole, professor of Middle East history at the University of Michigan; and others.

As this collection of grandees spoke on various issues such as "Best Case Scenario," "Most Likely Scenario," etc., it seemed an especially dour group. Nir Rosen declared, "There is no best case scenario for Iraq." Richard Clarke stated flatly, "All the things they say will happen are already happening. Iraq is already a base for terrorists. There is already a civil war. We've got 150,000 troops there now and we can't stop it."

Looking back, with the success of the surge in mind, one wonders why these very smart people didn't bother to notice who was in charge in Iraq—General Petraeus—and therefore didn't look into his former success in Iraq with the 101st Airborne, and his published papers on counterinsurgency. People like Clarke especially should have known, and one suspects, did know, what Petraeus could and would do. Willful denial of a record of success indicated the editors of *Rolling Stone* were in fact biased toward failure rather than success. The panel was loaded with doomsayers.

Scheuer, for instance, already considered the war lost: "No matter what happens now, the Islamists will have beaten both of the superpowers—first the Soviet Union in Afghanistan, and now the United States in the heart of Islam. The impact of that in Islamic civilization is going to be enormous."

Regarding al Qaeda in particular, Scheuer was especially gloomy; "We have made bin Laden a prophet. His organizing concept for al Qaeda was 'The Russians are a lot tougher than the Americans. If we can beat the Russians, then we can eventually beat the Americans.' Even more important, al Qaeda will have contiguous territory on the Arab peninsula to attack [Americans]."

McPeak, who seemed nettled by the fact his advice was being

ignored in the military circles he once commanded, predicted utter failure: "We're going to see a full-scale intercommunal war that may not burn out until one side is all dead, all gone. The Kurds would like to sit on the sidelines, but I don't see how they stay out, especially up in the Kirkuk area, where they sit on a lot of oil. This is going to be ethnic cleansing like we had in Kosovo or Bosnia—but written big, in capital letters. And we can't stop it."

Perhaps most outrageous, blowing away fierce contenders for the honor, were the statements of Charles (Chas) Freeman. He was ambassador to Saudi Arabia during the Gulf War and in the new Obama administration he would be touted as the likely pick to head the National Intelligence Council. He'd also come under fire from Jewish groups for his involvement in a publishing venture of a Saudi-sponsored school textbook, *Arab World Studies Notebook*. The schoolbook was controversial owing to statements it contained that ran counter to American policy toward Israel and Arab states. At the time he was making his statements to *Rolling Stone*, Freeman was waiting in the wings for an Obama White House, or some other Democrat.

"The most efficient way to avoid mass killings," Freeman said, "is to help the Shiites win fast, consolidate their damn dictatorship, and get the hell out. The level of anarchy and hatred and emotional disturbance is such that it's very hard to imagine anything except a Saddam-style reign of terror succeeding in pacifying the place."

This line was an outgrowth of one strain of Bush administration thinking, referred to as the 80 percent solution. The Shia, with 80 percent of the population, won the election. Period. Sunnis would just have to deal with minority status. Freeman's position took that line and extended it to an acceptance of death squads, genocide, rape, dismemberment.

The *Rolling Stone* panel was asked to describe their "Worst Case Scenario": "This could become the Islamic equivalent of the Thirty Years War between Protestants and Catholics in Europe in the 1600s—a religious schism that blossoms into overt mayhem and murder and massacres and warfare. The various Iraqi factions will obtain the backing of other Middle Eastern states as they conduct their ideological and ethnic struggle. It will be a free-for-all that spreads beyond the anarchic zone of Iraq."

One by one, the assembled experts piled on the doom and dread.

It was a wining formula. After all, hadn't the Democrats grabbed control of Congress, dishing out a steady diet of disaster, and didn't they have eyes on the White House using the same tactics—attacking the war, the people who started it, the people who were running it? The list of charges was bookended by two sacred concepts: it was a war of choice, and it was America's most humiliating loss.

Democrats had their face rubbed in war in Vietnam, now it was the Republicans' turn.

Rolling Stone magazine, a periodical of often insensible pop culture, presents pieces like this as big journalism, dramatic pictures, big type-set, stark graphics. This is a magazine that gives the same self important presentation to the words of P Diddy or 50 Cent. Its publisher, Jann Wenner, delights in conducting "big" interviews of big figures. Vapid, empty, fawning, these interviews add nothing but goo to the public debate on issues, and are transparently vanity devices for the inflation of the ego of Wenner. Since Wenner founded the magazine in San Francisco around the time of the Summer of Love, *Rolling Stone* has assumed the role of an authoritative voice exposing pop-culture readers to "heavy" thoughts from "heavy" people. On Iraq, *Rolling Stone* and Wenner made sure the people featured for their observations and opinions espoused intriguing visions of an Xbox nightmare world as the only possible result of the war. These were the narrative points that laid the foundation for thousands of jokes, from people like Jon Stewart and Bill Maher, both comedians with staffs of busy and obsessive Bush-hating writers, all working up comedic material based on the idea that the war was a blunder before and a failure now.

The narrative was also advanced in the traditional, that is, more credible, media. April 11, 2007, the news leaked that three retired generals turned down the job of coordinating Iraq policy for the White House. Nobody wanted the job of war czar because it all seemed so directionless. Evidently, none of the three were allowed to speak to Bush, who by this time was focused entirely on "What do we do to win?" By mid-April 2007, Reuters was reporting that Republicans were fighting back against the charge that the war was lost. But the bad news kept coming: Defense Secretary Robert Gates announced an extension of all military tours in Iraq to fifteen months. It was a bitter disappointment to many military families.

Bush was speaking in Ohio, where he was asked to compare Iraq to Vietnam, and the president responded that a premature withdrawal of American troops from Iraq would produce the same sort of chaos.

At the moment, Bush was threatening a veto of legislation he himself requested—$100 billion in war funding—if Democrats persisted in attempts to include a troop withdrawal timetable.

Bush spoke on a Thursday. The day before he had told Senate majority leader Harry Reid he would veto his own war-funding bill if Reid didn't back down on the withdrawal timetable. On that late afternoon Wednesday, in a private meeting, Reid had told Bush "this war is lost."

As Bush spoke in Ohio, Reid brought that private conversation to the Senate floor, April 19, 2007, where he said, "As long as we follow the president's path in Iraq, *the war is lost*."

Reid's quote—"this war is lost"—became a staple of talk radio, and an emblematic sound bite for Republicans and conservative war supporters to expose the truth about the new Democrat majority: it seemingly had no interest in winning the war, or even the lower threshold of "succeeding." They wanted to declare a loss and leave.

Senate minority leader Mitch McConnell said, "I can't begin to imagine how our troops in the field, who are risking their lives every day, are going to react when they get back to their bases and hear that the Democrat leader in the United States Senate has declared the war is lost."

That same day a car bomb in Iraq had killed 200 Iraqis, a particularly gruesome attack that shocked an American public so inured to reports of violence and mayhem.

By Friday, Reid was still under fire for the statement. He responded that highly placed people in the administration knew "this war is lost, and the surge is not accomplishing anything as indicated by the extreme violence in Iraq yesterday."

As Thomas Ricks reported in *The Gamble* during these days of pessimism in Washington, American troops were involved in some of the toughest fighting of the war, under attack by Sunni insurgents, and al Qaeda's suicide bombers. The arrival of the last of the surge brigades would not occur for two months, in June.

The Democrat congress was standing in the way of the new round of funding for troops, in the absence of a timeline. Democrats Diane

Watson and Zoe Lofgren of California wanted the Congress to enforce an end date of September 2007. That was the date at which
Petraeus was to report back to Congress on the progress of the war,
so in effect those radical California Democrats were willing to say to
the general trying to win the war, "We're done with this war even
before you tell us how it's going."

One of the key strategies of the surge was protecting the Iraqi
population from the sectarian death squads, the Sunni insurgents,
and the al Qaeda provocateurs. The technique employed by generals
Petraeus and Odierno was to put American troops in Iraqi neighborhoods, small outposts of approximately forty men, to combat
violence aimed at Iraqis. Even in 2007, the news was not always
good. In April a twin truck bombing on a U.S. outpost in Baqouba
collapsed a two-story building housing U.S. troops. Nine soldiers
were killed. The deaths were the single worst combat loss for the
82nd Airborne since Vietnam. Al Qaeda in Iraq, the organization of
the late Abu Musab al Zarqawi, took credit for the attack in a message that praised two "knights" who stuck the "crusaders."

The media was not heartened by the fighting that took place in
the first six months of the surge. It didn't see how fighting could be
"winning."

For the left, it was just more of the same. The very fighting that
made it possible for American troops to establish outposts in Sunni
areas, begin to protect the local Iraqis, and eventually flip them to
the American and Iraqi government side was dismissed as just more
American brutishness and futility.

Referring to that very attack, the antiwar Open Democracy Web
site, based in Britain but widely read among the American left, wrote
two days after the big Baqouba attack, "It is becoming apparent that
the insurgents are already finding the means to counter the strategy embodied in the surge, even if the process has been underway
for only a little over ten weeks. That is an unexpected and ominous
development for the U.S. forces in Iraq, and indeed for the Bush administration itself."

This very artcle, by Paul Rogers, had begun by citing several articles published in America and Britain that offered evidence the surge
was working. They were ignored or dismissed out of hand.

One of those had appeared in the *Weekly Standard* by Reuel Marc Gerecht, a former CIA analyst. Gerecht had cemented his bona fides as a hawk with the left, and therefore damned his reputation, by telling the often excitable blogger Andrew Sullivan that he personally approved of physically coercive techniques of interrogation. In his *Weekly Standard* piece on the surge, he opined with a shot directly at the left: "House Democrats should admit they are in a predicament: The electoral interests of their party are at odds with the interests of the country in Iraq." In other words, Gerecht was serving notice that the left's interest in losing in Iraq was becoming obvious.

Gerecht acknowledged that the full effects of the surge would not be seen until the midpoint in the year, then two months off, "But militarily the United States is finally waging a counterinsurgency that makes sense: We are focusing our efforts on securing Iraqi lives and property. Incrementally, in many quarters of Baghdad, daily life for Iraqis appears to be getting better."

Another claim of success dismissed by Open Democracy and the American left came from noted neo-conservative Frederick Kagan, published in the *Guardian*, in Britain.

"At this early stage," Kagan wrote of the surge, "the most positive development is a rise in hostility to al Qaeda in the Sunni community. Al Qaeda has responded with its own 'surge,' which so far as not revived support for the terrorists or reignited sectarian violence."

Kagan, of course, had put his finger on exactly what eventually did turn Iraq around: the rejection of al Qaeda by Iraqis, particularly the Sunni minority.

Unlike the left, which pronounced the failure of the surge and the war at every juncture, people like Kagan and Gerecht were writing in April 2007, that the surge might work, but there were no guarantees. "Can America succeed in Iraq?" asked Kagan. "Definitely. Will we? It's too soon to say. The most that can be said now is that we seem to be turning a corner."

Nonethless, in America the left-wing bloggers continued to condemn the surge and the war itself with a self-important expertise. The blogger epluribusunum, posting on the Daily Kos in May 2007, a full month before all the surge troops would be in place, wrote: "Thinking that a 'surge' in Iraq will solve the problems we face there is grossly mistaken and doomed to failure. Anyone who believes this does not understand modern warfare."

Comments like this positioned military amateurs on the left to later go after General Petraeus as if he were no more than a failing schoolboy.

In early May, al Qaeda's second in command, Ayman al-Zawahiri issued a videotape saying the U.S. congressional bill calling for a troop withdrawal from Iraq was proof of America's defeat. "We ask Allah that [the Americans] only get out [of Iraq] after losing 200,000 to 300,000 killed, so that we give the blood spillers in Washington and Europe an unforgettable lesson to motivate them to review their entire doctrinal and moral system." The American left seemed not very concerned that its desires to lose and leave Iraq were seconded by al Qaeda.

In June the Council on Foreign Relations published an analysis by Lionel Beehner that declared, "The surge is faltering." The headline said it all.

In fact, the temptation to doubt good news proved too strong to resist for many in the left media. *Time*'s Joe Klein went to Iraq and spent a few days with Petraeus and Odierno, visiting troops and seeing the turn against al Qaeda firsthand. He acknowledged the Sunni tribes were being flipped against al Qaeda, but was pessimistic that a Shiite-led government could ever make peace with its own Sunni countrymen. While admitting Petraeus' counterinsurgency techniques had worked early in the war in Mosul, he was quick to point out Mosul was ultimately a failure because U.S. troops were spread so thin. "Now it seems likely that Petraeus will suffer the same fate in Baghdad as he did in Mosul," Klein concluded, with an eye to Petraeus' scheduled report to Congress in September that year. "He doesn't want to be the fall guy," Klein quoted a Petraeus aide. "And he doesn't deserve to be," said Klein, but "It is hard to imagine . . . how this can turn out any other way."

With three months to go before Petraeus would appear before Congress, *Time* magazine was already declaring the general had another failure on his hands, and ultimately, an American loss.

Barack Obama was starting to maneuver. On July 18, 2007, he said: "My assessment is that the surge has not worked and we will not see a different report eight weeks from now." He was aiming straight at the heart of the American left.

The left's media march to losing Iraq continued all through the summer of 2007. The *Times* of London asked in July, "Iraq: Has America lost the will to win?"

The piece dutifully acknowledged "that there have been some notable successes, with U.S. forces teaming up with formerly hostile Sunni tribesmen to take on al Qaeda," but noted—correctly— "even if the war is still winnable in Iraq, it is now being lost at home," and while President Bush thinks the fight can be won, "increasingly, it is an argument between the president and everybody else." The article cited Republicans who were either privately already convinced the war could not be won, or were in open revolt against the Bush administration. "Historians might conclude that this was the week Americans lost the will to win."

Also in July, in Salon.com, former diplomat Peter Galbraith (a onetime paid advisor to the semi-autonomous Kurds in Iraq's north) declared, "The Iraq war is lost—Bush and his band of backers won't admit that, but their strategy is already defined by the specter of an American defeat."

In August, antiwar.com published a study by the leftist Center for American Progress and *Foreign Policy* magazine, both of which cooperated in a survey of a hundred former secretaries of state, top commanders in the military, senior intelligence officials, and academics to assess the surge and the Iraq War. Their conclusion: the surge and the War on Terror are failing.

All of this was building to a crescendo as an early September date Petraeus had with the Congress of the United States approached. Petraeus was to deliver his first progress report on Iraq, and Democrats in Congress were preparing to open fire.

As August unfolded into September, the early conclusions about the surge built to a cacophony of criticism, much of it informed by old news of the first half of the year. The surge was not working, it was a failure, it was a mirage, it was beyond America's reach, it was never going to work, and it couldn't have worked. In fact, Petraeus was preparing to demonstrate that the new strategy, which included the surge and related tactics, was working, and rather dramatically.

If Petraeus had any time to keep up with the news back home, he had to know he'd be walking into a hostile environment in which personal credibility would not necessarily repulse attacks.

On September 10 and 11, Petraeus and Ambassador Ryan Crocker were set to testify before the Senate Armed Services Committee.

The morning Petraeus was to begin his testimony, the *New York Times* carried a full page ad from MoveOn.org, an ultraliberal political action organization. MoveOn's ad was headlined "General Petraeus or General Betrayus?" and stated flatly, "General Petraeus is a military man constantly at war with the facts."

This was a military man the left should have loved. Petraeus was a leading proponent of the notion the United States could not kill its way out of the war. He was employing the very tactics the left should have embraced. Reason was rejected in favor of antiwar, anti-Bush passion.

It was a stinging personal attack on a distinguished military man who didn't deserve it. Petraeus was stunned by the bitterness and the sheer audacity of the assault on his character. He proceeded to give his testimony over the next two days in a calm and professional manner, but he was visibly shaken, and subdued.

The reaction against MoveOn was immediate and should have been expected. President Bush called the ad "disgusting." Even the left-wing blog DemocratUnderground decried the attack, not because it was inaccurate, or low, or shameful, but because it gave the opposition talking points. It also revealed the left for what it was: a collection of shallow, sophomoric name-callers who would sink to any level, even beneath the gutter.

There was a fierce backlash. The *New York Times* came under scrutiny for giving MoveOn what seemed to be an especially low rate, about half what would normally have been charged any other customer. The *New York Times* seemed to have been caught endorsing the political position of an advertiser.

Except for Senator Joe Lieberman, no Democrat senator condemned the ad. Suspicions were raised that some had been warned it was coming, however, by the appearance of a quote in Politico .com, a well-connected political news site, from an unnamed senator: "Nobody wants to call Petraeus a liar on national television. We expect outside groups will do it for us."

MoveOn's Eli Pariser had been quoted, famously, after the 2006 congressional elections in which Democrats swept to victory, in no small part with the help of money and advertising from MoveOn. org, "Now it's our party. We bought it. We own it. And now we're going to take it back."

When the far left embarrassed the Democratic Party by setting off an IED targeted at an American general with an unblemished record, the nation should have been able to see what was taking place. When not a single Democrat senator would object to the MoveOn ad, it was evident that they simply did not want to hear from an important American commander on his assessment of the most pressing issue in American life. The Democrats stood naked for the country to see, but the nation was wearing its blinders.

Petraeus gave his testimony, answered questions, and returned as quickly as he could to the safety of the war zone.

Perhaps Petraeus didn't realize what he was getting into. Looking back, he might have been able to see the broad outlines of the presidential campaign looming before him as he sat at the felt-covered table giving his testimony before the Senate.

A lame duck in the White House meant there would be a free-for-all in both parties, as men and women who considered themselves to be presidential timber maneuvered to show the American public their best stuff. On the Democrat side, it was easy to guess everyone would run against the war. By the time the primary season kicked off, it was Democrat dogma that the war in Iraq was wrongheaded, badly executed, and hurting the country more than it was helping. Democrats wanted out.

Barack Obama weighed in the day after Petraeus' testimony concluded, September 12, 2007: "Let me be clear. There is no military solution in Iraq. There never was. The best way to protect our security is to pressure Iraq's leaders to resolve their civil war and to immediately begin to remove our combat troops."

Neither of Obama's assertions was actually in much disagreement with Petraeus. But his words were crafted to sound like opposition for his left audience.

On the Republican side, support for the war was lukewarm to a bit warmer. Only John McCain tried to speak clearly about the impact of not winning in Iraq, and only McCain spoke enthusiastically about the surge.

Campaigning, Obama's tone before rallies that were grabbing headlines for the sheer size and enthusiasm of the crowds was growing sharper, and more critical of Bush, but also implicitly more harsh toward Petraeus: "We don't need any more spin about the surge that was supposed to see the Iraqis step up. We don't need any more spin about the surge succeeding in what it was supposed to do, which was get the Iraqis to stand up and take responsibility for their own future so we could bring our troops home. We don't need any more tough talk from George Bush or John McCain, because the Taliban's still fighting in Afghanistan, the terrorists who hit us on 9/11 are still at large. We don't need more leaders who just see what they want to see in Iraq. It's time to recognize where we are in Iraq."

In reality, at that moment the tide was turning, and Petraeus' troops and the Iraqis were cornering and killing al Qaeda by the hundreds.

For Petraeus and the United States military, if it wasn't exactly clear what was shaping up, it soon would be.

Throughout the presidential primaries, two important developments were underway: The surge was working in Iraq and that success was almost completely ignored at home.

A year from the looming Election Day in November 2008, Barack Obama appeared on *Meet the Press* with Tim Russert. He stepped up his criticism of the war and President Bush. "Finally in 2006 and 2007, even after we'd had an election, George Bush continued to want to pursue a course that didn't withdraw troops from Iraq but actually double downed, and initiated the surge. And I said at that stage, very clearly, not only had we not seen improvements but we were potentially worsening a situation there."

One of the longest pre-primary seasons on record was about to conclude as nine candidates on the Democrat side, and twelve Republicans raced through the holidays and toward the start of a blast of primaries.

The first big primary date, Super Tuesday, occurred February 5, 2008. Barack Obama nosed out Hillary Clinton on the Democrat side, and John McCain edged out Mitt Romney on the Republican side.

The primary season was beginning to shape up as a contest between the antiwar, anti-surge candidate Barack Obama, and the win-the-war, pro-surge candidate John McCain. Little would change through the primary and general election campaign, except the surge and the war were turning into successes for the United States, and the news was buried as if it were just another casualty of Iraq.

Hillary Clinton, hobbled by a vote to approve the war, was considered much too muddled on Iraq to suit the tastes of the left. The American left wanted clear, albeit irrational, opposition to the war, and that person was Obama.

Ten days after the first primary contest, February 15, 2008, AntiWar.com ran a piece by Ali Gharib, a longtime antiwar figure in the leftist blogosphere. Gharib quoted extensively from a report titled "Awakening to the New Danger in Iraq" from the Center for American Progress, the left-wing political action group funded by George Soros, and run by John Podesta, one of the most committed and focused leftists to emerge from the administration of former President Bill Clinton.

The CAP report stated, "The conventional wisdom among most conservatives and Washington policy elites is that the surge has 'worked.' This . . . ignores the fact that the fundamental objectives of the surge—to create a more sustainable security framework for Iraq and advance Iraq's political transition—have not been met."

Gharib and AntiWar.com declared, "The surge period has, in fact, quelled violence across Iraq to some degree, but critics argue that the drop in violent attacks has less to do with the increased number of U.S. troops and more to do with the newfound cooperation of Sunni groups who used to align themselves with the violent insurgency."

This line of reasoning was widely adopted on the left as a way to counter the obvious facts of the war—sectarian violence was down, and one of the strategies of the surge was working extremely well. That was Petraeus' aim, to turn the Sunni minority in Iraq from enemies to cooperating allies. The very tactic that was reducing violence and turning the tide in Iraq was neatly flipped into a criticism of the success itself.

Barack Obama, a Democrat primary candidate on a roll, made a significant concession February 21, 2008, in a candidate debate sponsored by CNN: "I think it is indisputable that we've seen violence reduced in Iraq." It was a bombshell statement, a headline-grabbing concession, but one for which he was forgiven by the left in its growing ardor for the transformative candidate.

Rolling Stone magazine published a piece by a young American-born reporter of Arab descent, Nir Rosen, March 6, 2008, titled "The Myth of the Surge." It criticized Petraeus' tactic of arming Sunnis to protect themselves from al Qaeda terrorists who were attempting to take control of the Sunni minority. Rosen was well down the path of defeat in Iraq. He'd previously published "If America Left Iraq: The Case for Cutting and Running," in the *Atlantic Monthly* in 2005, and had published a book about the occupation of Iraq called *In the Belly of the Green Bird*. Rosen was read widely by the antiwar left, and was committed to a line of reasoning that said America could not win in Iraq, so it should give up trying.

Polling showed that Americans were more than ever convinced the war had been a mistake and it was not panning out as promised. A CBS News poll released March 19, 2008, showed by a margin of 64 percent to 29 percent that Americans believed the war was not worth the cost to the United States. The Pew Research Center released an analysis of its own polling that same day showing that while more Americans had noted the war was going better, it was also true that more Americans now said the initial decision to go to war was wrong.

A few days later in March, the McClatchy Washington Bureau published a piece by Leila Fadel and Nancy Youssef that asked, "Is the 'success' of U.S. surge in Iraq about to unravel?"

The piece was posted on the left-wing *Huffington Post*, and quoted widely on other Web sites of the left.

The reaction among the left was perhaps predictable. "You cannot drink the Kool-Aid that is being shoved down your throat 24/7," one commentor wrote. "There comes a time when you can no longer tolerate propaganda and must face the truth, no matter what it is. And here is the truth: the government of the United States of America was seized by a group of pretenders who thrust it into a war of conquest for their own personal gain."

Many other comments followed along the same lines.

Beginning in March 2008, Nouri al-Maliki began taking personal control of Iraqi security, ordering three Iraqi divisions into Basra, to dislodge and defeat militias loyal to Muqtada al-Sadr, the firebrand Shiite cleric who had taken up residence in Iran, for his personal safety.

Maliki called Petraeus and asked for support as he and the Shiite government officials were going to lead an Iraqi invasion of Basra to root out Iranian-backed Shiite militias. The Americans had been waiting what seemed like forever for the Iraqis to seize the moment as Maliki said he would do, so Petraeus immediately agreed.

Backed by American troops and air power, Maliki succeeded, and the Iranians and al-Sadr conceded defeat in a negotiated settlement.

While Maliki was making his moves on the battlefield in Mosul and Basra, Barack Obama said on March 19, 2008, "In order to end this war responsibly I will immediately begin to remove our troops from Iraq. I will begin to responsibly remove one to two combat brigades each month. If we start with the number of brigades we have in Iraq today, we can remove all of them in sixteen months." Gone were the days of 2004 and 2006 when Obama was opposed to rigid deadlines and timetables.

Yet only a few days later, on April 8, 2008, Obama hedged again on the surge in a Senate hearing: "I also think the surge has reduced violence and provided breathing room."

Despite a lukewarm endorsement from the Democrat front-runner, Petraeus came back to give Congress another report April 11, 2008, evidently aware of the toxic public attitudes about a war that was succeeding, at long last. As was his style, he rejected triumphalism and victory declarations, evidently cognizant of the reaction that talk of "victory" would inevitably cause from the left, which was clearly driving public opinion.

"We haven't turned any corners. We haven't seen any lights at the end of the tunnel. The champagne bottle's been pushed to the back of the refrigerator," Petraeus said. True, modesty earned him a clean getaway from Washington back to the war zone, but it also emboldened his enemies at home.

A week later Alternet posted an interview with the British author Jonathan Steele, a correspondent for the leftist *Guardian* newspaper in Britain. His new book was called *Defeat: Why They Lost Iraq.*

Steele said, "Certainly, it is a defeat. If the neo-con project was to have secular, pro-Western, stable democracy in Iraq, it's very unstable, not pro-Western, not secular. And it's a defeat in foreign policy terms because far from being a launchpad for pressure on Iran, Iran has benefited from the invasion."

The left seemed not to notice or care that American troops were fighting at least three wars at once: against Iraqi insurgents, against al Qaeda in Iraq, and against Iran. Seventy-three percent of American troops killed during this period were from Iranian-made bombs. Called explosive formed projectiles, or EFPs, they were a sophisticated and especially lethal armor-piercing design, manufactured in Iran. Indeed, the leading candidate of the left was being lauded for his willingness to sit for talks with Iran with no pre-conditions. One pre-condition could have been a demand from the United States that Iran stop supplying these bombs to Iraqi insurgents.

Within days Gallup was reporting opposition to the war at home had hit a new high. Not only that, the new high in Iraq War opposition is also notable because it was the highest "mistake" percentage Gallup had ever measured for an active war involving the United States, two points higher than the number who said the Vietnam War was a mistake.

Gallup said opposition to the war had been "cemented" in the public mind.

It was the job of the Democrats and the left to make certain opposition would remain cemented, even if American commanders and troops were seeing success with their surge efforts.

To that end, despite his acknowledgment of the signs of surge success, Obama aimed his rhetoric at the bull's-eye of the antiwar left. On May 2, 2008, having secured the Democrat nomination, candidate Obama said many times on the campaign trail that he was the only candidate who opposed the war from the start—from 2002 and each year thereafter, and he promised that as president he would fulfill the promise of that opposition and finally bring the war to an end.

Viewing the politics from afar, Petraeus was faced with a paradox: The standard bearer of his Democrat critics knew the war was now succeeding, but was also promising to walk away.

Barack Obama, July 2, 2008, appeared on television for an interview with Wolf Blitzer of CNN: "The extraordinary work our troops have done there, they have performed brilliantly throughout the process, and obviously I am very pleased to have seen the reductions in violence that have occurred over the last several months. There is no doubt because of their heroism and their outstanding work we had the opportunity to salvage the situation in Iraq."

Four days later the *Times* of London reported Iraqis were leading the final purge of al Qaeda from Iraq: "American and Iraqi forces are driving al Qaeda in Iraq out of its last redoubt in the north of the country in the culmination of one of the most spectacular victories of the war on terror." Nouri al-Maliki, the Iraqi prime minister, proclaimed the death of a major al Qaeda commander, the capture of 1,000 suspects, and an Iraqi defeat of terrorism.

By this time Obama was no longer a man running for the nomination, but a man who had captured the nomination and was now running for president against John McCain, a longtime proponent of the surge.

On July 14, 2008, Obama published an op-ed piece in the *New York Times*, "My Plan for Iraq."

"Unlike Senator John McCain, I opposed the war in Iraq before it began, and would end it as president." He once again said the war was a "grave" mistake, that it distracted the United States from the fight against al Qaeda, and the Taliban, and that Iraq had nothing to do with the 9/11 attacks. "Nearly every threat we face—from Afghanistan to al Qaeda to Iran—has grown."

Obama and the left either didn't believe Nouri al-Maliki and the American generals when they had said only a few days before that al Qaeda had been routed in Iraq, or didn't believe the *Times* of London when it reported a "spectacular victory."

Obama had rushed to print because a day or two earlier Maliki had made the comment that a timetable for the removal of American troops would be good for the Iraqi government. Obama leapt on the apparent policy disagreement between the Iraqi and American governments. Bush was still insisting the removal of American troops would depend on the conditions on the ground.

Obama's concluding line was one he would ride to office: "It's time to end this war."

That same day, Obama's official campaign Web site purged his previous critiques of the surge. The *New York Daily News* reported an old Iraq plan in which he stated, "The surge is not working," had been wiped clean. Also disappeared was an earlier claim that improvements in Iraq security—especially in Anbar province—were due to Sunni sheikhs, not U.S. military muscle.

On July 21, 2008, Obama visited Iraq in a highly publicized tour cum photo op, and after meeting with members of the Iraqi government, he sat down for an interview with *Nightline*'s Terry Moran. He promised a troop phase out if he were elected, and he startled everyone—even his most ardent supporters—with a statement that seemed self-contradictory. Given the successes of the surge and the Sunni Awakening movement, would he look back and say if he would have supported the surge knowing then what he knew now. Amazingly, Obama said no.

Petraeus and the American public were then faced with the reality that the leader of the left was so committed to an antiwar position he would have chosen troop withdrawals, leaving a chaotic, deadly, perhaps genocidal Iraq, rather than embrace a strategy that had proven successful.

Was Obama committed to losing in Iraq?

The next day he was interviewed by Katie Couric of CBS News. She asked him what he had noticed about Iraq since his last visit in 2006—a full two years earlier. "There's no doubt the scary situation's improved," he said.

To her credit, Couric pressed Obama with four specific questions on how he could say he would still oppose the surge even knowing it would be successful. Obama meandered through a long answer about how the $10 billion a month war cost could have been put to better use at home, but she kept pressing. Finally, a cornered Obama sighed, and said, "Katie, I have no idea what would have happened had we applied my approach, which was to put more pressure on the Iraqis to arrive at a political reconciliation. So this is all hypotheticals."

Couric gave up and moved on, but Obama's naked willingness to accept defeat rather than take a chance on a win was exposed for all to see. This only endeared him to the left. Losing a war was a winning strategy to those on the left, and Obama would deviate from the formula for electoral success only at his peril.

McCain's people jumped on it. "Obama 'Would Lose a War' to Win an Election" blared a McCain campaign press release. They might as well have saved their breath. Hammering home this point would only help Obama with the left and its new camp followers in the American electorate.

However, the big brains of the left realized the now completely exposed contradiction that had opened their favored candidate to heightened suspicions from an American public, which might find itself suddenly pleased—and surprised—that the Iraq war was indeed turning.

Joe Palermo, a professor at Cal State University Sacramento, picked up the cudgel the day Obama was squirming under Katie Couric's persistent and skeptical questioning. "John McCain's 'surge' success story is a lie," Palermo headlined his piece on the *Huffington Post*.

"The United States destroyed Iraq in order to save it. Just look at Falluja, or Baghdad with its hideous blast walls and checkpoints. That place will never be the same. In a just world the United States would pay reparations to Iraq for a hundred years."

In the comments section that followed, someone named Lolliedot-com wrote, "It's gonna be a lot like Rwanda. Someday we'll make a movie about the truth of what's happening over there. It will win an Oscar. I used to be a real newshound. I trust it so little anymore that the only TV news I watch is on Comedy Central."

In fact, the left had broadly adopted comedians and sportscasters and theater critics as its leading political reporters.

Still, it was necessary to keep beating down the narrative of winning that would not die. The Associated Press moved an analysis piece by Robert Burns on July 26, 2008, that opened with this line: "The United States is now winning the war that two years ago seemed lost."

Immediately the left-wing blogs went to work. Noted Arabist Juan Cole wrote on Alternet just a few days later. Cole claimed that the surge was not a particular success, but that violence in Iraq was on a downward trend because deadly ethnic cleansing had been "brutally effective."

In mid-August Obama had the gall to attack McCain over his judgment on the Iraq surge. The occasion of the attack was a speech before the VFW in Florida, and Obama's desire to answer a charge made a day earlier by McCain that "behind all these claims and positions by Senator Obama lies the ambition to be president." The truth hurt, and Obama bristled.

Obama listed Senator McCain's positions on the invasion of Iraq, including his expectation the United States would be greeted as liberators, and that the cost of the war would be paid by Iraqi oil revenues. "Senator McCain now argues that despite these costly strategic errors, his judgment has been vindicated due to the results of the surge."

The last day of August 2008, the *New York Times* military reporter Michael Gordon reported that the background of the decision to surge troops in Iraq was a tumultuous debate inside the White House. Bush was opposed in his decision by the ambassador in Iraq, Zalmay Khalilzad, the State Department was opposed, the Pentagon had its doubts, and even the American general commanding forces in Iraq, General George Casey, opposed more troops. Gordon reported the internal debate had been underway for months.

On the same day that Bob Woodward's *The War Within* was published, laying out at book length what Gordon had reported in a fragmentary manner—the long, and often torturous process by which the decision to surge troops was reached by President Bush—candidate Obama appeared on the Bill O'Reilly program on Fox News Channel and admitted (after repeated and insistent questioning) that the surge had "succeeded beyond our wildest dreams." But he also said it was still too costly, citing the $10 billion or $12 billion a month the war required.

In support of the publication of his book, just two months before Election Day, Woodward published a headline grabbing piece in the *Washington Post* in which he stated flatly that the surge didn't reduce violence in Iraq, but credited the decision of Sunni tribes to switch sides from al Qaeda to the United States. The explanation was said to be Petraeus' generosity: he'd put thousands of Sunni fighters on the U.S. payroll at $300 per month, plus more for the fighters' tribal sheikhs.

As Obama coasted into Election Day, the left was in full repetition mode, touting the line that the surge was either a failure or irrelevant. Obama's tip of the cap to the troops was explained away as simply a requirement of a major American candidate, but that he didn't really believe it, nor would he behave as if he did if he were to win the White House.

Woodward's book was ignored. His conclusions about Bush's tardiness in realizing the war was going badly made headlines and, as those conclusions continued the narrative of Bush mistakes and misjudgments about the war, the public left it at that.

It wasn't until Thomas Ricks' book, *The Gamble*, was released five months later, after President Obama had assumed office, that the significance of Woodward's earlier reporting came into focus. Woodward's book established beyond a doubt that the surge was the right decision, and that it worked spectacularly well. But it wasn't until after a president rode to office denying the wisdom of the decision could that difficult decision receive the respect it deserved.

The left wanted no part of success in the Iraq War. That was not the path to election victory. Five years of war had proved that much, and having learned the lesson that loss leads to victory, the left was not about to waste bad news about the war, and not above creating bad news where it didn't exist in order to win an election.

It bears repeating that on Friday February 27, 2009, President Obama admitted the truth. Speaking before a subdued audience of United States marines at Camp Lejeune, North Carolina, Obama cut the legs out from under the arguments of the left that sustained an entire election campaign. "And I also want to be very clear," he said. "We sent our troops to Iraq to do away with Saddam Hussein's regime—and you got the job done."

A central point of the Bush war justification confirmed. Even Obama admitted at long last that the war was about Saddam Hussein, not WMD.

"We kept our troops in Iraq to help establish a sovereign government—and you got the job done." Bush's insistence that all people—even Iraqis—wanted to be free and self-governing was confirmed.

"And we will leave the Iraqi people with a hard-earned opportunity to live a better life—that is your achievement, that is the prospect you have made possible." Bush's insistence that the Iraqi's deserved our help to live a better life, confirmed.

The next day the *Wall Street Journal* declared the speech "Obama's Bush Vindication."

It should have been a moment of crashing humiliation. A two-year campaign to undermine a war with the American public had been exposed as a fraud by the very person who perpetrated the lie.

The left didn't care. It had won. Bush had been defeated. The left had seized power. It was moving on.

Chapter Eleven

What to Do When Swiftboating Lies About Bush Are Spoken in Your Presence

At the end of his two terms George W. Bush held a final news conference at which he was asked why he pursued his war policies so vigorously and so long after 9/11 when public support was slipping away.

Bush blurted out, "You remember what it was like around here after nine-eleven? I do."

It was a refreshing moment for people who'd been waiting for Bush to defend himself in a way that cut through the prepared remarks, the talking points, and the defensive spin. It was also a stark reminder of the atmosphere of anti-Bush recrimination that followed 9/11.

To the left, Bush had been exposed as a spoiled little momma's boy who was in over his head. He'd been a deer in the headlights reading the kids in Florida the book about baby goats as he learned of the attacks on New York. He'd flitted around the country like a coward, afraid to stay in one spot for fear Osama had him and Air Force One in the crosshairs. He was after Saddam because he wanted to show his daddy he was tough. Not to mention the finger-pointing about not seeing the warning signs right before 9/11 when he got the last presidential daily brief in Crawford, while on his ranch vacation. The insults and purposeful undermining of his credibility with the American public was calculated to do damage and the calculation paid off.

Yet despite this eight-year onslaught of attacks and criticism, the Bush administration never really defended its decisions. Indeed, many conservatives complained that George W. Bush and his spokespeople and surrogates did not defend the policies of the administration with enough vigor and determination. Too often Bush defenders repeated a predictable storyline about the Iraq war or 9/11 or Saddam Hussein that had already been repeated to death, and seemed not to be infused with the passion of true believers. Conservatives trying to defend what the administration had done, who believed in what the administration had done, often found themselves twisting in the wind, waiting for someone who had actually formulated the policies and believed they were proper and right to step forward and speak in a convincing way.

Not until former vice president Richard B. Cheney decided to speak out in the fourth month of the Obama presidency did we hear a stout defense of what was done, why it was done, and the life-saving results that were yielded. Cheney's detractors—and they are numerous and venomous—insisted he was lying about the interrogation results that allowed the United States to unlayer a plot to fly yet another passenger jet into yet another tall building, this time the Library Tower in Los Angeles.

But a reasonable person might wonder whether the fact that the Obama administration only belatedly released the memos that detailed the interrogation results did not indicate that Cheney was right, and releasing the memos would expose the lie of the so-called "torture" debate.

The swiftboating had been effective enough to swing an election, but it was eventually revealed for what it was: a campaign to undermine the credibility of a president with charges that were not necessarily accurate.

Owing to the effectiveness of these swiftboating tactics, it is almost not possible to remain welcome in polite company if one is not willing to admit that Bush was wrong, that the war was wrong, that everything that was done during the Bush administration to keep the country safe was a bundle of horrible blunders, and further that it was all based on lies. This reality can begin to grate. The fool wades into these discussions unprepared.

Still it may be asking too much of a thinking, reasonable person to hold a complete silence in the face of the calumnies which are casually thrown around these days. One might find oneself at a summer barbecue, or a dinner party, or a holiday gathering with the relatives. Everyday people don't write op-eds, they talk to their family, friends, co-workers, neighbors.

Someone, a neighbor, a brother-in-law, a nephew home from college, might say, "Bush sold us a war based on lies." A murmur of general agreement will rise up from the others gathered round. The prudent soul will get up for a refill of his wine glass. After giving serious thought to the possibility of being shunned for offering countervailing opinions, one could engage along the following lines.

Ok, you think Bush was wrong about Iraq, so let's start with the War of Lies. America wanted Saddam gone, and he is gone.

Would you prefer the United States had left Saddam on his throne? Have you read the human rights reports on Saddam's murderous regime? Would the world be better off with Saddam Hussein still in power—today—in Iraq? Would the world be better off with the evil Uday and the malevolent Qusay running wild, stealing brides from their weddings and forcing soccer players into an Iron Maiden? Would you be comfortable knowing that Saddam was about to throw off UN sanctions in 2003 and by now would be doing whatever he wanted with no international power to thwart his designs on his neighbors or the wider world? Would you prefer to have Jacques Chirac's France a major world oil power, courtesy of Saddam? Do you think the United States would have been better off ignoring (as it had for many years) the growing list of human rights crimes committed by Saddam against his own people and the foreign guest workers who took jobs in Iraq? (Egyptian guest workers returned home in boxes, without explanation.)

And what exactly were these lies? WMD? Saddam's involvement with terrorists? Or are you talking about the small stuff, such as "we'll be greeted with flowers and sweets," or "it will be a cakewalk," or "Iraq's oil revenue will pay for the war"?

The questions and challenges will continue.

Saddam had nothing to do with 9/11.

Well, the whole point was to prevent the next 9/11, not simply punish the guilty parties for the one that had already occurred. But beyond that, read the Senate Select Committee on Intelligence report of July 2004, and look over all the confirmed contacts between bin Laden and Saddam. Yes, the SSCI said there was no "operational cooperation," but wouldn't you expect a prudent president not to wait until the world's two nastiest men decided to cooperate?

What's more, read Christopher Dickey's 2002 *Newsweek* report recalling a 1993 visit to Baghdad in which he watched the all-star team of the world's terrorists gather for a conference convened by Saddam Hussein at the Al Rashid Hotel, and you tell me you're comfortable with Saddam remaining in power and consorting with the likes of Hamas, Hezbollah, Abu Nidal, Fatah, and more? Saddam tolerated the presence of Abu Musab Al Zarqawi, an al Qaeda terrorist, in Iraq after the Americans invaded Afghanistan and drove al Qaeda out. And you would prefer a president who let that situation fester, who would wait until we are attacked again before acting?

Saddam was suspicious of bin Laden, and bin Laden hated Saddam's secular regime.

So what? They both hated the United States, and Ray Robinson, a CIA man charged with deciphering millions of pages of Iraqi documents, found a diary that documented meetings in Afghanistan between the Iraqi vice president and the Taliban, representing bin Laden. They discussed mutual efforts against the United States.

There were NO WMD!

This is a phony argument. The world believed Saddam had WMD. The UN believed Saddam had WMD. The Germans, the French, the Brits, the Jordanians, the Egyptians, the Iranians, the Syrians—they all believed he had WMD. The Iraq Survey Group analyzed the papers of the Saddam regime and found that Saddam needed to convince his neighbors, even his own generals he had weapons of mass destruction. If Iran thought he did not have WMD, they might have invaded even before the United States. As the U.S. invasion moved closer to Baghdad, his own generals were shocked to learn they would not be using WMD on the invading Americans. Everybody thought he had some sort of chemical or biological weapons. Why should Bush have known better? After all, the CIA had nobody on the inside who was trustworthy, as we know from the belated discoveries of just how bad the American intelligence was about Iraq.

Colin Powell's speech at the UN used phony information about

Iraq's mobile bio weapons labs from a man known to be a fabricator. Bush lied to sell the war.

Bush thought it was patently obvious that Saddam had to go, and his administration had to come up with reasons to do what the whole world knew had to be done, even though no country could or would do anything to get rid of him. Only the United States could do it, and the left—in the United States and Europe—made repeated demands for "good reasons," claiming with a false pose of open-mindedness that "he still hasn't made the case," all the while ignoring their own vigorous anti-Saddam campaigns of the past decade.

But Cheney and Condoleezza Rice spoke about "mushroom clouds," intimating he had nuclear weapons.

For starters, the whole point of invading a country to stop them from acquiring nuclear weapons is to get there before they have the nuclear weapon. Why do you think an invasion of North Korea is off the table? Why do you think the international community is so determined to keep Iran from acquiring nuclear weapons? A nuclear-armed nation is impervious to invasion. It's called deterrence. What would be the point of waiting until Saddam had nuclear weapons before acting to disarm him? It would have meant the deaths of many thousands more American troops, and many hundreds of thousands of Iraqis (the United States would undoubtedly have retaliated against a nuclear strike on our troops.)

So no, he didn't have nuclear weapons, but he did have precursor materials (500 tons of yellowcake uranium at Tuwaitha), he did have the scientists, and he did have the blueprints for a weapon. Those blueprints were found among the millions of pages of Iraqi documents posted online by the U.S. government, and immediately taken down because they could have been used by someone else wanting to build a bomb.

By the way, the invasion of Iraq exposed the nuclear proliferation network of Pakistani scientist A. Q. Khan, hitherto unknown to Western intelligence agencies—a windfall from Bush's firm stance against the threat of nuclear terrorism. It also caused Libya to turn over its active nuclear program to the United States out of fear of an invasion, and Libya was quite close to having a nuclear bomb. So at least one nuclear-armed state was "stood down" by the American invasion of Iraq, even if it wasn't Iraq.

Bush didn't send enough troops, he tried to run the war on the cheap. Look at the looting that took place right after the invasion.

Sure, people went crazy. It was the first time in thirty years they had Saddam's boot off their neck. The looters were the people Saddam's regime was organized to oppress. Yes, they went batty when they learned he was finally gone. What did you expect? Plus, read the history of the invasion from General Tommy Franks and others. American troops were supposed to be heading home immediately after the invasion, after handing Iraq over to an interim government. Sending more troops might have been an answer for the insurgency that followed, but not the invasion.

Well, exactly. He didn't anticipate the insurgency, or the death squads or any of the terrible things that began shortly after the invasion.

Are you telling me that the insurgency and the Shia death squads were Bush's fault? You believe Bush sent the Sunni insurgents out to kill Shia and vice versa? That's absurd.

He didn't handle the post-invasion well.

No, he didn't. It took a long time to find the generals who knew what to do. Thank God for David Petraeus, who was trashed by the left, by the way.

Bush let Paul Bremmer screw things up.

Yes, he did. You can have that point.

Bush had lousy pre-war intelligence.

The CIA couldn't get people inside Iraq without needlessly endangering their lives. They had a couple of sources who were bogus and gave us bad information. Our bad. We should have had more people inside Iraq, but for one reason or another—and you might want to question some Democrats about this—we didn't.

During the waning days of the Clinton administration, CIA agent Bob Baer was working in northern Iraq, in the Kurdish area. Two rival Kurdish leaders (both later high officials of the post-Saddam Iraq government) were organizing an invasion/coup. Clinton National Security Advisor Anthony Lake demanded a halt to the operation and had Baer recalled from the field. Baer was accused of orchestrating the operation—an illegal U.S.-sponsored coup—and eventually retired from the CIA. He turned to writing, and published several books, one of which became the movie *Syriana*. How much better off would the world have been if the United States had sponsored a successful coup against Saddam in the late nineties?

Bush tried to silence a war critic by exposing his CIA wife.

No, he didn't. Valerie Plame exposed herself when she started a chain of events that eventually led people to ask, "Who sent Ambassador Joe Wilson to Niger to investigate an Iraq uranium buy?" At that point she had to be exposed because her husband had charged that the vice president sent him to investigate a key element of the case for war, and had then ignored his evidence and gone to war on false charges.

When Robert Novak was told—not by Scooter Libby—that Wilson's wife worked for the CIA, he simply looked her up in *Who's Who in America*. The entire saga was classic leftist swiftboating.

But Scooter Libby lied. They were trying to punish Wilson by telling the press information on a covert agent. Her sources were exposed.

Bush was being hammered with a lie, namely that Wilson had been sent on a mission and found the president's reasons for war were false. The charge had to be rebutted, so the truth came out that Ms. Plame sent her antiwar husband on a mission that allowed him subsequently to undermine one of the main reasons for the war.

Bush spied on Americans. Listened to their phone calls. Read email.

You're perfectly fine with having the most private conversations on your cell phone in bars, department stores, elevators, airplanes, and trains, which anybody within earshot can hear, but you object to the government scanning your calls along with millions of others for words that might be tip-offs to a brewing terrorist plot. Do you honestly think they are listening to you? You are not a terrorist; a computer is scanning your call. You are being protected, not harmed.

Bush killed 1.2 million people in Iraq.

That's two lies rolled into one. First, the number of people killed after the invasion and before the surge was a tenth of that, and the larger number was the product of a willful political lie. Secondly, Bush didn't kill those people. The Shia had been oppressed too long and wanted their turn to use cordless drills on Sunni skulls, and the Sunni insurgents meant to show they could cut off the heads of Shia apostates. Bush gave them freedom; if they used it to kill each other, it is not the fault of Bush or the Americans.

Al Qaeda wasn't in Iraq before the United States invaded.

The hell it wasn't. *Newsweek*'s Christopher Dickey, whom the Brits might refer to as an "old Arabia hand," went to Baghdad in January 1993.

Dickey's eyes popped out: "Islamic radicals from all over the Middle East, Africa and Asia converged on Baghdad to show their solidarity with Iraq in the face of American aggression," Dickey reported, referring to American president George H.W. Bush. "Chechens in Persian-lamb hats, Moroccans in caftans, delegates who hailed 'from Jakarta to Dakar,' as one Senegalese put it, poured into Baghdad's Rashid Hotel, where Saddam's minions urged them to embrace jihad as 'the one gate to Paradise.' And the greatest holy warrior of all? 'The mujahed Saddam Hussein, who is leading this nation against the nonbelievers,' they were told. 'Everyone has a task to do, which is to go against the American state,' declared Saddam's deputy Ezzat Ibrahim."

Saddam was up to his eyeballs in terrorists. Even the Senate Select Committee on Intelligence acknowledged there were multiple and repeated contacts between Saddam's regime and al Qaeda. And it really is impossible to ignore the fact that the leader of what became al Qaeda in Iraq, Abu Musab al Zarqawi, brought 200 fighters with him when he escaped from Afghanistan a full year before the American invasion. Saddam's intelligence service—the ruthless internal police who ran the real torture chambers—said they "couldn't find him." This is preposterous: Zarqawi received hospital treatment in Baghdad and spent two more months in the city recovering from his war wounds, yet at the same time evaded one of the world's best teams of secret police. Al Qaeda was in Iraq because Saddam didn't want him out.

Bush ran torture chambers, we didn't live up to our own values, the world hated us.

The world also won't take the prisoners from Gitmo. The world knows how dangerous they are and wants nothing to do with them. The world was hypocritically attacking Bush, hoping the American people would decide it was more important to be liked by the world than to be kept safe from terrorist attack.

Three people were waterboarded, under rules designed to prevent torture, and two of the three were al Qaeda planners of 9/11. What president would not make certain he or she had not extracted any future plans against America? Two dozen people were subjected to sleep deprivation. They were al Qaeda operatives, and the possibility was real they knew of future attacks or better yet, how al Qaeda operated and who else was involved in the organization.

Despite the ruckus raised by Frank Rich of the *New York Times* and a few others, Abu Ghraib was not part of the legally sanctioned tough interrogation techniques. It was criminal torture and the army personnel who carried it out were tried and punished. The very facts of what they did to detainees prove it was not part of the otherwise carefully thought-out and executed interrogation regime.

Bush wasn't even legitimately elected, he was selected by the Bush friendly Supreme Court.

Wrong. Al Gore won the popular vote, but lost in the Electoral College, which is how our system works. All studies and independent recounts put Bush ahead of Al Gore, and the correct decision was reached by the Supreme Court. Bush won. Like it or not.

Bush was a dolt, a joke, an embarrassment.

The left made him a joke. He had higher grades at Yale than John Kerry. He was, to borrow a phrase from Barack Obama, smart enough. He didn't speak well, and his verbal back flips were exploited by the left to undermine his credibility and authority. But he did the right things.

Bush was incompetent. Why was New Orleans such an embarrassment to the United States? We accepted relief supplies from China!

Yes—and several other countries also jumped on the opportunity to embarrass Bush. U.S. government crews pulled 30,000 people out of the attics of flooded houses with helicopters. The mayor of New Orleans and the governor of Louisiana were both unprepared, and fell apart during the crisis. Their failure led to thousands of people spending miserable days without food or water or safe and comfortable shelter. Bush's FEMA was overly bureaucratic and maddeningly unresponsive, but it was federal officials who eventually completed the rescue operation. Bush was blamed for staying away, and he would have been blamed had he shown up and disrupted emergency operations. It was a convenient pretext for the left to both allege and claim it had proved that Bush and Republicans didn't like black people. That was a lie.

I can't stand Bush. I don't like the way he talks, or the way he walks, or his religion or his claim to be the "decider."

This is where the rubber meets the road. At the bottom of all the criticism is a visceral dislike—hostility—for Bush and his supporters. Eventually the argument will peter out and it will come to this: I hate Bush.

For the more reasonable among us, and admittedly there were not many, there is the issue of always rethinking what we did, and whether it was right. It doesn't hurt to look at how the political opponents attacked and undermined what we did. And very few people who supported Bush policies, and watched in dismay as they were destroyed by an onslaught of charges based on willful twisting of both the facts and the truth, thought the president and his men and women defended themselves or their decisions very well.

But doing the right thing counts for something. As we see the new president adopt many of the policies of his predecessor, policies the new president condemned in the campaign, we should be able to see the outlines of the real story rising in the mists and fog.

Afterword: How Barack Obama Swiftboated His Way to the White House—and Beyond

Barack Obama and his Chicago team were in on the ground floor of swiftboating George W. Bush, the war in Iraq, and the efforts to keep America safe after 9/11. Howard Dean certainly blazed the Bush-hating trail, but it was the Obama team that inherited from Dean the Internet magic and the mantle of Bush challenger.

By the time the insurgent Democrats had retaken the congress in 2006, Obama was one of the leading participants when it came to the day-in and day-out swiftboating of Bush and the war. He certainly took advantage of the panoply of swiftboating arguments whenever possible on the campaign trail in 2008. He boasted that he had always opposed the war in Iraq, and constantly asserted that the president "took his eye off the ball" by leaving Afghanistan to its dusty, violent future and turning instead to Iraq. Obama played every one of the instruments in the anti-Bush band: against the war, against Gitmo, against tough interrogations (torture), against wiretapping, against the Patriot Act, against the very language of the war on terror. Obama took full advantage of the left's swiftboating techniques, almost laughing at his competitors, who either didn't understand how potent these arguments were, or had been boxed out of using them by, like Hillary Clinton, actually voting for the war.

Swiftboating the war and the president played to Obama's strengths, and he ceaselessly repeated the attacks against Bush formulated and distilled by the left, using those arguments to convince America's independent voters to swing to his side.

The conflation of fact and fiction, the foaming anger and bitter vituperation that were a font of lies about Bush, Cheney, and the Iraq War (along with a shocking stock market collapse late in the campaign) swept Obama into office. And it continued apace after he assumed the presidency.

Bush had a strange political life after political death. Frequently during his first six months in office, Obama reached for Bush whenever he was faced with trouble. He constantly complained that he had inherited a "mess" in Iraq and an economy in free fall, blaming the "failed ideology" of free-market capitalism for the financial collapse that helped elect him. These were new and (alas) highly effective coinages in the left's ongoing campaign of lies against Bush and the Republicans. The "mess" in Iraq was already in its last stages and the economy would heal itself in time as it always does, despite Obama's efforts to stampede a panicked American electorate into supporting a massive expansion of government.

But as the former president maintained his silence in Texas and President Obama delved deeper into his policy vault, swiftboating George W. Bush made less and less sense and proved far less effective than in its heyday during the campaign.

The continued swiftboating campaign against Bush also became a losing game as Obama began adopting a series of Bush policies that he had previously decried. After dramatically announcing on his second day in office that he would close the Guantanamo Bay detention facility within a year, Obama soon had to admit there were some people incarcerated there who would be too dangerous to release. After bashing Bush senseless for issuing so-called "signing statements" when signing a bill into law (indicating that the president had little, if any, intention of actually following the law), Obama issued his first signing statement within days of his inauguration. Obama also followed Bush's lead on Iraq, executing the plan signed by former President Bush and Iraqi President Nouri al-Maliki. Obama outlawed torture, more properly described as enhanced or harsh interrogations, and then promised that in a dire situation, such as interrogating a terrorist who has information on an imminent attack, "I will do what I have to do."

Some of Obama's most vocal supporters in the media harrumphed over these developments, and even dreaded left-wing figures such as Keith Olbermann suggested that he was becoming a little too *Bush* for his own good. Generally, though, the new president got a pass, even when he most affronted the left.

However, a far more serious problem now confronted Obama and his team: namely, who will we swiftboat now?

It was important to find a new enemy to subject to the same swift-boating techniques that had brought Obama to office. Political power was a direct function of the president's popularity, and that meant someone or something else had to be correspondingly *unpopular*.

The formula remained the same: stand up a lie as the truth, buttress it with whatever flimsy or false evidence you have at hand, and pour on withering fire, Chicago-style.

Such an opportunity presented itself one day on the radio.

Radio host Rush Limbaugh, addressing his approximately 20 million listeners, said he thought Obama was a socialist and that he hoped the new president failed. Great outrage ensued. Limbaugh was attacked mercilessly—usually festooned with snide references to his onetime drug problem and/or his weight. Limbaugh was both pronounced a pariah and held up as the ugly new face of the Republican Party.

That was the swiftboating version. The truth was something else.

A transcript from the Limbaugh program for January 16, four days before Obama's inauguration, shows him reading from a letter he had received from a major American publication. The brackets indicate Limbaugh's ad lib insertion:

Dear Rush:
For the Obama [Immaculate] Inauguration we are asking
a handful of very prominent politicians, statesmen, scholars,
businessmen, commentators, and economists to write 400
words on their hope for the Obama presidency. We would
love to include you. If you could send us 400 words on your
hope for the Obama presidency, we need it by Monday night,
that would be ideal.

Limbaugh continued, speaking for himself:

Now, we're caught in this trap again. The premise is, what is your "hope." My hope, and please understand me when I say this. I disagree fervently with the people on our side of the aisle who have caved and who say, "Well, I hope he succeeds. We've got to give him a chance." Why? They didn't give Bush a chance in 2000. Before he was inaugurated the search-and-destroy mission had begun. I'm not talking about search-and-destroy, but I've been listening to Barack Obama for a year-and-a-half. I know what his politics are. I know what his plans are, as he has stated them. I don't want them to succeed.

The cry went up across the nation: Limbaugh and the Republicans want the president to fail, and that means they want the country to fail. What kind of Americans are these? This, by the way, from Americans who had earlier cheered the prospect of the country losing a war.

Frank Rich and others on the left demanded to know whether a talk show host was now running the Republican Party.

Republican National Committee chair Michael Steele was asked if he or Limbaugh led the party. Steele replied that Limbaugh was merely an entertainer, and said that his remarks on the radio were unfortunate and "ugly."

Now, to the great joy of the left, a secondary explosion lit up the sky, as the right demanded Steele back off his assertion that Limbaugh was a *mere* entertainer. Steele called Limbaugh to apologize.

The Republicans were on the ropes for weeks with columnists, late-night comics, and cable talk show hosts hooting at the sight of a major political party forced to bow down to a talk show host.

But at the same time other issues loomed over the White House: What if the stimulus didn't stimulate, what if the housing industry didn't rebound quickly, and what if the freeze in bank-to-bank lending—the engine of the corporate economy—proved resistant to a thaw? Faced with all this, Limbaugh proved the perfect distraction.

On the first day in March, Obama's chief of staff, Rahm Emanuel, appeared on CBS's *Face the Nation*, and was asked who represented the Republican Party. Emanuel said it was Rush Limbaugh because Limbaugh had:

> called for President Obama to fail. That's his view. And that's what he has enunciated. And whenever a Republican criticizes him, they have to run back and apologize to him, and say they were misunderstood. He is the voice and the intellectual force and energy behind the Republican Party. And he has been up-front about what he views, and hasn't stepped back from that, which is he hopes for failure. He said it. And I compliment him for his honesty, but that's their philosophy that is enunciated by Rush Limbaugh.

As the Obama agenda unfurled in the coming weeks, the media continued to focus on Rush Limbaugh and the wreckage of the Republican Party. Meanwhile, bailout plans inherited from George W. Bush were transformed from bridge loans to auto companies into a complete government takeover of General Motors and Chrysler, as well as most major banks and dozens of smaller financial institutions. The stimulus bill Obama insisted the nation adopt on a track so fast that members of Congress who voted for it hadn't read it turned out to be a heaving load of pork and boondoggle that didn't produce jobs but piled up massive debt and devalued the dollar.

Those concerns were brushed aside. Instead the story was "Rush Limbaugh wants America to fail," and all Republicans and conservatives take orders from Limbaugh.

When ordinary citizens objected to the out-of-control spending, the ballooning debt, and the taxation required to pay for it, the gunsights of the left suddenly swiveled toward them. No longer was it enough for the left to attack Republican and conservative leaders, they now went after private citizens.

Beginning in the early spring and growing swiftly into a national phenomenon, people alarmed by the mounting cost of President Obama's agenda organized to hold protests they called Tea Parties. Several big events, some televised nationally, were scheduled for tax day 2009—April 15—in large cities around the country. Tea Parties were held in over 800 spots and some estimates put the total turnout

at over half a million. The *Christian Science Monitor* described the protests as "recalling the spirit of the country's revolutionary roots to
demand smaller, more responsible and more constitutional government." The *Monitor* reported that it was the largest national protest
since the immigration rights marches of 2006.

But the paper also quoted Jeffrey Kimball, a professor emeritus
of history at Miami University in Oxford, Ohio, who scoffed at the
movement. "We may have just seen the whole movement at these
protests," Kimball said. "I don't see it as a groundswell, but a mani-
festation by those people who form the core of . . . the extreme right
reacting both to the condition of our time and President Obama—
he's black and he's liberal."

This nascent charge of racism against anyone who opposed the
Obama agenda would later bloom into a full-blown swiftboating
narrative. In the meantime, Tea Party protestors were accused of
being tools of corporate interests, and were mocked as laughable
fools whose only contribution to public discourse and debate was
entertainment.

On MSNBC, Rachel Maddow and blogger-turned-*Time* magazine reporter Ana Marie Cox spent thirteen minutes making lewd
jokes about "tea bagging," referencing a sexual practice they had
perhaps learned from porn videos. Ms. Maddow called it a "double
entendre palooza."

Likewise, when CNN political analyst David Gergen noted that
Republicans were "searching for their voice" following two electoral
losses, anchor Anderson Cooper interjected, "It's hard to talk when
you're tea-bagging."

The jocularity was everywhere. At a White House press briefing, press secretary Robert Gibbs fielded a series of questions about
policy involving Spain when he was asked whether the White House
and the president were monitoring the Tea Parties. He dismissed the
protests. "I've neither monitored them nor spoken with the Spanish
about them," he said, to laughter from the press.

Some of the left media became so contemptuous of the Tea
Party protestors it slipped out on the air. Susan Roesgen, a CNN
reporter in Chicago, approached a protestor at an event in Chicago
during a live news report, reading signs that were in the crowd.
"Let's see, 'Drop taxes, drop socialism,' ok, let's see, you're here

with your two-year-old and you're already in debt, why are you here today?"

A man holding a toddler with a pacifier in her mouth replied that he thought the president believed in Lincoln's faith in liberty. Roesgen interrupted him and asked, "Sir, what does this have to do with taxes? Do you realize you're eligible for a four hundred dollar tax re—"

"Let me finish my point," the man interrupted her. "Lincoln believed that people had the right to share in the fruits of their own labor and government should not take it, and we have clearly gotten to that point—"

"Wait," Roesgen interrupted again. "Did you know that the state of Lincoln gets fifty billion dollars from this stimulus, that's fifty billion dollars for this state, sir."

The man began to answer, but Roesgen cut him off by stepping away. "You get the idea, here," she said to the audience. "It's antigovernment, anti-CNN since it's promoted by the right-wing conservative network, Fox. And since I can't really hear much more and since I think this is not really family viewing, I'm going to toss it back to you, Kyra."

And with that the studio anchor took over. Roesgen came under a torrent of criticism from the right for her rude treatment of the protestor (and her contract was not renewed), but the narrative was set: the protestors were mere puppets of a reactionary television network.

Left-wing actress, comedian, and sometime radio host Janeane Garofalo, interviewed in Canada, said the Tea Party protestors were motivated not by legitimate concerns about taxation and out-of-control spending but (somehow or other) by the reactionary fear of a black man in authority. "This is racism straight up and is nothing but a bunch of tea-bagging rednecks. There is no way around that." Her remark caused a stir on the right, and solemn nods of agreement on the left.

All of this was a warm-up for the health-care debate. Obama had talked about health-care reform throughout his campaign, and by the first spring of his presidency, he was promising to sign a health-care bill into law before Congress went home for its August recess.

As the Democrats in Congress began to work up various health-care bills, the broad outline of what the left wanted was beginning to become clear, and objections to some of the ideas that were being thrown around under the Capitol dome began to bubble to the surface.

The left decided it was time to make certain that Republicans could not stop Obamacare, and so a new narrative was put into play. CNN's Gloria Borger brought it up back in February during a TV panel debate on the fate of the Republican Party in answer to an assertion by GOP chairman Michael Steele that he was going to try to bring young black voters into the party. "Well, it's going to be difficult," she said, "because right now, quite frankly, the Republican Party looks more like the old Confederacy."

In other words, the GOP was a whites-only party that was dead set against progress, yearned for the grand old days of segregation, and had no interest in modern America with its diverse population.

The narrative came in handy when, quite to their surprise, Democrats were suddenly faced with an all-out popular revolt against an overreaching and debt-heavy health-care reform package that the president and the left were pushing as the most important legislation on the Obama agenda.

Republicans were not able to block or even slow Obama's health-care initiative—as it turned out, it was conservative, so-called "Blue Dog" Democrats who did that. But this didn't stop the left from blaming Republicans and their "southern populist" (i.e., religious redneck) base.

When Ohio Republican George Voinovich told a group of Ohio newspaper editors that the biggest problem facing the GOP was too many southerners, he presented a gift to the left. "It's the southerners. They get on TV and go '*errrr, errr.*' People hear them and say, 'These people, they're southerners. The party's being taken over by southerners. What the hell they got to do with Ohio?'"

The left leaped on the Voinovich quote as if it were an oasis in the desert. Even the Republicans say so! Opponents of health care were merely anti-Obama southerners whose racial animus was clear.

Nevertheless, support for the president's health-care initiative continued to drop and Obama and the Democrats launched a public-relations effort to sell the policy in a series of public meetings across the country. But as the August town hall meetings erupted in shouting and genuine anger, and the president's approval ratings slipped below 50 percent for the first time, the Democratic National Committee released an ad calling the protestors "thugs" and "mobs," whose only motive was to destroy the president.

Meanwhile, the White House asked its union allies to mobilize their membership to attend the town hall meetings, and "punch back twice as hard." The call was answered. The next day, five members of the Service Employees International Union were arrested for assault on a health-care protestor at a town hall meeting in Tampa, Florida. It mattered little that the protestor was black. He suffered a beat down because he dared to speak up against Obamacare. Meanwhile, others on the left stepped up the attack, insisting that the protestors were racist rednecks, GOP activists, or both.

In a two-week period at the beginning of August, this narrative came into full flower.

Cynthia Tucker, a Pulitzer Prize–nominated columnist for the *Atlanta Journal-Constitution*, told Chris Matthews on MSNBC that 45 to 65 percent of the people coming out to protest Obamacare "were not comfortable with a black man as president." Carlos Watson, another MSNBC anchor, said, "Socialist is the new N word."

Paul Krugman, the Nobel Prize–winning *New York Times* columnist, also weighed in. Describing the widespread protests, he asked, "Does this sound familiar? It should: it's a strategy that has played a central role in American politics ever since Richard Nixon realized that he could advance Republican fortunes by appealing to the racial fears of working-class whites."

Speaker of the House Nancy Pelosi and her second in command, Steny Hoyer, wrote in a *USA Today* editorial that the protestors were "un-American." Later she labeled the protests "astroturf"—not an authentic grassroots uprising—and claimed that there were swastikas in evidence, clearly intending to discredit this popular insurgency comprising a broad spectrum of middle-class Americans as a phenomenon of the lunatic fringe. Other liberal commentators speculated that the anti-health-care crowds drew from the same pool of right-wing paranoia as the "birthers," who claimed Obama hadn't really been born in Hawaii as a U.S. citizen.

Whatever the merits of Obama's health-care plan, none of this had anything to do with the real issues. It wasn't about what kind of health care Americans would or would not receive from a new government program. It wasn't about savings in Medicare or piling more debt on an already debt-ridden society. It wasn't about whether the many proposals might work out to be good or bad.

It was the politics of distraction. It was about attacking and destroying. It was about staving off defeat. It was about lies passing themselves off as the truth. In short, it was about swiftboating.

This swiftboating strategy worked against Bush; it helped get Obama elected, and the left has continued to use it—with the help of a compliant liberal press—to bully the right in the budget and the health-care debates. What's more, they will continue to do so in future debates, until the American public wakes up and starts paying attention to the swiftboating lies of the left. Already a groundswell is building against the liberal swiftboat brigade and their enablers in the media. Let us hope the day comes soon when ordinary Americans cry, "Enough!"

Acknowledgments

I would like to thank my editor, Adam Bellow, for guiding this book to publication. Any author would be lucky to have Adam's help with his work. Thanks also to my literary agent, Mel Berger, for all that he does. I would also like to acknowledge that many fine authors have risked their lives and labored thanklessly to tell the story of the Iraq War as they have witnessed it, and I have used dozens of accounts to form my opinions. To single out any individual author might seem to diminish others, which is not my intention, but I recommend to readers of any point of view Dexter Filkins's *The Forever War*, George Packer's *The Assassins' Gate*, and Donovan Campbell's *Joker One*. Dozens of other authors and journalists have informed my views of the Iraq War, but these three in particular have the effect of leavening the natural partisanship that arises from the politics of war with the reality of a faraway conflict.

Index